D1095114

Mothers and Sons

By Carole Klein

THE SINGLE PARENT EXPERIENCE
THE MYTH OF THE HAPPY CHILD
ALINE
MOTHERS AND SONS

MOTHERS
and SONS

Carole Klein

Houghton Mifflin Company
BOSTON 1984

Library of Congress Cataloging in Publication Data

Klein, Carole.
Mothers and sons.
Bibliography: p.
Includes index.
1. Mothers and sons.   2. Mothers—Psychology.
3. Sons—Psychology.   I. Title.
HQ755.85.K57   1984   306.8'743   83-22546
ISBN 0-395-31826-2

Printed in the United States of America

V 10 9 8 7 6 5 4 3 2 1

The author is grateful for permission to quote from the poem "The Last Hiding
Places of Snow," from *Mortal Acts, Mortal Words* by Galway Kinnell. Copyright
© 1980 by Galway Kinnell. Reprinted by permission of Houghton Mifflin
Company.

*Of course to,
and with infinite appreciation of,
William*

Acknowledgments

I am deeply indebted to all the mothers and sons who carefully answered my questions and volunteered ideas born of their own experience. Similarly, I am grateful to the many professionals who took time away from their own work to aid me in mine. In particular, I express thanks to Edward J. Sivasta, Jr., Dr. Alexander Lowen, Dr. Irving Markowitz, and Dr. Veva Zimmerman for their generous allocation of time and thought. Each person contributed a singular perspective that greatly widened the base of my investigation.

To Ms. Cameron Barry, the deepest appreciation. Her responses to the book as it developed were extremely important and are amply reflected in the final product. Every author should have a friend with such literary sensitivity and critical skills.

Thanks also to Elaine Goodman, who typed and retyped my manuscript, as it went through its evolutions, without a whisper of complaint or a lessening of dexterity.

On a personal note, thanks of course to my husband, Ted, who once again supported my efforts and understood my preoccupation. And finally, some words of celebration for my daughter, Emily. Clearly a woman is doubly blessed to have both a son and a daughter. When the daughter is Emily, that blessing is extended beyond any measure.

Contents

Mothers and Sons

Introduction

Henry James, in midlife, sent his mother a letter that began, "Dear Mommy." Lyndon Johnson's mother, in a rush of emotion at the news of her son's first election to Congress, wrote him, "My darling boy! How dear to me you are, you cannot know . . . take care of yourself darling. Write to me. You have justified my expectations, my hopes, my dreams. . . ."

The relationship between mother and son has been analyzed by a son named Sigmund Freud and vilified, in his well-known book, *Generation of Vipers*, by a son named Philip Wylie. Yet the story I want to tell lies somewhere between Freud's emphasis on psychosexual development and Wylie's on psychological damage. My concern is what it *feels* like for a woman to be the mother of a male child. And, too, what it feels like for a man to be "of woman born."

Mine is a study shaped by contrasts, enriched by differences. The spate of writing on the mother-daughter relationship has emphasized the parallels of the female experience from generation to generation. Little attention has been paid, at least publicly, to the other mother-child bond. What is it like for a woman to give birth to, and raise, a child who is her opposite, not only biologically but culturally? What is it like for a boy to come to life in a woman's body, to know an infant's extraordinary fusion and identification with his mother, and then have to define himself as "man" by denying his need of his mother and of what she, as "woman," represents?

I have come to feel that this is the most private story any mother or son has to tell. It is a tale of such intense complexity that we cannot easily find the words—or the courage—to tell it. The prism through which a mother views her son is colored by a poignancy and passion that make her falter in the attempt to express what she sees.

To make these issues public at last, I employed several different methods of research. I interviewed extensively more than thirty psychiatrists and psychologists. Along with providing specific theoretical material, all agreed that it takes a very long time for their male clients to "get to the mother part" when presenting an account of their lives. Unlike women, men seem to find it difficult to share feelings about their mothers that go beyond studied reverence or facile expressions of antagonism.

I also thoroughly researched the professional literature, examining established theories of male and female development, as well as the most current sociological and psychological data on issues related to my investigation. I paid particular attention to such topics as how boys are socialized into society, how traditional Freudian theory is being re-examined, and how feminism is affecting the way mothers raise their sons. My graduate work in psychology and sociology guided my investigative methodology.

These explorations confirmed that many layers of defense must be stripped away before a man can allow himself to touch the central place his mother occupies for most of his life. For example, in a major study that followed men's lives over a thirty-five-year period, one subject was forty-seven years old before he could finally admit how profoundly his mother had angered and frightened him when he was a little boy. Until then, during the most "exhaustive projective testing," the researchers reported, he had never revealed the slightest hint of his rage and sense of deprivation.

With the guidance of experts in the preparation of psychological questionnaires, I devised a set of questions to be sent to more than five hundred women, and supplemented many of the responses with personal interviews. After I had accumulated all the data, I had additional assistance from these social scientists in assessing the results and defining their implications and conclusions. I also prepared an interview guideline for two hundred men, whereby carefully planned, open-ended questions were answered in writing or, much more often, during individual face-to-face meetings, which allowed the men to answer the questions in even greater depth.

These interviews form the basis of this book. The respondents represent a cross-section of age, geography, and ethnic background. However, they do not technically meet one of the criteria of a truly scientific sampling, because they are not a controlled segment of the general population. It seemed important with so elusive a subject to give priority to the search for central themes. I needed men and women who thought deeply about their lives and who were willing at least to try to translate their thoughts into words. Thus, these seven hundred sons and mothers are a particularly articulate group.

There are fewer male respondents than women, because when I began, I intended, feminist consciousness running high, for the book to be primarily a mother's story. It was only after I started my research that I realized how circular and intertwined the tale really is: a son's experience of his mother is not a supplement to the story of mothering sons; it is a vital, inextricable part of it. The degree to which I understand his longing, joy, anger, or pain relates directly to my clear comprehension of hers. And, although they came into my research later and are fewer in number, my interviews with sons were most often considerably, even remarkably, revealing. Once he begins—whether through correspondence or personal meeting or even when stemming from a casual encounter—it seems extremely difficult for a son to stop talking about the first and most important woman in his life.

For example, one middle-aged man I was introduced to at a cocktail party was absolutely appalled at my only half-serious suggestion that we discuss his relationship with his mother instead of making the usual small talk. Five weeks later, he called me from his hospital bed, where he was recuperating from an episode of vascular insufficiency. After reminding me of our meeting, he cleared his throat and said, "Look, I actually do want to talk to you about my mother." At his request we arranged an early afternoon meeting to take place only two days after his release from the hospital. Not the sky darkening outside the windows of his apartment nor my worry that he was getting overtired could stem his need to explore long-buried memories and feelings about his mother.

During the last ten years, I have also taught in women's studies programs and led workshops for women who are trying to achieve greater self-understanding. I ran an ongoing group for mothers of sons throughout the course of my research and writing. This enabled me to observe mothers and to participate in their discovery of the commonality of their experience with sons. I gained firsthand knowledge of how their lives touched at a seemingly infinite number of points.

In a related but less comprehensive process, I periodically gathered together groups of little boys and girls in order to observe the differences in the ways each sex views a mother, and also to try to discover the particular shapes boys' and girls' lives take around a mother's omnipresence. I should note that during this investigation I deliberately chose not to point out occasional resemblances between the relationships of mothers and sons and those of fathers and daughters. There are some, of course, but for the clearest understanding of the mother-son relationship, I focused my inquiry solely on its components.

To illuminate further the nature of the mother-son bond, I also looked to poets and writers. The attachment between mother and son has informed literature down through the ages. Indeed, the artistic son or mother has often dared to venture into territory other men or women have avoided. Since a gifted writer's vision is generally more encompassing than most people's, a line from Proust about his mother, or a sonnet written by a poet to her adolescent son, can often illuminate the truth of our own lives.

Finally, perhaps the most important source for this book has been my own experience. I am the mother of both a son and a daughter. While I love them equally with a passion of stunning intensity, I know the love takes different shapes. My son is now in his middle twenties, and I have been conscious of a growing need to understand more than I do about what our effect has been on each other's lives. Some years ago, the critic Theodore Solotaroff described a certain kind of writing as a "necessary inquiry." He said, "The necessary inquiry is one that the writer, quite literally, has to write, or, what comes to the same thing, has been saving up to write." He also said that in such a joining of writing and issue, the writer is "as much a witness . . . as a commentator." This definition goes very far toward explaining my decision to write a book about mothers and sons.

So, out of all these elements, the themes of the mother-son experience began to emerge. Whether a mother is in her twenties or her fifties, when she talks about her son, she is talking about power and status, about vulnerability and intimacy and sexuality, about her feelings toward men and her own femaleness. When a fifty-year-old man or a fifteen-year-old boy grudgingly or wistfully speaks of his mother, he often suggests a sexual motif, a fear or need of love, self-doubt or egocentricity, his comfort or lack of it in being a man, and what masculinity implies to him.

More than I had ever suspected before I began this book, I realize now that a mother mirrors the world for her son. She is his guide through the high country of feelings and values and relationships. What also emerged from my interviews was that a son is the clay with which many women will fashion their most intricate life designs, no matter what other challenges compete for their attention. Such sublimation no doubt offends the reader who thinks it is wrong to place any male, even one's own son, on a pedestal. Yet what is precisely so fascinating and controversial about this subject is how difficult it turns out to be to check conditioned reactions to giving birth to and raising a male child.

We are living in an era of transition, which means that yesterday's values pull us one way, tomorrow's another. It is not always the most comfortable position to be in, nor is it always possible to know which way we want to go. Consequently, just when a mother feels she is forging new ground in raising her son, she may find, much to her dismay, that she has slipped back into a traditional set of responses. What further stems her stride into the future is one aspect of society that remains quite unchanged: the general reluctance to admit how astonishingly powerful the mother-son bond truly is.

Other cultures acknowledge this truth more readily. A man is sometimes expected to maintain the intensity of the relationship for a lifetime (for "of course" no other relationship, whether with his wife or his own children, could ever replace it). In southern India for example, Havik Brahmin sons are expected to stay with their mothers forever and to bring their brides back to their mothers' homes. In one study of Hindu families, of the 157 people in the sample who were asked to measure the power of their various emotional connections, 115 said that the strongest tie was between mothers and sons. In other countries, there are rituals practiced early and designed precisely to weaken the power of the hold a son and his mother have on each other's lives. Sheila Kitzinger, an anthropologist, reports that the idea that a boy must forget his mother in order to become a man is common to many more primitive societies.

In our own culture, we are considerably confused. Mothers are told to remain emotionally involved with their sons so that the sons have enough psychological support to fulfill society's expectations of them. Yet as a woman embraces her male child, some voices will rise in ominous warning that she may create a "mamma's boy," the ultimate crime. As a result mothers often seem to live with their sons on the edge of pain, wanting to stay close, afraid not to pull back. Nor do sons escape their own bewildering conflict. The battle between establishing distance and clinging to dependence takes hold of a boy almost at the moment that he learns to differentiate himself from his mother or sister as a male, rather than a female.

But amidst all this confusion, beyond the myth and the denial, lies a connection impossible to refute or even to alter significantly. As Oliver Wendell Holmes put it, the bond between mother and son outlasts all other phases of life; it is one that holds fast as "youth fades, love drops," and even "the leaves of friendship fall." How well that bond supports us, why we choose to cling to it, and how generous or selfish we are when we do are only some of the questions I will now, as witness and commentator, begin to explore.

FORMING THE BOND

Pregnancy and Birth

In many distant, primitive societies, giving birth to a son was a woman's only way of achieving status. Myth and mysticism, and often magic, infused with extraordinary meaning the idea of having a son. Discomfiting as the idea of male significance may be to a contemporary consciousness, the notion persists. Feminists will quite rightly decry a society in which a woman gains esteem through bearing and raising a son, but if we are ever to unravel the intricate lacings of the mother-son bond, we must accept the idea that having a male child has a unique social and psychological meaning for a woman. Even women who led the movement to break out of the passivity and sublimation of the female role were deeply influenced by the belief in superior masculine power. For example, the distinguished anthropologist Ruth Benedict began her training and career only after her marriage failed and she had given up the hope of ever having children. One cannot help wondering what path Dr. Benedict's life would have taken had she given birth to a son. In her girlhood diaries she noted how "a sense of personal worth" and an "enthusiasm for one's own personality" seemed to be primarily the destiny of men. She concluded her reflections by declaring, "It seems to me the one priceless gift of this life: of all blessings on earth, I would choose to have a man-child who possessed it."

Because the male child can, more easily than his mother, possess the world she brings him into, because he is a sexual "other," he will evoke feelings and conflicts in her that are instantly and permanently woven into their relationship. All the half-told stories of her female life so far, all her unresolved feelings about men, will influence how she both shapes and reacts to her son's developing maleness. And there appears to be no greater influence on a woman's current and continuing psychology than the feelings she experiences in response to a son.

Studies also show that more of the normal conflicts of pregnancy are also, if only unconsciously, associated with having a male child. Indeed, despite the romantic, rosy portraits we see of pregnancy, it is often a time of intense stress and ambivalence. When we move from one life stage to another, there are pulls backward as well as forward. Talk all we will about the excitement of passages and transitions, the stubborn wish to stay put beats in all of our timid hearts. So, as much as a woman may long to be a mother, she may find herself terrified at crossing over the line of her girlhood, which is what having a child seems to symbolize. In many other parts of the world, and for a long time in our own, marriage, not the onset of sexual activity, was the point where the line between childhood and adulthood was crossed. More and more, however, childbearing is being postponed, and marriage itself puts fewer restrictions on a woman's independent activities. Today even a woman who has been married for several years maintains the sense of freedom and lack of responsibility that we traditionally associate with being young. But this baby inside her is turning her into a grownup, with all the duties and restrictions the term implies, and she's not at all sure she likes the change. The permanence of the soon-to-be-born child's place in her life may overwhelm a woman who finds comfort in emotional independence. For some women this is particularly true when the child is a boy.

Jean, a thirty-three-year-old editor, was seven months pregnant. She was bewildered by her anxiety about a decision she thought had been so carefully considered.

"I'm beginning to think that my conflict has to do with the idea of having a son. Not that I don't want one," she hastily added. "Just that it frightens me. You see, awful as I guess it sounds, I realize that I've never felt one hundred percent committed to any relationship with a man . . . that it's always been important to me to know if I don't like the way things are going, I have the independence to walk out. To imagine 'owning' a male, with all the commitment 'possession' implies, of being irrevocably connected to him, no matter what kind of person he turns out to be, seems an idea beyond my comprehension."

Jean's anxiety reflected her ambivalence about male-female relationships. These conflicts were appearing more and more frequently in her dreams. The themes of her restless nights, it turned out, were remarkably similar to the dreams of other pregnant women. Perhaps because these sleeping confrontations with hidden feelings *are* so common among pregnant women, the dream is often used as a creative tool by writers in fashioning stories about motherhood.

In Doris Betts's "Still Life with Fruit," the heroine, Gwen, is going through labor with her first child. The experience is violent, both emotionally and physically. When Gwen drifts off into a fitful sleep, her dream reveals some of her fears about men and the relative powerlessness of women.

She dreamed she found her baby hanging on a wall. Its brain had grown through the skull like fungus; and suspended from its wafer head was a neckless wet sack with no limbs at all. Gwen started to cry and a priest came in carrying a delicate silver pitchfork. He told her to hush, he hadn't opened the membranes yet. When he pricked the soft bag, it fell open and spilled out three perfect male babies, each of them no bigger than her hand, and each with a rosebud penis tipped with one very tiny thorn. The priest began to circumcise them in the name of the Father, Son and Holy Ghost; and when a crowd gathered, Gwen was pushed to the rear where she couldn't see anything. . . .

In the dreams of the women I interviewed, there was often a strong subplot of male dominance, with more than half of the women reporting that their most violent nightmares during pregnancy involved a son. Several remembered dreaming (in the exquisitely terrifying detail Mrs. Betts describes) the same dream: each gave birth to a full-grown boy, who stretched her body beyond repair as he forced his way into life. Similar strains of dominance and submission are easily seen in the quite usual dream of a solidly built baby boy pushing his way up, not down, the birth canal, choking off his mother's breath as he insists on taking his own.

The uncovering of these long-buried and unresolved conflicts about being a woman in relation to men feeds our fears about mothering men. Nevertheless, most of the women I studied were traditionally triumphant when their sons were born. Indeed, one major study of pregnant women's dreams proved that those who sail through the nine months, never spoiling their sleep with nightmares, often suffer terrible pain in labor and delivery. Frequently, they are susceptible to postpartum depression, as well. This evidence led researchers to speculate that the sleeping battles with buried fears allow pregnant women to do the "psychological work" necessary to meet the challenges of childbirth.

However, there are some women whose feelings about men are even more turbulent, and whose dreams during pregnancy may therefore be unhappy portents of how their sons will come to feel about themselves. These women do not simply dream of their sons ripping them apart at birth. As the psychiatrist Gregory Rochlin confirmed in a study of masculinity, such women are convinced, medical records to the contrary, that the maiming actually happened. One mother in my research told me (while her eight-year-old son gazed sullenly out the window) how excruciatingly painful the boy's birth had been for her; how, in comparison to his sister's delivery, his had "ripped her apart." To this mother, the son's birth seemed to have elements of violent attack: she, a woman, was already victim to his, a man's, inherent sadism.

I carried the boy's image in my mind when I interviewed some grown sons who brooded over their inability to form intimate relationships with women. More often than not, they blamed themselves for the barrenness in their lives.

"I know it's my fault," one man said. "Somehow I can't seem to measure up to a woman's standards. I seem too harsh or impatient or demo nding, even when I don't want to be, when I really want to be a sensitive partner." Perhaps I was unduly influenced by my memory of the eight-year-old's expression as he listened to his mother's insistence that his life had begun with her suffering. But it seemed to me that a number of these men were struggling to make sense of the anger they had suspected, as they grew up, lay behind their mothers' dutiful care. They had glimpsed the connection their mothers unconsciously drew between masculinity and brutality. Now, they were almost asking how much love they really deserved, given their mothers' view that they were inherently barbarous.

However, despite these unfortunate extremes of response, most mothers will not envision a son as holding them hostage to masculine power. Instead, a woman will probably

look on this new relationship as the most potentially fulfilling of any she has ever known. Her welcome to her son,
its degree of warmth, is profoundly influenced *by* those
earlier relationships, for she hopes that with this baby boy
may at last come the resolution to much of the past's lingering pain.

My attempt to understand why a boy is still so overwhelmingly a woman's child of preference was like looking
through a bulging family album. Generations of parents
reach through time to shape a prospective mother's welcome
of a male child.

Barbara, the mother of a three-year-old son, was, like
Jean, a woman in her early thirties. As I arrived for our
appointment, one winter afternoon, her own mother was
just leaving. Their farewell was as frosty as the day, in
marked contrast to Barbara's warm affection toward her little
boy.

"All I can say," Barbara soon announced to me, "is that
I was as happy with the birth of a son as a native woman
in a tribe that kills its daughters. Because that's what I feel
my mother almost did to me. Until I work out my rage
against her, I can't *imagine* being a mother to a daughter
myself!"

An actress, Barbara tends toward the dramatic. But her
feeling that it would be too confusing to mother a daughter,
because of her lingering conflicts *as* a daughter, is a remarkably consistent factor in many women's wish to have
a son. Even women who felt far less anger toward their
mothers than Barbara did still preferred sons, perhaps out
of an intuitive feeling that the old resentments and fears
they felt about their mothers would be reactivated if they,
in effect, gave birth to themselves. Their guilt they said,
would be unbearable if they found themselves repeating
behavior that had marred their own childhood. With a son,
they might avoid this negative legacy and feel less frightened

by the crucial question all pregnant women consciously or unconsciously ask: "Will I be a better or worse mother than mine was?"

A daughter's distress over her mother can, on the other hand, have a negative influence on the idea of having a son. Many thoughtful women who said they *didn't* prefer sons felt that their attitude could be traced to their sense of displacement from their mothers when a baby brother was born. For a small group of women, this is a difficulty that got seriously out of hand. One thirty-five-year-old mother, Sarah, painfully retraced earlier problems in raising her little boy.

"He's very precocious, but instead of being proud, I found myself being outrageously critical and very, very harsh. I'd promise myself to be kinder, but I seemed absolutely unable to praise him, no matter what he did."

At the urging of her worried husband, Sarah sought help to relieve her obvious hostility toward her son. While the child was certainly not the only cause of her behavior, she made a clear connection in therapy between her current belligerence and the swallowed rage of childhood, when happiness had been irrevocably shattered by the arrival and accomplishments of her venerated brother.

"I felt my mother just lost interest in me," Sarah remembered. "Nothing was ever the same. I adored her—and she adored my brother." The birth of Sarah's son reignited sibling resentment toward her interloper brother, obscuring a gentler maternal response.

I found this trick of the unconscious that turns son into brother particularly common in women who had several sisters. In the traditionally male-oriented society they grew up in, the birth of a male child after "only" daughters often brought special grateful pleasure to a mother and made the bevy of little girls feel virtually eclipsed.

For some mothers of sons, such bitter memories create a

somewhat different defensive response. The mother doesn't feel hostile toward her little boy, but she is fiercely protective of her daughter, who as she'd once done, must move over to make room for their brother inside their mother's embrace.

"My girls are just so lovely and bright. I don't want them to feel outshone, the way I always did," such a mother may say, too often not realizing that her concern may make her somewhat guarded toward the son she really does love. I was to be told by a number of grown sons that they frequently had felt left out of the constellation of mother and daughter, or that their mothers' praise of them always seemed meager in comparison to the response to a sister. When a specific memory is offered as proof of a son's right to feel deprived, his resentment is as strong as if it were the night before, rather than twenty years ago, that he had sat alone, reading a book, while his mother and sisters giggled together behind a closed door.

The way a woman is valued by her mother crucially affects how she will respond to having a son. I expected this when I began my investigation into why mothering a son has unique significance for a woman. What I was not prepared for was how a woman's desire for a son is shaped by that other male figure in the family album—her father. More than 70 percent of the women I spoke with listed their fathers as the principal "other" in their wish to have a son. This was a considerably higher percentage than those who wanted a son in order to please their husbands. Thoughts of Daddy's stern or smiling face, feelings about his love and a daughter's comparative worth, play themselves out as a woman fantasizes about giving her male parent what is, ideally, his first male grandchild.

As the poet Adrienne Rich wrote, "I wanted a son, also, in order to do what my mother had not done: bring forth a man-child. I wanted him as a defiance to my father, who had begotten 'only' daughters. My eldest son was born, as it happened, on my father's birthday."

Adrienne Rich seemed to be challenging her father by bearing a boy, but many women in my study hoped to please their fathers by the act. Fathers in our culture have long been invisible men to their daughters. The limitations imposed by so-called appropriate male behavior make many men emotionally and physically self-conscious around female children, especially when their daughters are no longer little girls. I was touched by the wistfulness in many women's voices when they spoke of their fathers. Their companionship had seemed so elusive. Catching and holding a father's attention was terribly difficult to do—especially if there was a brother to compete with.

"I knew my father loved me," one woman said, "but it was my brother's life he paid real attention to, my brother's accomplishments he had the real investment in."

Even when there was no brother, the male image seemed to many women to have superseded their own, for it made their female selves a disappointment in their fathers' eyes. Over and over I heard women describe their uncertainty about their fathers' love: "I was the third daughter, the one 'supposed' to be a boy." Or, "I tried to do all the things a son would do. I was a terrific athlete, but I know playing ball with me or taking me fishing never meant to him what it would have if I'd been a son. Well, now he has a grandson to do these things with, and it's *my* doing. I get a terrific kick out of that idea. It's why I prayed all through my pregnancy to have a boy."

At first glance, these comments seem uncomfortably self-effacing. It made me uneasy to think of a woman's son being the source of her sureness about her own father's love. But experts say there is no act or attitude that doesn't reflect some inner longing shaped by the past. What matters is whether such longings control, rather than just influence, current choices. After all, it does seem possible that the accident of birth that allows a woman a second chance to form a love bond with her father, through delight in a boy who shares their genes and is part of their family history, can have important aspects of redemption. The loneliness and pain of her own childhood may recede beside the happy continuity of generations that she has made possible.

Clearly, then, many feelings mothers have about their sons stem in large part from living in a society where men are more valued than women. Consistently, mothers admitted to a special soaring exultation when they voiced the phrase "my son."

"It's completely incompatible with my views on equality," a divorced thirty-nine-year-old Chicago lawyer, who has taken huge steps away from her upbringing as a Southern belle, said with a grin. "When I was a little girl in Tennessee, I dreamed of growing up and having a cluster of handsome, brilliant sons to show off to the world. Well, I had only one son, seventeen years ago, but I greeted his birth with all the extravagant pride of that little flower of a girl's fantasy. No matter how fiercely dedicated I've become to the notion of women's independent achievements, the truth is that when I introduce my golden boy to someone, I'm absolutely triumphant!"

Having a male child also evokes a flush of sexual response that will both confuse and enchant a mother. When we mother sons, all the old anxieties about the differences between the sexes emerge from the dark recesses of our minds. Many a woman recalled being "stunned" by the first sight of her son's sexual organ. Although clearly in proportion to the rest of his body, the penis seemed to obscure all other parts.

Some mothers spoke, with considerable embarrassment, of how nervous they felt when bathing their baby sons. Largely this was because, as the infant smiled up at his mother's face, he frequently experienced an erection. In some distant peasant cultures, mothers fondle their sons' genitals, delighting in the excited response of the babies' bodies. In our own world, we not only reel in horror at the very idea of such sexual play; we are threatened by any sensual overtones in the chaste coupling of mother and son. Ironically, although modern men and women may see themselves as sexually liberated, the cultural belief persists that a good mother is an asexual person. The image of saintly Mama frowns at stirrings of sensual pleasure between a mother and a naked baby boy.

Many mothers were at first reluctant to admit (I suspect even to themselves) that the sexual aspect of the mother-child relationship is in any way different with a boy from what it is with a girl. Nowhere was their discomfort (usually masking intense delight) more evident than when they described breastfeeding. In truth, breastfeeding sons is highly erotic. William N. Stephens, an anthropologist, reported that studies of nursing babies in less inhibited societies than ours (where a mother is given to fondling a son's body and allowing him to play with her own) show that the "erotic manifestations" and "libidinous pleasure" of nursing were seen, "with no doubt whatsoever, more often with boys than with girls." Suckling boys were much more likely than suckling girls to indulge in "active, passionate manipulation of the mother's breast," and later would find the weaning process an infinitely wrenching blow.

Researchers have extrapolated from such studies general conclusions about the behavior of a nursing mother and a baby boy. Because a mother is sexually aroused by nursing her son, she further stimulates the infant by kissing him, caressing him, and being especially playful. Although she does not want in any way to be overtly incestuous, the intensity of her feelings is in itself sexually exciting to the infant male. (Apparently some women who are too unnerved by this mutual arousal neatly solve their dilemma by having their milk dry up.)

A somewhat whimsical aspect of this shared sexual dynamic is that many women are especially susceptible to a son's passion at this time, for after pregnancy and delivery a new mother often feels quite unattractive. Her stomach is still distended from birth, or she may have, in this breast-obsessed culture, always thought of her own breasts as either "too big" or "too small," but to this male person she is perfect, totally appealing, magnificently voluptuous. While nursing a baby of either sex generally makes a woman feel quintessentially female, with a son there is the added dimension of sexual awareness. Thus, whatever regret a mother may feel about having to renounce her girlishness, her baby boy compensates for it by making her feel irrefutably a woman.

Whimsy aside, nursing gives a woman a sense of herself and of her son that can be remarkably gratifying. For example, an artist-mother wrote about how it felt to nurse her son.

> The soft pressure of that warm sweet body against my own.
> The steady, steady, steady sucking, is astonishingly stimulating. I like to have us both undressed, so that we touch each other in as many places as possible. My mind creates the most exotic images and, sometimes, elaborate sexual fantasies. I feel a little embarrassed, although I've checked it out with my doctor and he tells me it's not unusual. I often come to orgasm, sometimes quite spectacular ones!

In fact, as a mother's color heightens, and her breath grows raspier with peaking feeling, her sucking son may be experiencing a similar spasm of fulfillment in an infant framework. It is a sight of mutual desire and delight that can deeply stir the emotions of the person we have not yet mentioned—the father of this son, the mother's mate.

The birth of a child, particularly a first one, is, in its way, as emotionally eventful for a man as it is for a woman. Donald Bell, a social historian, recalled his response, as a young husband, to the news that he was going to be a father:

> I found myself seized by a wide range of feelings. Elation rapidly gave way to uncertainty, and I wondered with increasing doubt how I could actually be a father. How would I know what to do? Would I suddenly need to think of myself as part of an older generation? I had enough trouble, I realized, just struggling to find myself as a man, and now I was suddenly faced with accepting yet another sense of self. I was no longer to be merely a son, a breadwinner, professional man, and a husband, but a father as well. How could I possibly do all that?

Research into the reactions of expectant fathers documents that their wives' pregnancy may indeed be a period of substantial stress. Several studies revolve around the idea of "psychological couvade," a condition in which a variety of physical symptoms connected with pregnancy, such as nausea, fatigue, or even swelling breasts and abdomen, are experienced by the husbands of pregnant women. Ample evidence exists that once the baby arrives, a man's stress may continue, no matter how joyous he is about the birth. Under his pride and pleasure may lurk a worrisome sense of displacement from his wife's affections. He is no longer the sole focus of her attention. He no longer has special claim to her love. When he gazes across the room to the rapt oneness of nursing mother and child, jealousy and fear may surge through his comparatively isolated body.

Nearly every man I interviewed who had both a son and a daughter substantiated the fact that the man feels far more conflict at the sight of the son at his wife's breast than he does at the sight of his nursing daughter. Out of his unconscious come all the confusions and passions he once felt in relation to his own mother. He may find himself wrestling uneasily with feelings of deprivation and competitiveness as his wife's breasts become his son's, rather than his own, objects of pleasure, and as his wife becomes confused with the mother who once held *him* to the breast.

While he watches the infant boy suckle, incestuous fantasies and unresolved needs may create a tension that he very likely will communicate to his wife. For some couples, these regressive responses can cause quite serious problems. About 15 percent of the women I interviewed had gone through a period of markedly reduced sexual activity after their sons were born, and about 3 percent of the group felt that their sex lives had never returned to what they were before their sons came along.

"I couldn't wait for the doctor to give us the go-ahead," a woman told me. "My husband has a really high sex drive and was chomping at the bit those last few weeks of my pregnancy. And then, there I was, ready to make up for lost time, and zilch! For the first time in our entire sex life he was impotent; and for several months afterward, if I didn't absolutely seduce him, he would never have made a move. And even when we did make love, it was, to be kind, perfunctory."

What most likely had turned off this boy-turned-man-turned-father was that he had made too deep a connection between the image of "woman" and the image of "mother." With a baby at his wife's breast, those images merged into a portrait that is terrifying in its Oedipal overtones. It suggests such dangerous taboos that passion can be instantly abated until the son-man is able to make the emotional transition to father.

Other women, however, report a quite different, though not unrelated, response from their husbands. The mother's feelings about her breasts change. Breasts do become a life source to her son as well as organs for sexual play with a lover. A man, sometimes to his own horror, may find himself vying with his baby son for possession of the mother's breasts and feel intense excitement in the battle.

"I was really shocked at Roger's behavior at first," Barbara, the actress-mother, said about her husband. "We got into this bizarre routine, where I felt I was in some kind of sex show. He'd sit there, watching me nurse. A look would come over his face, and I'd know damn well what was going on in his mind *and* his body. He'd start for me the minute I put Jeffrey down, and the first thing he'd do was squeeze my breasts and suck on them." Flushing at the memory, she added, "And if he got any milk, he practically shot off the bed with excitement. It's weird, I guess, but I have to admit, the sex was fantastic afterward."

Clearly, the mystery of birth evokes fears and fantasies and consequent responses that few mothers or fathers can anticipate. What's more, however well a new father manages to deal with his feelings of loss and masculine rivalry, or however lovingly the mother and baby make room for him in the new family arrangement, there is a truth so universal that almost every major artist in the world has tried to express it. Whether the statement is made by Michelangelo, Renoir, or Picasso, whether we glimpse it on canvas or in stone, we immediately understand that even without father, mother and son together are remarkably complete.

Oedipal Myths and
Misunderstandings

A very moving novel entitled *Call It Sleep*, written in 1934
by Henry Roth, tells of an immigrant family living on the
Lower East Side of New York. The story, that of a six-year-
old boy and his parents captures a vision of motherhood not
often found in contemporary literature:

> Friday. Rain. The end of school. He could stay home . . . and
> do nothing, stay near his mother the whole afternoon. He
> turned from the window and regarded her. She was seated
> before the table paring beets . . . her hands were stained with
> [them]. Above her blue and white checkered apron, her
> face bent down, intent upon her work, her lips pressed
> gravely together. He loved her. He was happy again.

This image of mother and son sounds innocent, yet to
psychologically attuned ears, the child is clearly in his Oedipal period. Psychologists see, behind that pure little face,
a boy's vision of ravishing his mother's body on the shabby
kitchen table. And to them, surely the mother's hands seemed
to move as much through incessant anxiety as through the
need to prepare the stuff of dinner. The neurotic potential
of the passionate connection between mother and son has

been amply documented in the professional literature. Nothing less than a son's entire social and sexual life is at stake in the way his mother acknowledges his ever-growing love.

Perhaps no theory of Sigmund Freud's continues so heavily to influence psychoanalytic thought as the Oedipus complex, although there has been a re-examination of some of its basic premises in recent years. In Freud's view, unresolved Oedipal feelings are at the core of all neuroses. He divided the Oedipal stage into two phases. The first, the pre-Oedipal, runs from infancy through the fourth or fifth year. Many developmental tasks challenge a child during this time, primarily within the framework of his relationship with his mother. Through his interaction with his mother, a boy begins to learn, among other things, whether the world can be trusted, how to balance gratification and frustration, and how to love, and to understand his capacity to hurt or anger a loved one.

As he begins to have a sense of himself as a distinct person in an expanding world, he also begins to form a sense of sexual identity. Throughout these early years, he has satisfied himself sensually by such oral, anal, and genital pleasures as sucking on a nipple and feeling the warmth in his diaper. When he enters into the Oedipal stage, at about the age of five, however, sexual arousal and wonder and exploding awareness well up in a rising arc of passion that seeks a partner's response. Suddenly his mother, that awesome creature inside of whose body he once lived, and who has continued to nourish him with body and soul since the exile of birth, becomes a focus of intense sexual excitement. He not only needs her as he has in the past; he wants her, and he would like, in his mounting passion, to vanquish anyone who competes for her attention. Thus, according to the rest of the theory, a little boy's father, no matter how loving a parent he is, will be transformed into a bitter rival by a son in his Oedipal phase. Furthermore, because the son does wish his father harm, he is terrified of his father's reprisal. His terror, in Freud's view, is transformed into a fear of being castrated by the more powerful male. Resolution of the Oedipal complex, at about the age of six or seven, involves accepting the father's supremacy and identifying with him instead of the mother. The boy now tries to become part of the male world and suppresses his incestuous instincts.

Freud called this developmental story the Oedipus complex because, in the ancient myth, Oedipus unwittingly murdered his father and married his own mother, Jocasta. When Oedipus eventually learned the truth of his incestuous love, he blinded himself in a symbolic act of castration. Jocasta, despairing over her part in the tragedy, took her own life. Mother and son, by their incestuous impulses, were agents of each other's doom.

To Freud, Oedipus was every son. On him lies the urgent need to escape the destiny of incestuous yearning. But "a myth," wrote the sociologist Philip Slater, "tells us something about the people who listen to it," and we should bear this in mind as we wrestle with the theory of the Oedipus complex. There can be significant disadvantages to the consciousness of self influenced by a psychoanalytic age. Explanations of psychological pitfalls that leap off the pages of books meant to guide our behavior often make the reader more fearful than enlightened. As a consequence, the very suggestion of incest can freeze instinctual rushes of love. That most primal intimate connection, the joining of mother and son, is often tainted by a nervous and far too literal acceptance of Freudian theory.

This is not to suggest that Freud's revelations about a boy's powerful attachment to his mother and his rivalry with his father do not remain among his most important contributions to human understanding. One need only observe a little boy during this Oedipal phase of development to see how clear these stages are.

"Mommy!" shrieks Ginger's five-year-old son, Jason, when she leaves him alone with me in the living room to go to greet her husband. Before I can assure them all is well, the parents are racing back. The terror on their faces tells me they expected to find nothing less than their little boy lying in a deepening pool of blood. Instead, they see only his fierce, flushed face, which he immediately buries in his mother's abdomen, clasping her hips with tight little fists. It is apparent, as one looks at Jason, that only here, with Ginger's body exclusively his, can he find release from the burning new mixture of love and need and sexual tension.

Even so, Jason's passionate longing for his mother goes beyond sexual craving, and it is in this larger aspect that we find some of the re-examination of Freudian theory. To the philosopher and psychoanalyst Erich Fromm, for example, Freud's principal error was in placing too strong an emphasis on the sexual aspect of a son's desire for his mother. As a boy tightly grasps his mother's hand, he does not simply want to draw her to an incestuous bed. Far more important, he wants to follow her back to the safe, paradisiac state he knew inside the womb and during the first months of life. Like Oedipus before he learned the truth, he yearns for a time when he did not know the terrors or responsibilities of consciousness and when his mother's loving protection was magnificently complete.

Wolfgang Lederer, a psychiatrist, offers a personal memory of this yearning. As a boy, he says, he and a good friend discovered they performed the same little ritual when they were tense or frightened. If a teacher scolded them, or some older child seemed menacing, they would bury their noses into the hollow of their clenched hands. Dr. Lederer wrote that the act brought with it "a sense of peace and completeness, comparable to immersion in a warm, long forgotten ocean; a stage of being before thought and before pain . . . related to the mother: the visit home, the only way we can go home again."

Literature, too, abounds with poetic illustrations of a son's longing for the security of his mother's presence. A well-known example is found in Marcel Proust's *Swann's Way*:

> My sole consolation when I went upstairs for the night, was that Momma would come in and kiss me after I was in bed. But the goodnight lasted for so short a time; she went down again so soon, that the moment in which I heard her climb the stairs, and then caught the sound of her garden dress of blue muslin, from which hung little tassels of plaited straw, rustling along the double-doored corridor, was for me a moment of keenest sorrow. So much did I love that goodnight, that I reached the stage of hoping that it would come as late as possible, so as to prolong the time of respite during which Momma would not yet have appeared.

As the young boy lay waiting to slip from consciousness into sleep, his mother's image — its anticipation and its fulfillment — sustained him. But these suggestions that a son's Oedipal longings are more than sexual are not meant to imply that sexuality doesn't play a part in a son's conflicts. Many men I interviewed described a recurring dream of childhood in which they tied their mothers to a fence or tree. Invariably they woke up at the point when she was safely captive. Freud called a nightmare "a dream that failed," a story the dreamer cannot pursue to its too-terrifying conclusion. These sons had to short-circuit their incestuous fantasies because of an inability to face the unbounded anxiety of a wish fulfilled. A boy's sexual longing for his mother always has ominous as well as glorious implications. Should he try to make love to his mother in his dream after successfully tying her up, he may confront the shattering horror of sexual failure.

Karen Horney, one of the analysts who expanded on Freud's work, once described an experiment that relates to these truncated dreams. After cutting a slit in a rubber ball, a researcher asked each member of a group of boys and girls to place a finger inside it. Both sexes were uncomfortable with the idea, but the little boys were obviously far more fearful, to the point where many simply couldn't obey the instructions. A boy's anxiety is father to the man's. Research into the self-perceptions of men (my own study included) show that it is quite common for a man to think his penis is too small. In Dr. Horney's view, this anxiety is rooted in the same fear that made plunging a finger into a spongy slit so terrifying. The idea of smallness and of alarming depth both suggested to Horney a son's sense that he is childishly incapable of filling his mother's sexual needs. The potential humiliation and rejection of his incestuous fantasies can contribute to a generalized fear of women that may become a lasting resistance to love. "Woman" is perceived as both dangerous and seductive. She is a bottomless hollow that can never be filled and in which a man may become helpless and lost. The inherent threat in a woman's attraction, said Dr. Horney, was "a typical ingredient in the analysis" of every man who came to her for treatment.

If all analysts do not share this view of the relationship between a son's incestuous fantasies and a lasting fear of women, most do accept the premise that, one way or another, a man's mother greatly affects his romantic life. With the unconscious image of his mother at his side, a man searches out love along a highway whose double lanes at times hopelessly confuse him. It is a grown-up son's dilemma to resolve his childhood longing for his mother (a longing Erich Fromm called "one of the deepest emotional desires rooted in the very existence of man") and his fear of losing her by, on the one hand, seeking her in all other women and, on the other, trying to escape his need for her by finding someone completely different. That no woman can both be a man's mother and not be his mother is, in the opinion of many professionals, the true cause for the disintegration of many marriages and otherwise rewarding relationships.

In his autobiographical novel of mother-son love, *Sons and Lovers*, D. H. Lawrence showed his protagonist, Paul, obsessively alienating Miriam, his first real sweetheart. As he attacks her smallest mannerism (reminiscent of his mother's contempt for the girl), he thinks to himself, "He scarcely knew what he was saying. These things came from him mechanically." Finally, he tells Miriam that they had better break off, and he returns home, leaving her, as well as himself, abject and confused. Wrote Lawrence of Paul, "He had come back to his mother. Hers was the strongest tie in his life . . . nobody else mattered. . . . Everybody else could grow shadowy, almost non-existent to him, but she could not. It was as if the pivot and pole of his life, from which he could not escape, was his mother."

There is also general agreement among most professionals that the other part of the Oedipus complex, a boy's rivalry with his father, is a legitimate psychological conclusion for Freud to have drawn. In my own study, many men, when remembering their boyhood dreams, recalled one that is a significant variation of the dream in which they held their mothers captive. In this one, somebody else has tied her up, and it is the son who heroically rushes to her side to "save" her from the approaching danger, which is, in the view of most analysts, the boy's father. Analysts typically interpret such dreams as a boy's wish both to best his father and to convince himself that his mother is with his father only because she is afraid of him. Without force or fear, a mother would certainly remain chaste, saving herself for her preferred son. Such resistance in a son to the idea of his mother as his father's willing sexual partner can create enormous wakeful stress as well as sleeping dreams. The pain of these scenes also lingers long in a son's memory.

"My father adored my mother," said Robert, a law professor in a major university. "I gradually began to feel very shut out by his devotion to her. I remember one incident that seems to sum up that whole period of my childhood. We had gone out to a special restaurant for my seventh birthday celebration. My mother was wearing a new dress that I'd helped her shop for, and I thought she looked absolutely beautiful. When we sat down, I insisted on reading the menu myself. . . . It wasn't easy, but I struggled until I put together a meal I really wanted. I looked up, smiling, to tell my mother what I'd chosen, and I couldn't wait to see how proud she'd be of my being so grown-up — and saw that she and my father were holding hands under the table. Immediately I felt excluded and enraged. I picked up my fork to throw at my father's suddenly evil face, but I was too terrified to do it. . . . Instead, I put down my menu and made some whiny plea for my mother to read it to me because I couldn't do it myself. That, of course, meant she had to drop my father's hand, but I didn't feel very triumphant. I just felt guilty and still very afraid, and of course miserably jealous. Needless to say, my birthday was ruined."

What stopped Robert's hand was a son's fear of castration for his forbidden sexual yearnings. Unresolved, this genital anxiety can also persist into adult life, bringing in its wake a joyless host of phobic avoidances or other troubled sexual responses.

Not surprisingly, "fantastic" fear of genital harm will

again work its way into the less censored atmosphere of a boy's dream life. At some time in their development, over one third of the men I interviewed had dreamed that their penises began to grow wildly, finally getting in the way of an approaching car or stretching over a windowsill just as someone unknowingly tried to shut the window. Those men who had been in therapy now looked back on the dreams as "obvious" expressions of Oedipal guilt and of the fear of a father's vengeance. Again, even Freudian critics do not quarrel with the idea of a son's hostility toward his father and his fear of retribution. Where they part company with Freud is likely to be, once again, over his belief that the rivalry is primarily sexual.

As postulated by Erich Fromm, the father-son struggle is, rather, a cultural matter. "Freud gives a universal meaning to a feature that is characteristic only of patriarchal society," Fromm said, explaining that, in a world where powerful men dominate, young men must subject themselves to their fathers' rule. In their submission, most likely, begin a festering resentment and a wish to affirm their own manhood by toppling the father from his controlling perch.

In this area, too, literature is full of expressions of what can sometimes be a lifelong struggle. Particularly notable is Franz Kafka's bitter recounting of a son's oppression, "Letter to My Father." In the personal diary that often served as counterpoint to his literary themes, Kafka wrote, "As a little child, I had been defeated by my father, and have never been able to quit the battlefield all these years, despite the perpetual defeat I suffer."

Thus, the competition between father and son seems to have more to do with authority and rebellion than with incestuous desire. Indeed, we are reminded by Fromm that Oedipus never actually fell in love with Jocasta, but was married to her as a privilege that accompanied the throne, after he had saved the widowed queen's kingdom from destruction.

Thinking about Jocasta reminds us of one aspect of the Oedipal tie that has been virtually overlooked: the passion directed *at* Oedipus rather than that which stirred inside his own heart. I am speaking of the extraordinarily powerful attraction a mother feels for a male child. If a son wants nothing more than to be one with her, for her part a woman feels a compelling and lasting need to surround his identity with her own. When women talked to me about their sons, I was struck by the completeness of the identification their language expressed.

"We couldn't get into a good college. . . ." "We don't know what sort of career would really make him happy. . . ." Even when a woman seemed closely involved with her daughter or with her husband, she rarely encircled their lives as completely as she did her son's. The single pronoun was used to separate other family members from each other and from the plural person called *motherandson*.

In his maleness, a son opens up feelings in his mother about being a woman. It is wonderful to share the mantle of common experience with a daughter, but by his contrasting image a son singles out his mother to herself, and in his ardor she finds additional affirmation. Even today, when being a man's "prize" is a questionable value for many women, there is a lingering excitement in being perceived this way.

"When my son looks at me with worshipful seriousness and says he wants to marry me when he grows up, in spite of myself I feel like preening," a thirty-five-year-old mother said about her youngest child and first son. "Especially," she added wryly, "when his father, dear as he is, has long since stopped thinking of winning me as such a terrific victory."

There is additional stimulation in the idea that a son is

a sexual "other." Because he is a member of the more powerful sex, venturing into his world can be especially titillating. A broadcaster and writer, Sherrye Henry, expressed for many women the particular satisfaction of being close to the experience of a male child. "After all," she said, "it is just impossible to imagine knowing any other male so intimately." The British author Margaret Drabble recalled that when she had her first son, she was extremely pleased, because "it seemed 'exciting' to have a boy."

In the way that we relish the idea of finally knowing in exact detail the secret, male existence, our innocence of the male experience makes the secret wonderfully fresh. The majority of women who had both sons and daughters reported that, while they loved their children equally, they "enjoyed" their little boys much more. A son seemed to bring to the mother the delight of surprise. His responses were intriguing. He was a captivating foreigner on the familiar, female landscape.

Perhaps even more important, this provocative sense of difference sweeps away the years, bringing us back our own childhoods, where we re-enact our own impassioned Oedipal dramas. In their important study of family life, *Secrets in the Family*, the distinguished team of social worker Lily Pincus and psychiatrist Christopher Dare wrote that, although being a parent is considered by many to be a necessary stage of adult development, "the expression of this need is colored by unconscious wishes to re-enact . . . sensual enjoyment of bodily contact" with their own parents. To my surprise, many mothers were quite conscious of this sensual time flow and, more often than not, found that it lent a shining luster to their feelings for a son.

Rose, a mother in her early thirties, who admitted to finding her passion for her six-year-old son "astonishing," gently handled the little boy's reluctance to go off with a neighbor so that she and I could have our interview.

"It's all connected for me," she said after he had left. "Past and present, my father and my son. You see, I know just what my son is feeling when he cuddles in my lap. It's the most extraordinary level of intimacy to feel the memory in my body of what he's feeling now in his. The way I would love how my father's body felt, and how he smelled such a 'man' smell, so different from my mother's. I'm not a very introspective person; till I stopped working, I was office manager for a group of lawyers, and I tend to deal with things intellectually rather than emotionally. But since I've had my little boy, I find myself all caught up in sensory memory and feeling. I'm convinced," Rose added firmly, "that this sort of ebb and flow of remembered and current sensation is a major part of any mother's connection to a son."

Other women recalled scenes from their early adolescence, when incestuous pressures were awakened by their fathers and joined with the maturation of their own bodies.

"I remember how my father would half undress as he tried to beat me to the shower after our tennis game," a woman said, smiling shyly. "And how I'd find some excuse to hang around the hall, fighting off the picture in my head of him standing under the water. It was terrifically exciting *and* incredibly anxiety-producing." Yet even when these memories evoked the repressed anxiety, the vast majority of women agreed with Rose that such sensual memories were indeed an important link in the binding tie they felt toward a son.

But, having finished my research, I am convinced that there is an even more powerful aspect to a mother's enchantment with a son, one that has a separate, singular force of its own. In all of my interviews, no triumph rang so loudly as when the mother of a son declared, "He is so much like me . . . we are so amazingly in tune." There is a rich, wondering delight in a woman's voice when she speaks of her son as an extension of herself.

"I cannot tell you how my son complements me," one

mother said, and another most tellingly offered, "It's as if, through him, I've found the missing half of myself." So frequent, so strong, was this idea of a son as "found half" that it must be regarded as central to the intensity of feeling a woman has for a male child.

Conventional psychoanalytic theory would see this as meaning that the mother envied men. Warnings would be issued about the emotional fallout on a boy who must make up for his mother's lack of self-esteem. Yet despite this psychological wisdom, large numbers of apparently well-adjusted women, with apparently well-adjusted sons, told me that their sons "completed" them in a way no adult male ever did. The idea that the son as the "other self" comple-ments a woman's female identity, while also being part of her flesh, joins them in a sliding-together fullness. Sun and shadow, yin and yang, mind and body—all those qualities we try to balance in order to attain the richest expression of self—seem to find their most powerful fusion when a woman reaches out to a son. It is an attraction that will pulsate inside a mother throughout her son's life.

Still, most mothers accept, however ruefully, the idea that their passion must gradually be muted as their sons mature. Unfortunately, mothers also report that their at-tempts to release a son gently are sometimes hampered by a husband's insistence that the release happen too soon and too sharply. For example, when Jason screamed and clung to his mother, his father was extremely impatient, once he realized that his son was unharmed. It appears that all sorts of unconscious stirrings contributed to the father's intol-erance of the demanding, dependent little boy. The feeling that a male shouldn't be so needy is one, and unconsciously playing back his own need for his mother may be another. Oedipal memories, lying deep inside a man's mind, of the too-early loss of his own mother will affect the tolerance he has for his son's reluctance to let go of the woman who is now the father's mate.

More and more experts believe that Oedipal theory should also be adjusted to acknowledge that masculine and feminine identification are not true opposites. Nonetheless, a boy does get through the Oedipal phase in part by beginning to identify with his father rather than continuing to view him as a rival. If his father does not welcome that identification, if he *is* intolerant or rejecting, the transition will be difficult for a son to achieve. Certainly, the Oedipal obstacle looms immeasurably larger when the father is not around to participate actively in family life.

Studies show that boys in the Oedipal period have a more difficult time in coping with their parents' divorce than does a girl of the same age. With no father around to encourage the repression of incestuous fantasies, the boy may find that his feelings are alarmingly free to flow. Lying in his bed on the other side of the wall where his mother sleeps alone, a boy can picture her bed's empty space and his imagination may concentrate on filling it. Again, it is a picture that is likely to fill the ambivalent seducer with dread. One most unfortunate way for a boy to deal with the terror of unrestrained yearning is to drive the longing so deep underground that sexual energy can be virtually extinguished—in some rare instances, all his life.

Although such tragic effects of Oedipal conflict *are* relatively rare, single mothers, even more than their married counterparts, are extremely concerned about the outcome of ongoing intimacy with a son.

"He's always wanting to climb into bed with me on Sunday morning," a divorced mother named Doris said about her five-year-old son. "If my husband were still on the other side of the bed, I know I'd have no compunctions about it. But I find myself so torn, between wanting to be extra-affectionate to compensate for his father's being a thousand miles away and his being an only child, and at the same time not wanting to be too stimulating. I *love* to cuddle with him," she said with a sigh. "It makes *me* feel less lonely too. I wish I could let myself enjoy it more. . . ."

While it is reasonable for a single mother to feel such apprehension about life with her son, an attraction as mutual and intense as that between mother and son has the potential for trouble, even with a father around. Interestingly, some mothers are reluctant to admit not only to this possibility, but to the validity of the Oedipus complex. The chauvinistic and sexually centered "blindspots" of Sigmund Freud enrage these women, and much of their criticism is well taken. Nonetheless, my research convinced me that the myth of Oedipus and Jocasta continues to explain many of the subleties of the mother-son relationship. That a boy is profoundly attracted to his mother, that she opens up the world and sensual awareness to him, that mother as well as son will feel stirrings of incestuous yearnings, remain truths, however well buried, about the life a mother shares with her male child. It seems to me that the principal challenge in the Oedipus myth for a modern Jocasta is not to deny these truths but to obviate the myth's threat of doom. The horror of incest has made generations of mothers unreasonably terrified of what Drs. Pincus and Dare call the "primitive aspects" of mother-son love. They suggest that the best way for a mother to control her incestuous fantasies is to acknowledge freely that they exist. Only by being as alert as possible to the dimensions of her feelings can a mother monitor her responses without unnecessary anxiety or guilt. To help a son move on from the longing that binds him to his mother, she must be free to admit how very painful it is for both of them to let each other go.

Growing Up Male

Buying the Cultural Bias

> ... blest the Babe,
> Nursed in his Mother's arms, who sinks to sleep
> Rocked on his Mother's breast; who with his soul
> Drinks in the feelings of his Mother's eye! ...
> No outcast he, bewildered and depressed. ...
> —William Wordsworth

The infant's satisfied breathing as he peacefully falls asleep speaks of emotional as well as physical hunger appeased. Poets have always known that the darker side of love is the wrenching anxiety of wondering whether the "we" one desires so desperately will split apart, making two separate, lonely selves.

Wordsworth suggests that the security of the mother's love shapes her son's sense of belonging in the world. But there are cultural influences that affect a boy's achieving such security. From the earliest days of his life, a male child receives different treatment, which deeply colors his vision of himself, his mother, and the world. It is not necessarily a treatment females should envy, despite all the problems attached to "growing up girlish." For, in truth, the road to masculine power has more than its share of hurdles.

In the beginning stages of life, the crucial process all children engage in, regardless of sex, is called "attachment." The desire to be close to a loving person is one of the distinguishing characteristics of infancy. John Bowlby, a pioneer in the study of attachment, has explained that during the infant's first few months, he is learning to discriminate a particular figure, usually his mother, and is developing a strong liking to be in her company. After about six months, he shows his preference in unmistakable fashion. Throughout the latter half of his first year, and during the whole of his second and third, he is closely attached to his mother figure, which means that he is content in her company, and distressed in her absence.

The mother-child attachment continues for a lifetime, but it gradually diminishes in intensity from that initial skin-tight connection. For two months or so, there is really no difference to a baby between his mother's body and his own. She is his whole environment, and, in the most literal sense, he feels blissfully attached to her. Where does her nipple end; where does his mouth begin? When he grasps his mother's finger, there is no break in the connection that links hands. But slowly, dimly, some time around the second month, his bodily sensations tell him there are differences. The hand he moved across his face to his mouth, as he lies in his crib, has a different taste from his mother's breast or finger. And the life-sustaining nipple may disappear from view, even though his stomach feels alarmingly empty.

By his fifth or sixth month, the baby has some understanding that a person is responsible for appeasing his needs. Usually that person is his mother, and her reaching out to soothe his discomfort binds him to her. This developmental period, called "separation-individuation," will last until the end of his third year, and during that time her reassuring image will gradually separate from his own. Relinquishing the magnificent comfort of merger, and accepting instead that he and his mother are two separate people, form the major challenge of early childhood.

Although this stage of development has a built-in timetable, it is very sensitive to disruption. Absolutely nothing will alter its course more dramatically than a mother's not being available to reassure her child that she can be counted on to protect him from his own extravagant strides toward independence. The more certain a child is of her continued support, the less frightening seems the beckoning of the larger world. The mother serves as a frame of reference, a "beacon of orientation," while the child shapes a separate self.

According to the psychiatrist Margaret Mahler, who gave us the term "separation-individuation," the earlier in a child's life that this timetable is interrupted, the more problems lie ahead for him. For example, studies of children who spent their first months in institutions, without the chance to form a strong human connection, show that they rarely develop a capacity to love or a full sense of their relationship to the world. They may stay rooted in the earliest form of experience, basic-need gratification, listlessly accepting anyone who supplies it. The world looms uninvitingly on the horizon. Nothing about it or anyone in it seems attractive enough to reach out to.

Of course the scars of such intense deprivation are not the exclusive province of any sex, both boys and girls suffer profoundly from a lack of early attachment. But even in a loving home, special hazards exist for a son engaged in the process of first becoming, and then enjoying, his life as a separate person.

From the beginning, there is a rather malevolent twist to a boy's experience. During his first weeks of life, he may get even more Eden-like attention from his mother than a baby girl does. For, as in breastfeeding, a mother seems to hold and touch a son with special and stimulating frequency. Then, as if his expectations have been raised only in order to plummet, his mother's attention appears to wane. Research shows that as he moves further into his first year, his mother is likely to be more cautious in her response to his cries. Far fewer swoops of rescue from the lonely crib. Instead of cuddling him to her bosom, she may lean over the crib with a smile, and then leave again, to let him cry it out. My interviews indicated that, whatever other reasons may prevent her from giving more lavish solace, a mother's dutiful adherence to ideas about masculine self-control and invulnerability are a major factor in this response to her son.

The Educational Testing Service performed a related experiment in its Infant Laboratory. Two mothers, with approximately the same mothering style, and their year-old children "interacted" under an observer's trained and watchful eye. The first sketch is of a mother and son.

"Baby walks away from mother," the observer noted; "he trips and falls. Baby returns to his mother, fretting. Mother touches baby and baby touches her. Mother takes out plastic ring, shows it to baby, rolls it across the room, saying 'See the ring! Bring the ring to Mommy! Can you get the ring?'"

And now the observation of mother and daughter . . .

"Baby walks away from mother, trips, and falls. Baby returns to mother, fretting. Mother picks up and hugs baby. Mother, still holding baby, offers baby a stuffed animal."

We are told in the report on this experiment that the first mother's goal was to encourage independence. After briefly comforting her son, she discouraged further contact by tossing the ring to the other side of the room. Finally, she prodded him to forget his discomfort and take off on his own again to claim the toy. The mother of the little girl, on the other hand, "prolongs the physical contact, by picking her up and hugging her." What's more, by offering her the stuffed animal, she entices the baby to stay close by and avoid any further distress from separate exploration.

When the mothers in my interviews displayed or described to me similar sex-typed behavior, it was almost always with a self-conscious apology for "overprotecting" their daughters and for encouraging the dependence that "I should know by now" cripples female autonomy and self-esteem. I suggest that the apology might be better offered to our sons, who very likely may not feel protected enough.

The conflicting wishes for freedom and for safety, for autonomy and for fusion, haunt every child's ambivalent heart. Sometimes, as children sense the immensity of what it means to become a separate person, to manage life on their own, menace seems to lurk in every corner, and the only peace of mind lies in a hand to grasp or a sheltering embrace. But, once again, heirs to the cultural bias that says they shouldn't be dependent, boys are expected to conquer their need for emotional protection much earlier and more fully than girls.

Traditionally, we urge a boy onto the path of growing up much sooner than we would his sister, and as a result he gets hurt earlier and more often than she does. Life's dangers may therefore present themselves before he feels ready to cope with them. (It is interesting to speculate how much sibling and sexual rivalry has at its core a sister's envy of her brother's looser rein and a brother's secret desire to be more tightly bound to his mother's side.) In any case, studies have established that little boys are more prone to "inconsolable states" and are more vulnerable to the anxieties of separation than girls are. While not categorically matters of cause and effect, we certainly know that separation problems are more intense for a child who is frightened. The simple truth is, we expose our sons to more situations in which they will be afraid.

The anthropologist Margaret Mead wrote that a boy often feels he must "act up to—and a little beyond—his full strength, and he is always a little anxious, for fear the strength that is demanded isn't there." As a devoted fan of Dr. Mead's, I was therefore not surprised when so many men remembered experiencing exactly this kind of tension while growing up.

"I always felt pushed just a little bit beyond what I could handle," recalled a thirty-five-year-old executive named Howard. "I had a vague, though sometimes very clear fear that this would be the day when I'd get in trouble, hurt myself badly, or wander too far from my mother and get really lost. I remember when I was very small, I used to like her to wear bright colors. She had a purple sweater that I'd tell her to put on whenever we went to the park. She got a kick out of my being so interested in her clothes, but the truth was, I liked to be able to pick her out easily when I'd go off to play and something went wrong. Sometimes," he added pensively, "it was enough just to turn and see her there, but if I got really upset about a kid or messed up a game and was being teased, I'd need to get back to her physically. Absolutely nothing was more terrifying, has ever been more terrifying, than seeing that bench empty as I ran toward it. Locating her again was locating my lifeline."

Underscoring Howard's recollection is the fact that over 80 percent of the men in my study remembered a recurring childhood nightmare of coming home from school and finding their mothers gone. With mounting terror, the little boy would run from room to room, looking for his mother or at least some sign that she'd be returning soon. Interestingly, although the dream was frightening, the prevailing mood most of the men described was of deep loneliness, a feeling of being totally helpless. Several child psychologists claim that little boys are particularly prone to dangerous behavior in order to force their mothers to show that their protective reflexes are still functioning. A sudden dash into the street or onto an unprotected ledge brings her flying to his rescue and makes him feel less terrifyingly on his own.

What's more, the physical world the little boy is being pushed to master doesn't seem at all eager to receive him. It is hard and cold and bruising, a place of pain, where his body, so tentatively claimed as his very own, is threatened by bumps and falls and injuries to his ego. The distrustful, defensive stance so many men assume in relation to the world is believed by more and more professionals to be influenced by the stored-up anger of these early encounters—when they couldn't understand why the environment was so hostile and why they weren't being given "enough" comforting for their distress.

To examine this assumption, I ran storytelling sessions for two groups of boys and girls. I quickly discovered that being hurt and getting into serious danger were the boys' dominating themes. They created their stories out of assaultive words, like "banging," "crashing," "smashing," and "bumping." The violence of nature looms large in the fantasy world of the little boy who is asked to wander unaided inside it. Storms sweep him up, and tornadoes blow his house down. Huge waves wash over him, and leaping fires disfigure a security-giving face.

Their own aggression also ran through the boys' stories, frequently (revealing the development of another masculine pattern) tied to a contest, where victory comes at someone else's failure. Aggression is of course a common defensive response to feeling vulnerable and underprotected. That many of these children were seven and eight years old, an age when aggression should be muted by the ability to empathize, reinforces Dr. Mahler's theory of the disrupted developmental timetable. In the early stages of separation-individuation, aggressive bouts of hitting and throwing are often observed in children who haven't been given enough emotional fuel for the journey away from a mother's side. In Dr. Mahler's opinion, the energy these children use up in resentful acting-out "drains so much of the energy available for development . . . as to hamper psychological growth."

When he feels vulnerable, a boy often directs his anger at his mother. Since she is his primary protector, her lack of availability confuses and enrages him. This was verified in the nervous tales of retribution I heard from several of the little boys: "I squirted a big hose of ice cold milk in my mother's face . . ." "I dreamed I put a fish in my mother's coffee pot . . ." and the recurring "Once upon a time, a little boy locked his mother up in a big dark jail for being bad. . . ."

Many professionals believe that this sort of anger translates itself over the years into hostility or, at the least, distrust of all women. In apparent confirmation, many men admitted having a tendency to look at new relationships with a watchful, measuring eye, not for the potential for happiness, but for the possibility of frustration and hurt. Nearly every man also said that he was always the first to end a relationship when he felt it going sour, even if he wanted nothing more than for it to continue. Pride intact, vulnerability masked, he would walk away rather than admit his deeply ingrained fear of being left.

If he did stay, his demands were often insatiable.

"Men who haven't dealt with attachment and separation when they are small spend their lives trying to achieve it," said Dr. Eve Lazar, a New York analyst. "They want primarily to feel a woman will take care of them, so they marry caretakers, not sexual or emotional partners, and their insistence on a mate's attention is outrageously excessive."

Dr. Lazar was implying that being "taken care of" can increase rather than lessen a man's dependence. A good number of men who had grown up in male-dominated homes supported this view. The father's behavior had proved that no matter how old a man got, he might expect his wife to baby him.

"My mother did everything but cut up my father's meat for him," said Lewis, a thirty-four-year-old businessman. "And, in fact, sometimes she even did that! She'd monitor his dinner like a royal servant, always passing second helpings or the first cup of coffee to him before he might—God forbid!—have to ask for it himself."

Lewis also confirmed the experience of other men in revealing how his skewered boyhood image of male-female relationships was proving to be an obstacle in his own search for love.

"I find myself comparing the behavior of women I meet with my mother's response to my father. It's absurd, really, because when I go home to visit, it embarrasses and angers me to see my mother still waiting on Dad or consoling him about a problem that affects her life as much as it does his but that she wouldn't dream of asking his comfort for. Yet when I meet a woman, part of me feels cheated if I don't get exactly that kind of special care. More than cheated; scared. It's not just that I want such continuing babying; I really feel I *need* it!"

Paradoxically, it seems to be the boy whose dependency needs were satisfied in childhood who is able to become more independent and less emotionally demanding of others as a man. The delicate balance mothers of sons must achieve is between encouraging a boy's steps toward a separate self and still being available for those pauses which make the rest of the journey seem less terrifying. It was touching to listen to men who were otherwise mature and self-sustaining as they recalled their happiest memories of their mothers. From even the most nonchauvinistic male and the strapping figure of masculine strength came descriptions of staying home from school with a cold and being deliciously indulged by her.

"My mother would sit near my bed, after she brought me lunch or a snack on a tray," Howard recalled, still sounding dreamily content, "and we'd listen to soap operas together. I guess she loved to have the excuse to do something so mindless, but for me it was an incredible sensory treat, eating food she'd prepared especially for me, listening to grown-up programs, having my mother right there beside me to look at and talk to. When I went back to school, it was as if I'd been completely revitalized."

Interestingly, most adult men still find that the only way to escape the masculine restriction on dependency is to get sick. Even a moderate failure of health brings the most immoderate demand for a wife's attention. For those few blissful days when a cold makes it permissible to admit the need for nurturing, there is seemingly no end to a man's capacity for being coddled or waited on.

Yet it is more than being asked to stand on his own emotional feet that makes a boy's life both with his mother and separate from her so comparatively complex. His major dilemma is that he has to give up his identification with his mother. Traditional theory dictates that to be a man one must be not like a woman—not, then, like the woman who has been the focal point of so much that is good in the little boy's life.

A little girl must also become a separate person, but she is allowed to retain the infant's identification with her mother. Because she, like her mother, is a female, elements of the wondrous fusion of early life will be with her forever. A boy, on the other hand, is expected to make a total, wrenching split. It is not enough to separate; he must exorcise any aspect of his mother from his own personality. When he can't, he is often secretly ashamed. Thus, says the psychoanalyst Nancy Chodorow, "masculinity becomes an issue" for a boy in a way that femininity rarely does for a girl. He must become "someone apart" from the woman he is still so profoundly attached to if he is to meet the harsh requirements of becoming a man.

No wonder that, as a son represses his powerful feelings of identification with and dependence on his mother, he may feel the stirrings of "masculine anxiety," a condition many experts believe haunts men forever. One dominant form of masculine anxiety that begins in childhood is "ambiguity," said a sociologist, Jeffrey Hantover. The boy is "unclear about what kind of person he is to be, what he is expected to do." Actually, he "is told more what *not* to do," said Hantover; for there is always the possible "accusation of femininity" that he nervously tries to avoid by curtailing his behavior and denying certain feelings.

Other societies often treat a male more kindly than ours does. It is perfectly permissible for a boy in Buddhist society to admit dependence or a desire for nurturing, and men will be valued by others as much for their gentleness and sensitivity as for their courage and strength. By contrast, we subject our sons to immense confusion and sadness by making them uncomfortable about the qualities that link them to their feminine source. Ironically, if these qualities were allowed to flower, they would greatly ease the pressures a man feels in our culture.

Although some of these pressures and attitudes are changing, they persist more than we may be aware of. Novels by R. E. Delderfield and other writers chronicle life in the English boarding school, which functions on the premise that a boy must be separated from his mother by the time he is eight years old if he is to grow into a proper man. Once away at school, he frequently suffers brutal treatment from his classmates that will likely go unchallenged by the headmaster. After all, the boys are there precisely to purge themselves of "feminine" softness.

In America, said Ruth Hartley, a sociologist, boys of the age for kindergarten are already aware that they shouldn't be "sissies," which means admitting feelings of uncertainty, dependence, or attachment. Masculine loneliness deepens as this injunction is taken to heart.

Many psychiatrists describe male patients who feel "ghost-like," "not able to be close," and who brood that "nobody really knows me." I heard similar complaints from the men in my study. There was a deep longing to connect with a woman who would allow the man to drop the mask of masculine toughness and with whom he could conquer what Sidney Jourard, an analyst, called the "dread of being known." Many men hoped that if they found such a woman, they would also find themselves through her. These were men who had become so blocked off from feeling that they believed only the guidance of an emotionally expressive woman could help them reclaim their own emotional life.

A striking dramatic example of this is seen in an early film by Mike Nichols, *Carnal Knowledge*. Jack Nicholson and Candice Bergen are having an affair, but she forms a friendship with Nicholson's friend, played by Art Garfunkel. Garfunkel confides to Jack Nicholson that Bergen is so insightful that she uncovers feelings and thoughts in himself he had never known he had. It is Nicholson who is sleeping with her, but this revelation enrages him and makes him bitterly jealous. In an especially vivid scene of confrontation, he accuses his lover of cheating him. "You tell him his thoughts!" he cries, and then furiously demands, "Now, you tell me MY thoughts!"

Not surprisingly, men who were able to stay in touch with what they thought or felt said they had been close to their mothers when they were growing up, although there had been times, even for them, when the demands of masculinity made that closeness, in the words of one man, "a carefully képt secret."

Both mothers and sons marked a son's adolescence as the time when a new self-consciousness entered their relationship. To a large extent, along with the son's need to establish his (alleged) impatience with childish attachment, the intruder in intimacy between mother and son is the son's insistent sexuality. When a boy's Oedipal feelings are reawakened at adolescence, they are not only against those body changes which heighten feelings, but against the possibility of acting on those feelings. To gain the momentum finally to resolve these alarming yearnings, a son may whirl furiously out of any orbit that brings him into contact with his mother.

Here we see again how girls are allowed greater respite than boys from Oedipal conflict and ambivalence about growing up. In particularly vulnerable moments, they can, without losing face, return to the warm solace of the little girl's dependence on her mother.

"My sister is two years older than I am," a man said. "And I remember how upset I used to be that, at fifteen, she could sprawl out on the floor when the family was watching television, and put her head in our mother's lap, and Mother would stroke her hair. Not only couldn't I do that at *thirteen*; I despised myself for the impulse."

Mothers are also denied such respite with a son. Margaret Drabble rather ruefully mused that "it is good to have a daughter, because as she grows older one can go on hugging and kissing with more abandon." Such displays of physical affection begin to seem "odd" with a son who already looks

like a grown-up man, she wrote. I remember similar confusion over trying to decide whether it was all right to pull
my teen-age son to me when he looked, but clearly could
not admit to, feeling hurt at not being invited to another
boy's party. In the end, I held back, and felt I had failed
us both.

When the sex-role impositions become overwhelming,
girls are allowed a lot more cross-over behavior than boys.
A teen-age girl can sweat out sexual tensions on a baseball
field much more easily than a boy can over a kitchen stove
or in a ballet studio. Research conclusively confirms that,
even today, there is far more pressure on a boy than on a
girl to stay within the stereotypic limits of gender behavior.

Yet, in truth, although a girl is thus better able to quiet
the relentless demands of her developing sexuality, it is the
boy who is felt by many psychologists to be more in need
of the respite. In general, a boy's emotional development
is far less likely to keep up with his body's changes than a
girl's. By the time the girl's breasts develop, her emotions
have usually also matured, at least more so than the boy,
whose bulging jeans may fit awkwardly over a little child's
uncertainty.

Here of course we arrive at one of the most overt reasons
that adolescence is, in many ways, more turbulent for a
boy: the demands of his body are painfully transparent. If
he can't let himself think of his mother as a sexual being,
how can he confront her with the inescapable evidence of
his own sexuality?

"God, how I remember trying to wash the sheets myself
after a wet dream," said Howard, "and how mortified I was
when my mother noticed that I had changed the bed. But
the really awful memory is of a family wedding we went
to. There was a terrific-looking second cousin there whom
I hadn't seen for years. I asked her to dance, and almost

immediately got an erection. She was mortified, but I was ready to die on the spot. The music stopped, and I just didn't know what to do. It was horrible! My mother was seated directly in my line of vision. . . . There was no way not to face her to go back to our table. She was looking at me as I sort of sidled over, and then there was an imperceptible response, and I knew she'd seen. She got up from the table on some excuse and covered for me as I sat down. . . . I was terribly grateful, but it was weeks before I could look at her directly again."

There is a similar note of desperation in most men's recollections of teen-age sexuality. Even the elegant George Bernard Shaw once wrote, "At fifteen, I began to have sexual passions of almost intolerable intensity." It was a period when he lived in a state of almost constant "sexual preoccupation." Additionally, the confusion and frustration a young man feels at this time, and in this state, is intensified by the ever-present terror of sexual failure. If he has little control over the arousal of his penis, he has equally little control over its shriveled retreat from erotic adventure. It is a fear that, set against the social pressure to prove his manhood, can keep a young man thrashing around his life in a compulsive sexual frenzy.

The feelings that no longer fit in terms of his mother, and that humiliate him in front of his mother, are now directed, in the white heat of erupting feelings, toward almost any other available female.

"I was a real predator," one man remembered, with a sigh. "My head was filled with a floating collection of body parts—asses, breasts, legs. Girls were erotic bits and pieces that I could grab on to. I realize now that it was impossible for me to conjure up a whole person whom I might feel some responsibility for, and who, very likely, might find me inadequate."

A young man may find these chaotic emotions at war with his more generous, sensitive instincts. Since these are often instincts he identifies with his mother, he may feel even more guilty toward her and estranged from her.

"I did a perfectly hideous thing," Howard said, when recalling his first experience of sexual intercourse. "The girl had sort of a 'reputation,' but she wasn't in any way what we then called a tramp. I was absolutely beside myself when she invited me to her house one night and hinted that something might happen. I stole a condom from my father's drawer (which made me feel very odd). Pretty soon, though, I wasn't thinking of my father and mother's sex life; I was too busy obsessing about my own. . . . Well," he continued, with a mocking smile, "everything went off okay; hardly great, but okay. The best part was that I really performed. I wasn't a virgin anymore, and I wasn't a failure at getting it up. We didn't know what to do with the condom, though. We were afraid to flush it down the toilet, in case it plugged up, so I wrapped it in some tissue to throw away outside. But when I left her house, I got this surge of primitive pride, and then I had what seemed at the time the most sensational idea of declaring my manhood. I took out the condom and attached my handkerchief to it like a flag and hung it on a tree right in front of her window. She found it the next morning before her parents saw it, but she was terribly hurt, and I felt like a total rat when she lashed out at me in school. Even then, I knew I had violated every value I had been taught by my mother, and kept thinking she must see and hate what I'd become."

If the young man isn't being driven by his body's need for release, he may find himself swept away on rhapsodic waves of romantic love. From my research, I conclude that there are significant differences between the female and male experience of first love. Surprisingly, females do not recall feeling as vulnerable and bruised when these relationships ended. This may be because the boy brings to his first partner the same yearnings he has been trying to give up feeling about his mother. His need for being cherished, delighted in, approved of, hover around the space his mother has always filled, waiting now to fasten tightly to the first girl who really seems to care about him. When she stops caring, the memory of his other recent "loss" compounds his uncertainty and pain.

The author Graham Greene captured some of this youthful intensity in writing about his boyhood. During a family vacation with his parents, Greene fell wildly in love with an older girl. "For me," he remembered, "it was an obsessive passion. . . . I lived only for the moments with her. . . . Indeed, she began to be a little scared of what was happening." For months after they parted, he wrote to her every week, and so fixed was she in his memory that thirty years after they had ceased to correspond, "I received a letter asking me to get her seats for my first play." Without a moment's hesitation he recognized the hand on the envelope, and his heart leaped inside his chest, exactly as it had thirty years before.

As a boy comes out of adolescence, he is expected to become more stable and self-assured than he has been, not just in his romantic life, but in all the goals he sets for his future. In his study on masculine anxiety, Jeffrey Hantover wrote that "a lack of self-confidence is defined as unmasculine" among a young man's peers. It is another regrettable aspect of men's experience, continued Hantover, that, because of the absence of intimacy between males, "each boy dwells in ignorance of the other's doubts." In lonely certainty, he "knows" he is the only one who is so unsure.

In truth, how can any young man not be consumed with doubt about what lies ahead of him? He has been bounced back and forth between conflicting expectations and been given little support or preparation for the transitions that continually confront him. First, there are the wonderful days when he is merged as one with a mother who idealizes him and offers perfect intimacy; then he is weaned and pushed away. As he becomes aware of the expectations society has of him, and of the bias in his favor, he finds that this special status only heightens his insecurity, for he fears being exposed as the uncertain model of masculinity he feels he really is.

As he approaches manhood, he feels, understandably, like the victim of repeated assaults on his identity. He has been clubbed by the rigid demands of his social role, which greatly tempers the joy he is supposed to find in its promise of superior status. Very likely, too, he is thoroughly confused about what sort of partner will accompany him on his journey. Is he really prepared to take on an adult romantic life? Will he need to dominate women in order to control those feminine parts of himself that he has been taught by society to fear? Will he avoid commitment because he worries that a woman will make demands he is inadequate to meet? Will he dread dependence on a woman or greedily insist on it? Will he spend a lifetime trying to recapture the primary bliss of maternal love or refuse to be close to a woman lest such unity enable her to swallow him up?

As males are allowed a broader definition of masculinity, such conflicting attitudes toward love, and anxiety about their masculinity, should become less urgent. But until that time fully arrives, it seems inevitable that aspects of the mother-son bond will continue to reflect the tensions as well as the joys of becoming, and helping to shape, a man.

ASPECTS OF THE BOND

Mother and Son Equal Guilt

A number of questions in my survey dealt with whether and, if so, in what ways mothers and sons cause each other to feel guilty. The responses overwhelmingly confirmed that guilt, which Freud considered "the most important problem in the evolution of culture," is an inescapable component of the mother-son bond. Mother and son come to the feeling in different ways, but certainly they are alike in that the very intensity of their attraction for each other invites a sense of failure. The aspirations of love are so grand that they cannot help suffering the bruises of a recurring fall from grace.

Almost any definition of guilt is based on a self-evaluation that is harsh and unforgiving. Shame seems related mainly to someone else's judgment, but the accusing finger of guilt is usually found in one's own hand. An element of the suffering does involve other people's contempt, but our own remorseful voice can always be heard above the convicting chorus.

With mothers, this self-abasement seems particularly intense, perhaps because its seeds are planted very early. It may take the boy some years to suspect he isn't living up to his mother's (and therefore his own) expectations, but by the time he was born, his mother's head was already filled with ideas about her "responsibility" for preparing a son to be a man. Will she be able to raise him to meet society's demands? Can she *bear* to raise him that way?

The conflicts a mother feels are intensified by another of our cultural preoccupations, the pursuit of happiness. Earlier generations of women did not see it as their job to make a child "happy." In effect, the mother was an agent of society, and her primary task was to prepare her son or daughter to obey the rules of the larger world. In our own psychoanalytic age, however, it is not enough just to get children ready for life in the prevailing culture. It is a middle-class mother's task—she may even feel it is her obligation—to see that her children are also free of emotional stress. Instead of teaching her children to adjust their responses to meet her demands, a woman is expected to monitor her own maternal reactions carefully. If she doesn't, she may know the unspeakable guilt of having made her children unhappy.

A leading psychiatrist, Fritz Redl, has said that a modern mother often lives her life "as though a psychiatrist just flew by her window." And indeed, many mothers appear to have been victimized by psychological fallout. They seem to be constantly worrying that the very next maternal misstep may be the one that will irrevocably damage a fragile young psyche. Each move they make becomes a carefully considered detour around disaster, and even the most thoughtful, knowledgeable woman loses all objectivity at the very suggestion that she has an unhappy child.

"I went to my son's first-grade conference," said thirty-year-old, highly educated Alice. "Smilingly, his teacher skipped down a list of all his achievements and positive adjustments to achool. Then, really just as a quick aside, she said that she noticed he sometimes had a little trouble playing with the other children. And bam! Every positive thing she had said evaporated into thin air. All I could hear was that I had a sad son with no friends."

Ironically, a mother's need to know that her child is happy more often than not compounds rather than corrects any problems the child is having. After all, there are significant stresses in growing up, even in the most idyllic childhood. Mothers who cannot accept this truth subtly encourage their children to repress and deny their real experiences, and rob them of the chance to be comforted.

Common as this unfortunate pattern is, the tyranny of happiness is particularly oppressive when the child in question is a boy. Even a woman who genuinely wants to ease the cultural pressures of growing up male may unwittingly reinforce such injunctions when her son shows emotional pain. The staunchest feminist or career-minded mother may find something terrifying about a troubled son, and she is especially vulnerable to this ultimate measure of her maternal worth. That even a very young boy will sense such anxieties in his mother, and adjust his responses to meet them, was stunningly obvious in my interviews with sons.

"Mommy doesn't like me to be sad," a five-year-old said to our assembled group of little boys, and heads nodded in understanding. They knew immediately that this was more a guilty confession than a simple report. When they contributed their own experiences to the discussion, the stories confirmed that a mother's obsession with her son's happiness can make him feel more lonely than cherished. Grown sons' memories of childhood are also laced with images that reinforce the fact that little boys learn to hide natural feelings that mothers believe carry implications of their own failure.

"I went to summer camp when I was eight," said a college senior. "I really didn't want to go, but all the other boys my age in the neighborhood were going away, and I sensed that somehow it was very important to my mother that I be as self-sufficient as she thought they were. I hated camp from the minute I arrived, and I was miserably homesick. But I simply couldn't tell her. I'd sit down to write about how I felt, and instead, I'd make up outrageously cheerful stories about the terrific time I was having. When she came up with my dad on visiting day, I had a smile stretched across my face like a rubber band. I ran around with them all day, participating in everything, and I could see how happy it made her. I didn't have the courage to disappoint her by telling her how lonely I was. Being homesick was failure, was being culpable, was something you didn't admit."

That a loving, intelligent mother will contribute to a son's self-estrangement by denying him expression of his full range of feeling again relates to the problems of a transitional age. The traditional notion that a boy's tears or moodiness is "unnatural" is very hard to shake, and resists almost any intellectual insight or argument. A son's trauma and frustration suggest a deviance from society's expectations, and the mother then feels guilty about her failure in her most important social role. Not to guarantee that the potential of a male child has been fulfilled has implications of waste and failed responsibility that fill her with dread. Guilt because of an "underachieving" or unhappy son sits like a stone in her heart. The pain is so stubborn, unyielding, and immobilizing, it is no wonder that she is reluctant to acknowledge the boy's failure or despair.

Mothers agreed overwhelmingly (however ruefully) that they felt much greater pressure in fostering a son's worldly success than they did a daughter's. As one woman commented, "When my daughter took a year off before college, I wasn't at all upset. I wanted her to have time to work out some of her confusions. But to be truthful, I have to admit if my son wants to do the same, I'm going to worry the entire year. What if he should decide not to go to college at all? Is it my fault that he doesn't have more initiative? What did I do wrong that he can't meet the same kinds of challenges his friends do?"

Many experts now believe in the theory of the "good enough" mother, which posits that a woman does not have to be perfect to raise a reasonably well-adjusted and successful child. But it was the rare mother who was willing to settle for being good enough in relation to her son.

It is more than the internalized belief in male significance that makes mothers of sons so vulnerable to guilt. A mother's sense of accountability is enforced by everyone around her—her husband, the larger society, and, most terribly, her son himself. Over the years, the father's influence on the family has declined. Job performance pressures and work that frequently involved long commutes were only some of the competitive demands on the father's attention and energy. As the father gave less of himself to the family, sons began looking to their mothers for support and even salvation. In a world that was often fragmented and alienating, they held their mothers responsible for their unhappiness. Erik Erikson wrote that the troubled American man clearly "blames his mother for having let him down. . . . His father, he claims, had not much to do with it."

I found this to be true in my interviews with grown sons. A man was often angry with his father, frequently bitter over a lack of closeness, but the person who was held responsible for not giving him "enough" love and security was always his mother. This is the maternal paradox: because the mother is at the center of her son's life, he comes to believe in her omnipotence—a belief that only dooms her to disappoint him.

Mothers also seem to believe in this impossible omnipotence and will accept nothing less of themselves in their treatment of sons. When I suggested this to the group of women I had assembled to talk about mothering sons, it set off a hum of unanimous agreement.

"Of course! I feel responsible for *everything* that has to do with Peter," one woman said. "You name it: his school work, his social skills, his problems. It's all my doing and all my fault!"

I was surprised to see just how heavy a burden this responsibility can be for some mothers. A sizable number of women had sent, or were contemplating sending, their sons to boarding school, for reasons that were not purely academic. Rather, there was a generally uneasy feeling, expressed by one woman when she said, "I just don't want to mess him up; he's too important to me to make mistakes with." Another mother put it more tersely: "I'm tired of daily confrontations on what I'm doing wrong."

A woman's husband *can* greatly reduce her enjoyment of mothering her son by exacerbating her fear of failure. Unwilling or unable to take over the task of molding his son's life, the father may still have high expectations of him, which he expects his wife to assure. Again, this pressure is sometimes intensified by those unconscious journeys back to childhood which our children inspire in us. If a man felt undervalued by his mother, he might project his sadness and anger onto his wife and become highly critical of her responses to their son. As he attacks her for not doing enough, he may in reality be attempting to assuage his pain at the deficiences in his own childhood. Whatever his motivation, his criticism stings. Even mothers who protested their husbands' "autocratic interference" in their relationships with sons often worried that they were as incompetent and inadequate as they were accused of being.

"My husband and I have awful fights about our thirteen-year-old boy," one woman told me. "But the truth is, despite my resentment over getting blamed if Jed gets a lousy report card, I really feel at those times that I'm letting both my husband *and* my son down."

Another mother, in discussing her dreams, shared a repeated nightmare: "My husband leaves me because our son is such a disappointment to him, and, to my horror, my son blames me too. He tells me that if I had been a stronger mother, his father wouldn't have gotten so angry that he abandoned him."

Some of the guilt mothers feel toward their sons relates directly to such marital friction. Since a son's problems can be a major cause of husband-wife dissension, a woman may resent her son for being the cause of the grown-up discord. Yet as she admits her anger, she feels guilty: it seems so wrong to feel unloving toward this prized male child she is supposed to adore.

In general, said the psychiatrist Elaine Heffner, "mothers are not prepared for the kinds of negative feelings they will have toward their children." Yet there's no doubt that all kinds of anger and "conflict about giving and taking" will arise in a mother who has a relentlessly demanding child. As Dr. Heffner explained, "The unceasing nature of a child's needs can be experienced as an assault on the self." This seems a warning especially applicable to the mother of a son. However much she loves this baby boy, on some level and, to a degree, shaped by her own experience with men, a woman is conscious that her son belongs to the oppressor group, and she knows that even in his crib he is already valued more by society than she is. These political perceptions, however dim, coupled with the frustrations of child-rearing, occasionally create sharp *and* guilt-producing hostility in a mother.

However, the majority of the women in my study felt less guilty about resenting their sons than about failing them. Their anxiety frequently seemed to put them in a double bind. Because her son's mental health is so vital to her personal esteem, a mother is often tempted to overstate her mission, and she may apply herself relentlessly to the fulfillment of even the boy's smallest need. Far too often, mothers say, as their sons grow to see them as all-giving, and all-sacrificing, they seem to become insatiable. Then the mother worries that she has done her son a disservice, by inviting such excessive demands. Yet not to fulfill the demands also makes her feel guilty. And so, commented the renowned sociologist Dr. Jesse Bernard in disheartening summation, "there is no escape."

This damned if you do, damned if you don't mothering of sons was an issue raised often in my discussion group.

"I feel so terrible," a mother ventured when the topic came up. "I give him my absolute all, and he still seems to need more. He's such an awful malcontent, and I'm sure it's my fault. Now I worry that he's never going to sustain any pleasure in his life."

The room immediately echoed with similar anxieties. One mother told of a son who "intimidates me by inflicting guilt. I don't ever do enough for him, and what I do is usually wrong. If I'd behaved differently, *he'd* be different, he'd be happier . . ." She had been imitating his whiny tone of accusation, but her voice broke with remorse as she spoke.

To a surprising degree, such regret is connected to the relationships between men and women. Just as it's hard to accept a husband's criticism (because he is a man, whose approval defines female worth), so it is with a son. Small and dependent as he is, a son stirs a mother's anxiety when he, a male, judges her lacking.

Still, much more than I'd anticipate, mothers *do* blame themselves for a son who seems cheerlessly overindulged. And they worry that, despite a contemporary consciousness, they are producing a man who, like far too many men of previous generations, will see women as existing only to serve him. For this reason, many women in my study, particularly the younger ones, were trying to moderate their maternal attention. It is, however, easier said than done.

For example, even mothers who worked often found it impossible not to feel threatened by a son's distress or resentment. Luci, a nursing supervisor and mother of a twelve-year-old son, illustrated the difference between paternal and maternal guilt in this regard. "My husband can go to the office after a breakfast row and put it all behind him. I take the picture of how upset Tony was right along to the hospital. I worry about whether it's affecting his behavior at school and whether he'll be there, and in what mood, when I get home. I'm too committed to my work to let these preoccupations interfere with my duties, but at the end of the day I'm totally exhausted from the tension. Then, when we all come together again, my husband will apologize for losing his temper and that will be the end of it, while I'll carry a sense of failure around for days and go out of my way to be extra loving and solicitous. And mind you," she added, with a sigh and a smile, "this has absolutely nothing to do with whether Tony's behavior was the real cause of the original scene."

Because little boys are considered by many professionals to be highly sensitive to separations, the mother's leaving even a peaceful breakfast table to go to work can be fraught with conflict. Her taking an extended vacation, even when her son is left home with adoring grandparents or a totally competent nursemaid, also limits her chance fully to enjoy her holiday. "Leaving my son" took high honors on the list of guilt-provoking situations for every mother I spoke with.

Indeed, since women have been taught not to be "selfish," especially in relation to the men they love, they feel enormously guilty if they put any self-interest ahead of the wishes of their sons. Rose-Ann, a divorced mother of a five-year-old son, summed up her very typical dilemma about a social life this way: "He cries when I drop him off at day care every single morning. I can count on it as certainly as the sunrise. And if I'm five minutes late when I pick him up, he's either hysterical or sulking in a corner. I'd really like to begin dating, but I don't even consider it, because I couldn't go through leaving him again in the evening. His miserable little face would be superimposed over even a man who looked like Robert Redford!"

My investigation revealed intriguing information on the subject of divorce: not only was a son often the cause of marital conflict, but marriages sometimes ended because of a mother's evolving response to the tension. Among my respondents were a good number of women who had moved from feeling guilty about raising sons who disappointed their fathers to feeling guilty about being unable to protect their sons from the punitive consequences of that disappointment.

Said one mother, "My son was being asked to pay too big a price for not living up to my husband's expectations. I never thought I would have the courage to walk out of what was always a bad marriage, but I was so ashamed of my inability to protect him from his father's rejection that I finally found the strength to do it."

On the other hand, a frequent source of divorce-related guilt is the worry over the effects of the loss of a full-time father on a son's adjustment. In the first flush of what Elaine Heffner called the "liberation mystique," lots of women packed in their marriages to strike out on their own, confidently carrying their little boys in tow. A little while later, a surprising number seemed to reconsider their decisions. The tenacious belief in a male child's "rights," and in a mother's obligations to make her son happy, may make a woman surprisingly anxious about her decision to end an unsatisfying marriage. She begins to scrutinize the boy's life for signs of deprivation and blames only herself for what she finds.

It is an anxiety that takes many forms. For instance, an unusually large number of nonmaterialistic women seemed very concerned with material comfort.

"There is never enough money, no matter how many budgets I sit up till dawn creating," one mother complained wearily. That her husband may be punitively withholding money, and that she continues to get paid a lower salary than a man, do little to alter her feelings of guilt. She *should* be able to buy her son the bike he wants or send him to the private school his friends from intact families or with "better" mothers can attend.

Other mothers worry that their sons are lonely without their fathers' companionship, even if it was the fathers' choice to withdraw from the scene. "It's insane, that's all, just insane," a woman muttered in self-disgust. "My ex-husband is the one who prefers playing with his young girlfriends on weekends, rather than with his son, yet I'm the one who feels guilty about Bobby being without a father on Sundays." The specter of homosexuality also frightens some mothers when they think of raising a son alone. In a split-custody arrangement a mother is more likely to surrender her son than her daughter, but the research indicates that it is rarely a case of loving a son less than a daughter that leads to that decision. Rather, the intensity of the mother's concern and her terror of "failure" force her to make what often seems her life's most profound sacrifice.

There are a seemingly infinite number of ways in which a mother's passion for her son invites guilt feelings. But the intensity of a mother's devotion to her son also has guilt-producing effects outside the mother-son relationship. A mother may feel guilty toward her other children, whom her son seems to have overshadowed in her mind. She may get so swept up in her own ardor that she unintentionally but gravely hurts her other children (forgetting how a brother may once have displaced her in her mothers' affections). More than a few women acknowledged the painful realization that their imbalanced attention could easily be called bias and could leave a sister, or even a less accomplished brother, lonely and aggrieved.

"I didn't mean to single out my older son," a typical mother told me. "It's just that he's so obviously a gifted child, with such special talents . . ."

Shortly before our interview, this woman had suffered a dreadful confrontation with her adolescent daughter, which had left her raw and shaken. How could she have been so blind? she raged at herself. How could she ever make amends for the girl's feeling of neglect? What long-term damage had she done? Yet, although she was genuinely contrite, I found myself wondering whether she would be able to break the lopsided pattern of her love. The impulse to invest in a son, especially a gifted one, is so remarkably compelling that even the deepest level of regret may not be able to induce a mother to alter it.

When we study the lives of famous men, over and over again we find the son who has been singled out by a fiercely determined mother. One of the most dramatic examples is that of the musician Pablo Casals and his mother. For more than a decade, the mother left her husband and her ten other children for extended periods of time in order to travel with Pablo to distant cities where he could study with master teachers. In an analysis of Casals' development, the psychologists Victor and Mildred Goertzel wrote, "Until Pablo was twenty-two, the home was fragmented, burdened, impoverished by the weight of the mother's consuming drive to see the talent of her son actualized and recognized."

The mother did not record any conflict she may have felt over the effect the pursuit of her dream had on her other children. Casals himself, however, made no secret of his regret. "My father thought that all these schemes did not make sense," he wrote in a memoir, "and attributed them to what he called my mother's *folie des grandeurs.* They argued with such bitterness that it pained me terribly . . . and I felt very guilty."

Despite the father's anger toward his wife, he retained close and loving ties with Pablo. But in many families the father-son bond does not remain intact. A mother may discover (often after her husband's bitter accusation) that her adoration for her son has built a protective fence around his life that has unwittingly served to keep the father out.

"I never meant to take over our boy," Becky earnestly reported. "I just enjoyed doing things with him and being with him; it always seemed so natural. Yet I know my husband resents our closeness, and deep down he feels I've stolen his son."

Becky seemed puzzled by something I heard frequently from mothers with similar father-son stories. The split in the family seemed to be widened by the fact that the boy was much easier to get along with when he was alone with his mother than when he was with his father.

Although there are many complex explanations for the inconsistency of a son's charm, there is one that is among the most basic truths about human nature: we tend to prefer the people who prefer us. Thus, a son who knows that he is his mother's proudest triumph will very likely behave in ways that foster this evaluation. Her unconditional admiration erases all need to argue or rebel. He may very well be "different" when he is with his father, away from the self-fulfilling prophecy of his mother's adoration.

There is yet another kind of guilt a mother may experience, and the problem it presents is a contemporary one. It is the guilt a woman feels in relation to herself. Underlying many of the responses of women was the disturbing question of whether the mother had paid enough attention to her own development while investing herself in her son's interests. Must she face the truth that, in her desire to be everything to this boy, she is virtually nothing without him?

Many women said sadly that they wouldn't know where to begin to look for jobs. They'd gotten married right after graduating from college and had never worked outside the home. They could not imagine that anyone would pay them to do anything but menial work. Other mothers felt boring, especially when they were in the company of women who were accomplishing things in the outside world. "I've reached the point where I hate to go to a dinner party with new people," one woman said. "There's bound to be some other woman there with a fabulous career and who looks terrific for her age, and all the men in the room gravitate to her. I sat at the right of one of my husband's partners last week at a dinner, and this new woman in the neighborhood who's a lawyer and involved in some community action project sat at his left. He and I have always liked each other, but suddenly everything he said to me sounded so patronizing, as if he were giving me the obligatory five minutes of female chitchat before turning back to the really interesting talk. She has the same number of kids as I do, but I didn't hear him ask her about them at all, though that's just about all he and I talked about, our children. It was obviously his view of what my principal identity is, and of course he's right. If you asked me to define myself, I'd immediately tell you I'm the mother of two sons, and start bragging about them. Who I am beyond that role, and being a wife of course, I don't have a clue. And I'm forty-four years old!"

This woman went on to say that she felt like a "cliché," and foolish besides. Indeed, in the 1980s a mother who is selflessly committed to her children seems to be the target of attack rather than the object of praise. As Dr. Heffner wrote: "The horror story was once told about women who failed to become truly feminine, natural mothers. Today, the same warning is sounded for women who remain 'imprisoned' in child care."

Another prominent social scientist, Pauline Bart, in her important study of depression in middle-aged women echoed the despair of this category of mother and linked the painful feeling to "the scorn with which the larger culture treats emotional closeness or dependency." A humiliating sense of having wasted her own potential exacerbates the particularly critical opinion society has of the woman who "smothers" her son. In addition, her all-consuming involvement in the growing boy's life produces a terrible paradox. His mature accomplishment may vindicate her passionate investment, but it may also leave her feeling useless and rejected. Over and over, women bemoaned abandoning earlier visions of their lives that would have precluded their becoming so vulnerable. "I was tops in my class at college," one mother said. "All my teachers encouraged me to go on to graduate school, but there were no part-time Ph.D. programs in those days, and by the time the boys were old enough so that I really could have gone back to school on a full-time basis, I had lost my confidence and drive." Other women deprecatingly recalled years spent in artistic volunteer work while talents in music or art became rusty by any professional measure. "I played piano for every school function in my children's school careers, from kindergarten through high school," was one typical statement of regret. "Some of the people I once studied with are famous now. I used to brag about having started out with them. Now I'm tormented with envy and disgust with myself every time I see their names in the newspapers."

The degree to which a mother does feel abandoned and frightened by a son's lessening need of her sharpens his own sense of guilt. The novelist and playwright Anatole France brooded that his mother "would have preferred that I should not grow, so as to be able to press me to her bosom. Everything that brought me a little independence offended her." The sons of such a mother will wrestle with a sense of obligation about how much responsibility he bears for his mother's pain and feelings of loss. How much harm had really been done to the mother by the son's need to pull back from her? What does the son "owe" his mother for her years of selfless sacrifice? These questions, I discovered, can have a powerful influence on a man's life.

Michael, a forty-five-year-old roving foreign correspondent, told me that he had planned his career around his mother's need to have him close by. "I tried to go abroad shortly after college," he said, "because I had always dreamed of combining work and travel. But as an only child, I felt so guilty about abandoning my mother after she had dedicated herself to me while I was growing up that I came back to New York. It was only when she died, when I was in my middle thirties, that I felt I could pursue the career I really wanted."

More typical than the need to stay physically close to his mother is a son's uncomfortable sense that it is his obligation to vindicate her life. If an anxious mother sometimes makes her son feel guilty about being unhappy, an unhappy mother may cause a boy considerable torment.

"I remember my mother as always being slightly depressed," said one man. "Even as a very little boy, I felt sorry for her. We didn't have a lot of money, but that wasn't it. She was very bright and considered herself above the other women in the neighborhood. They bored her, and she made no bones about it. She should have had a career, but for a woman of her day and class, it just could never happen. I was her favorite child, which made me feel guilty about my other brother and sisters, but I felt worse about the feeling that somehow it was up to me to make her feel good about her life."

The columnist Russell Baker, in his Pulitzer Prize—winning memoir; *Growing Up*, also spoke of how a mother, disappointed with her life, may look to her son for vicarious achievement.

> She would spend her middle years turning me into the man who would redeem her failed youth. I would make something of myself, and if I lacked the grit to do it, well then, she would make me make something of myself. From now on, she would live for me, and, in turn, I would become her future.

Despite his accomplishments, Russell Baker was apparently never convinced that he had made enough of himself to satisfy his mother. The men I interviewed frequently described the relentlessly nagging guilt that comes from such a feeling.

"No matter what I did, what accomplishments I laid at her feet, I always felt it wasn't enough," a very successful salesman told me. "For a long while, I thought it was because I wasn't going after a profession with real prestige, but now I understand there was no way to really satisfy her, because her own ambitions had been so frustrated."

This man's insights came after several years of therapy. It takes considerable social and personal awareness for a son to understand that a mother's need to live through his achievements often stems from her feeling that she has not been allowed to achieve on her own. That she is so insatiable suggests that nothing the son can do *will* really satisfy her.

The most perfect son cannot compensate for a mother's missing self.

Perhaps the most extravagant literary expression of this dilemma is Philip Roth's novel *Portnoy's Complaint*, in which the protagonist, Alexander Portnoy, becomes nearly hysterical with frustration at the unending demands his mother makes of him. Imagine, screams Portnoy to himself, after all Sophie Portnoy sacrificed for her little boy, "it turns out that I still won't be perfect. Did you ever hear of such a thing in your life? I just refuse to be perfect!"

There is no doubt that a mother's hovering attention and exalted aspirations can cause a boy some moral conflict. Even so, if she is not a deeply frustrated and unhappy person, his responses to her influence can produce significant accomplishment.

The psychiatrist Selma Freiberg suggested that there are worse things to do to our sons than spawn some moral conflict. Such neuroses are, after all, essentially curable. "In contrast," Dr. Freiberg pointed out, "there is nothing one can do to overcome the diseases of nonattachment created when there is no bond to begin with." One can even illustrate her view with the fictional Alex Portnoy, assistant commissioner of human rights, who might not have been drawn to his vocation without a mother who had shown him, albeit in exaggerated form, the power of commitment and conscience.

Actually, only a minority of the mature sons I interviewed seemed to feel seriously oppressed by their mothers' ambitions. A far larger number had, like Russell Baker, overcome their initial resentment and had come to see maternal influence as a positive shaping force.

"Without my mother's determined convictions about my destiny," one college dean told me, "I think I would have gone off completely half-cocked. I had a thousand fragmented interests, and though I fought her constant efforts to pin me down, I know now that my reluctant giving-in to that pressure moored me to a central focus."

Famous sons offer further examples. The writer André Gide said that he bitterly protested his mother's moral and behavioral impositions throughout his youth. Yet after her death he felt himself sink "into an overwhelming abyss of liberty. The very liberty which during my mother's lifetime I had so craved, frightened me. I felt dazed, like a kite whose string had been suddenly cut . . . like a drifting wreck at the mercy of wind and tide."

Why one son finds a mother's ambitions for him oppressive, and another encouraging, seems to have a great deal to do with whether or not the mother is finally able to accept him as a separate person. Prodding a son to make something of himself becomes seriously problematic when a mother will not relinquish goals that run counter to the boy's genuine talents and needs. Another mother may let her son know that she would be thrilled to have him become a doctor, but that she is also able to understand that this vocation may be absolutely incompatible with his own dreams. In such a case, the son may still feel some guilt at having disappointed his mother, but he would not be tormented by the thought that he had no right to do so.

To sum up, the stresses of guilt can be minimized if a mother acknowledges her expectations for her son but does not impose them to the degree that they cripple the boy's life. It is imperative for a mother to accept her son for who he really is. To do this, however, we must look to—and know—ourselves. We must ask the difficult question of whether, in expecting so much of our sons, we are not facing our lost hopes for ourselves. For his part, the son must realize that he as well as his mother suffers when the mother's individuality is sacrificed in his behalf. Such an awesome debt spawns a guilt that, whether consciously wrestled with or repressed, inevitably lessens a man's pleasure in living.

Interestingly, although the possibility of disappointing his mother weighs so heavily in many a son's mind, it is his mother he looks to for forgiveness when he commits his very worst transgressions. Research shows that when the death penalty was enforced, the majority of men about to die asked to have their mothers as their last visitors. More than wife, lover, or even children, it was a man's mother whose presence and forgiveness was needed before his life ended. And more than any other person, it is a mother who answers such a request, who will put aside her life to travel to a suffering son's side.

How deeply embedded the idea of maternal acceptance is in our collective consciousness was illustrated by the tragic story of John Hinckley, Jr., the young man who attempted to assassinate President Ronald Reagan. It is apparent by the accounts of public response to the horrifying event that even people who felt Hinckley should not be absolved of his crime, simply because he was declared insane, were shocked that when Mrs. Hinckley drove her son to the airport, for what was to be his most terrifying journey, on the advice of his psychiatrist she told him, as he left her car, not to come home or ever again ask for her aid. This act of rejection by the mother of a troubled son obviously seemed a haunting contradiction of the common idea of maternal love.

This does not imply that the ideal mother is one who refuses to admit that she has a pathologically ill son or who will never reject his request for support, no matter how outrageously he has behaved. It is, however, part of a mother's dilemma that even in extreme cases she retains a sense of obligation toward her son and feels acute guilt over denying him her help or her solace.

Perhaps a mother feels this guilt because she believes that her singularly intimate knowledge of a son does oblige her to reach out to him when no one else will. After all, she alone knows the full range of his fears and vulnerability, those aspects of self he has felt compelled to deny with other people in the name of masculinity. No matter how aggressive or demanding or even destructive he is as a man, she can remember the helpless, dependent little boy who needed her to protect him. (Mrs. Hinckley, in testifying for John, recalled, in tears, his sensitivity, his loneliness, his lack of friends when he was a little boy.)

A mother's exceptional knowledge of a son's vulnerability also gives her great power over him, a power that is another intrinsic and often anguishing part of the mother-son relationship.

Power—The Hidden Agenda

A remarkably insightful Swiss psychiatrist named Alice Miller read in Henry Moore's memoirs that the sculptor, as a small boy, massaged his mother's back with oil to ease the pain of her rheumatism. Miller wrote: "Reading this suddenly threw light for me on Moore's sculptures; the great reclining women with the tiny heads. . . . I could see in them the mother through the small boy's eyes, with the head high above in diminishing perspective, and the back close before him and enormously enlarged."

I find this image a startlingly graphic illustration of a mother's powerful presence in her son's life. The only element lacking is the description of how the mother feels when looking down on her child. How does her sense of strength and control develop as a child's eye wonderingly travels the sweep of her body?

No matter what emotion brings two people together, and no matter who the two people are—workers, lovers, husbands and wives—the element of power affects the design of every relationship. We can talk all we want to about equality and fairness, but even the most benign among us wrestles with the wish to influence and dominate the "other" in our life. For example, marriage counselors confirm that problems of power eat away at even those unions based on adoration. Similarly, the most devoted mother cannot help being affected by the issue of power constraints on a woman's life. Few women have reached the realms of public power or have been allowed to think of themselves as people of influence and strength. When a person does *not* feel personally powerful, he or she develops a tendency to search out the fulfillment of such feelings inside a role that carries authority. For most women, this has meant taking on the most significant role offered by traditional society, that of being a mother.

Locked out for so long from larger spheres of influence, a mother can satisfy her need for power in her relationship to her children. She is drawn to an image of herself that does not resemble the weak, infantile creature who needs men to guide and protect her. Instead, like Henry Moore's sculpture, she grandly imposes her presence. Alone with her child, as most mothers in Western society are, without the help of fathers or nearby relatives, without the means to find or afford good surrogate care, a mother's influence is great. However, a hazard of such a cloistered atmosphere of power, wrote the sociologist Philip Slater, is that "every maternal quirk, every maternal hang-up, and every maternal deprivation is experienced by the child as heavily amplified noise from which there is no escape."

A further complication and potential hazard of a woman's feeling powerful through motherhood is that the power she feels is vicarious and involves an indirect rather than self-directed route to self-esteem. Not only does the child have to live out the mother's dreams and goals in order to establish her influence; if her power comes from giving, then the child must continue to need to take from her.

The novelist and social commentator Elizabeth Janeway, in a discussion of this convoluted tie, used a religious illustration:

> It is peculiar . . . to all major religions that the myth of female power presents women not as goddesses . . . but as

typified by the Mother of God. Her divinity is no longer her own, but depends on her motherhood. It has become reflected and vicarious. Power and weakness meet, and the necessary mother is dependent for her sacredness on her son.

Indeed, the idea of the power in motherhood is most complex in relation to a son. It is an exhilarating experience to mother a child who belongs to a more powerful sex than your own. In Freud's view, this realization affects a woman's passion for a son positively; it helps explain why "only the relationship to her son can bring a mother unlimited satisfaction." For, said Freud, she is able to transfer to this male child "the ambition she had been obliged to suppress in herself."

Critics of Freud refute this male-supremacist concept. In Erich Fromm's opinion, for example, it is "the only idea in his thinking which seems to be without the slightest redeeming feature," except, he added, as a manifest example of Freud's own male chauvinism. Freud's writings certainly show that a society in which women and men have the same ability to achieve public power and external success was unthinkable for him. When John Stuart Mill, whom Freud otherwise greatly admired, spoke out on the equality of women, Freud wrote in a letter (in prose that seems not completely professional), "On this point, Mill is simply crazy."

Considering the recent defeat of the passage of the Equal Rights Amendment, it is hard to believe that women have come very far from Freud's narrow view of their potential. To be sure, increasing numbers of women are raising their voices in protest against the idea of male supremacy. They give much less weight than older women to the notion that "appropriate" female adjustment means that they must sublimate any aspirations for their own achievement to those of their sons. Yet the lingering values of the past continue to lend a special headiness to taking charge of a male child's destiny. No matter how she may dislike the knowledge, a woman knows that, even today, his success will be easier to imagine, more accessible, and more universally respected than a female child's will be.

"To put it simply," said Gloria, who at thirty-five was just beginning to have some success as a photographer, "I feel as if I'm investing in a winner. I know I should be ashamed to admit that, but you see, I'm not sure how to guide my daughter toward becoming a successful person, or whether anything I say or do can really help her surmount all the obstacles to female achievement. With my son, though," she continued, "I know that if I nurture his mind and talents, nothing can stop him. I'm sorry, but I find that certainty enormously compelling."

As I did my research, I discovered that a great many women, like Gloria, connect most fully to their daughters through a feeling of shared victimization. This can create its own strong bond, in which a mother fiercely defends her daughter against society. She wants, at any personal price, to shatter the restricting limits placed on her own development. Yet even as she charges out in front of the little girl to insist on equal opportunity, and teaches her daughter to be assertive on her own behalf, a mother knows the obstacles that lie ahead. This knowledge can dim the triumph of maternal power. Dr. Irving Markowitz, a psychiatrist who heads a family service clinic in northern New Jersey, reflected on this: "In a way, a mother knows she and her daughter are bound to let each other down, no matter how they mutually support and respect each other. It's a perception, and—because she wants so much to help her daughter—a frustration, that can actually exacerbate a woman's feelings of powerlessness."

No matter what the sex of their children however, all women share at least an initial sense of tremendous personal strength when they first gaze down on a helpless infant. The feeling can be breathtaking, flooding a mother with unexpected responses. Many women reported having dreams during their babies' infancy in which the mother had moved into the baby's crib or playpen. "I dreamed I was crying in the carriage," or "I dreamed I was terribly hungry and lying down and couldn't talk or move my body to get someone to give me food. Then I realized I was in my son's crib." The sociologist Richard Sennett, who has written about dreams like these, calls them dreams of "doubling," where the mother identifies with her infant "by half." She understands what it's like to feel helpless and dependent, yet she still has a sense of her mature and increasingly significant self. These are dreams of empathy from women who have suddenly discovered themselves to be protectors. In short, as Sennett says, "doubling is one initiation through fantasy into a new context of power."

These power dreams are not *necessarily* prompted by a child of either sex, but certain other wakeful and sleeping fantasies that also deal with power do appear to be triggered by a son. Being in charge of a male child's life can be extremely unsettling, particularly for women who not only are unfamiliar with this image of personal dominance but are vulnerable to the idea of responsibility for their sons' success. Every woman I interviewed had had recurring nightmares of her son (many more than of a daughter) being in serious trouble from which she could not save him. He runs into the path of an oncoming car; the carriage handle slips from her grasp and he races down a precipitous hill; he is suddenly lost in an airport or a maze of streets; he does not come home from school as the day ominously darkens.

Such anxiety can persist even when a son is older. The

broadcaster Sherrye Henry was puzzled by her own fear for the safety of her eminently capable and physically strong young adult son. Perhaps, she mused, it was just because he seemed to have such an important contribution to make to the world that she worried about her ability to protect him from any threat to fulfilling that promise.

Because we allow ourselves to be more protective of daughters, it is possible that we don't perceive of them as being in as much danger as our sons. Our familiarity with female experience also helps to make a daughter's world seem less threatening. The very differences that make a son seem exciting can also leave us uncertain about what perils lie ahead for him and whether *we* are really strong enough to face them.

Such apprehension notwithstanding, as she gets used to her new role, it is not uncommon for a mother to have thoughts about her little boy that may seem frighteningly perverse. The realization that she holds the reins of a male person's life in her hands can send malevolent thoughts racing through her horrified mind. Hostile impulses insist on being recognized, so many women fear that they live only one raised hand away from seriously abusing the little boy they adore. It is a paradox that mothers find terribly bewildering.

In the discussion group, the women aired this confusion and found much relief in seeing how common these conflicting feelings actually are. Of the eleven women present on one representative day, nine "confessed" that they didn't ever spank their sons, because of a secret fear that they would lose control and seriously injure them. Why they felt this way more with sons than with daughters was again owing in part to identification with the helplessness of a female child. More important, the difference appears to lie in the inability of most women to accept the depth of their anger at men. We haven't had nearly enough experience in being able to acknowledge anger toward the important men in our lives. And since we do deny these feelings, we don't know how angry we can feel without being driven to destructive acting-out. Because of this uncertainty, when we suddenly grow resentful of a son's demands, our belligerence seems fraught with dangerous implications, giving rise to fantasies of our abusing our maternal power.

Afraid as we are of losing control, we are equally terrified of losing his love. Women have traditionally linked the expression of anger toward a man with the fearful possibility of being emotionally abandoned by him. That the man in question is only a small boy doesn't seem to lessen the strength of this restrictive, anxiety-producing taboo. When facing a resentful son, we are suddenly no longer strong; we are utterly vulnerable, our potency swiftly eroded by his disapproval.

A young mother named Liza shared a dream that expresses this dilemma precisely. Her son was eighteen months old, and Liza had already been back at work at her job as a chemist for nine months, although she had originally intended to take a leave of at least a year and a half. "I was terribly torn," she said. "I loved being with the baby, but I just wasn't prepared for all his pulls on my time. It was important to me to at least keep up with the professional literature, but it seemed that every time I sat down to read, he would start to cry. Also, I really was anxious about taking such a long period off, of letting my colleagues get the jump on me. Then, when Timmy was about five months old and I was really facing up to the truth that I wanted to go back to work, I had this dream. He *walked* into my bedroom and just stood in the doorway, looking at me incredibly harshly. I knew he was telling me I was a bad mother, because I hadn't changed his diaper when I heard him crying. I'd stayed in bed, instead, and ignored him. I can still see him, standing there and staring at me, able to walk, when he couldn't even crawl yet. And," she added, her bright green eyes narrowing, "talk about power! I felt he had so much power over me in the dream. He could not only walk and seek me out; he could hate me!"

Unfortunately, a son may recognize very early in life that his mother's fear of losing his love gives him extraordinary power over her, and with precocious skill he may play on her concern. A long face when a request is turned down, a monosyllabic conversation at dinner, a slammed bedroom door or a sulking afternoon behind it, are the tools of the growing manipulator who has learned the sorry lesson that his love is a weapon of control.

Somewhat surprisingly, though, these power plays seem to please a son no more than they do his mother. One man's recollections indicate that among the least satisfying memories of his childhood was that he could "wind my mother around my little finger." Another particularly thoughtful son commented, "As a kid, I could always win out in a contest of wills with my mother, which made me feel underprotected. As a man, I feel emotionally underdeveloped; I still have a lot of trouble dealing with any kind of limits or frustration imposed by a woman, even if intellectually I know they're fair. I need to dominate, always."

However, if this son felt underprotected, many others feel exactly the opposite. The idea of their mother's omnipotence is so hard to shake that they are tempted to cling to her well past a time when it would be better to start letting go. This is especially true if a mother attempts to preserve the status quo. Although we tend to push sons out into the world too soon, a large percentage of women do find it difficult to give up their intoxicating dominance of a son's life.

Studies of overprotective mothers show that their principal motivation is to maintain the central role they enjoyed when their sons were infants. It is these women who may develop in their sons the quintessentially restricting idea that their independence is a sin against the mother, that to stray too far from the bench where she sits, guarding the son's life, is both dangerous and disloyal.

Most women do manage to suppress their need to dominate a son's experience, but we still can overplay our need to take charge. As a son goes about his own life, we may be threatened by any of his independent activities.

"I know some people would think I impose too many rules," a mother said defensively. "My son is sixteen and a very responsible person. Yet I insist on a curfew, because I can't go to sleep unless he's home, and he calls me if he's going to be even a half-hour late. He always has to tell me exactly where he's going and who he's going to be with. It makes me too uncomfortable to have him just sort of walk out of the house into the night. I need to *know*—to have a picture of what's happening to him. Otherwise, I get very anxious."

Other women described their often unexpected difficulty in adjusting to a son's being away at college, and, again, their discomfort was related to the blurred image of the boy's newly separate life. "Sometimes I wake up in the morning," one mother said, "and I think—where is Tommy now? Is he having breakfast? Is it raining in Boston? What is he wearing? What's he going to do today? And that I don't have the answers almost makes me cry."

Experts say that the reason these mothers feel the need to dominate their sons' experiences, and are so threatened when they can't, is a merging of boundaries between the mother's identity and the son's. Similarly, sons who are part of such overly close relationships may have considerable difficulty adjusting to an appropriately autonomous life.

"I was extremely close with my mother when I was growing up," said a thirty-three-year-old architect. "My father traveled a lot, and my sister was considerably older. I got to the point where I wanted my mother involved with everything I did. She should sit there when I did my homework; she should cheer me on at a swimming meet. . . . When I went away to college, I called her every week, telling her the most minute details of my daily life. It was only when I was out of school and began having serious relationships and was trying to put together a career that I realized I'd gone through life calling out, 'Look at me . . .' and only when my mother — or, later, someone I put in her place — *did*, could I feel okay. I simply had never really learned to validate my own experience."

When the maternal presence is felt to be so powerful, it seems to many sons that it will continue forever. The idea that a mother will always be there, always be a source of approval or its opposite, was amazingly common in my research, even among sons well along in years.

"I don't even have a clear picture of what my mother looks like," a fifty-year-old man said. "I mean, in my head, she looks exactly the same way she always has. I don't feel I'm excessively close to her, but certainly when something special happens in my life, I immediately let her know, and I can't imagine the emptiness that would be there if she weren't around to respond to my news."

In fact, a mother's presence is often felt, and the idea of her judgment is an influence even when she is no longer alive. Frank Mason, a well-known portrait artist, described a "vision" of his mother that crucially affected his life. He was contemplating remarriage to an American woman he had met while spending a year in Rome, but somehow he couldn't make a definite commitment.

"Then one day, shortly before I was due to come home," he told me, "I was working at my easel, and I looked across my studio and saw my mother sitting in a chair. She smiled and told me how much she liked Ann and what a good idea she thought it was for us to marry." He grinned sheepishly and said, "Believe me, I'm not at all mystical, but the fact is, a weight seemed to lift from my shoulders, and I ran out the door and down the stairs and across town to where Ann was working and asked her to marry me."

Sixty-five percent of the men I interviewed whose mothers were no longer alive had experienced day or night dreams in which the mother seemed to give the son her blessing at an important moment. Even when their mothers lived a considerable distance away, unmarried men who were seriously ill frequently went "home" to be taken care of by their mothers. Married or not, they quite commonly dreamed of their mothers healing them when they were very sick.

Sometimes, however, this long-term faith in maternal omnipotence has unfortunate results. I heard from a number of mothers that their grown sons became unreasonably angry when their "magical" healing powers didn't work.

"I'm convinced," said the mother of a twenty-nine-year-old man with a chronic ulcer condition, "that the fact that I couldn't make him better when he came back home after his last attack has made him angry at me, even though he doesn't know it. We were so fine together before his illness, and now there's real distance. He was so depressed when he came home, and he wanted me to be herculean, to 'take the sick away,' the way he used to ask me to do when he was a little boy. That I couldn't do it seems to have made him almost hate me."

As if to confirm how omnipotent and omnipresent a mother can seem to her son, the language and images used by sons of various ages were remarkably consistent when I asked them to create metaphors for their mothers' connection to their lives.

"I am a house without doors . . . there's no part of myself she can't enter without knocking," wrote a college sophomore. A twelve-year-old boy said, "I live in a transparent room, where my mother can see every move I make."

In its extreme, the sense that a mother invades every corner of the private life can lead a son to grow up needing to avoid any semblance of female control. A man's freedom from female (maternal) power may lie in never allowing himself to need a woman in any way. Merely consulting a woman for advice or guidance seems to bring him a dangerous step closer to being engulfed by her. This seems to be why many otherwise liberated men said they could never work for a woman. "I did once, and it made me extremely anxious," a publishing executive admitted. "Intellectually, I'm all for the idea, but, in reality, it can't work for me."

Men are similarly guarded in their personal lives. One man, who was ending a two-year affair, explained carefully that "no matter how close I feel to a woman, there's a part of me that is only mine, that I won't share. I never raise any woman's expectations about total intimacy; it's the only way I can feel unencumbered by love."

These responses *are* extreme, and, generally, if the mother does work at not taking too much control, there is reason to defend her impulse to stay involved with her son's life. She is, after all, only accepting the cultural arrangement, in which even the most powerful father has been as happy to turn over his son to her care as she has been ready to accept the power in the charge. Although from a wide range of backgrounds, most of the sons I interviewed named their mothers as the dominating presence in their childhood, even if they understood that their fathers had had the final say. There is a difference between authority and power. We may honor the awesome court of last resort, but in the day-to-day influence on our experience, it is the person whose nurturing presence is our security who makes the biggest impact on our lives. For sons as well as daughters (if not more so), a father is often a far less dominant presence in the family than a mother.

Perhaps not surprisingly, I found this to be true even with regard to parental ambitions. Although many of the men in my study had fathers who wanted them to enter a family business or follow them into a profession, the fathers' plans for them were rarely as ambitious or grandiose as the mothers'. These results fit neatly into the findings of Victor and Mildred Goertzel on the childhood of eminent men. In these instances, too, fathers were often concerned with what route a son chose to success, but it was "the mother," the Goertzals' study concluded, "whose dreams for the boy were more often infinite."

One father of famous sons who deviated from this pattern was Joseph Kennedy. His plans for his sons were on a majestic scale. Still, even in his supremely patriarchal home, it was the hand of his wife, Rose, that he expected to steer their boys steadily toward "greatness." Rose Kennedy shared her husband's vision for their sons; indeed, many observers felt the vision was the principal bond holding their marriage together. Whatever the case, we must remember that the role of a great matriarch was one that Mrs. Kennedy's contemporaries had been reared to assume and in which they found enormous reward. Consequently, Rose Kennedy applied herself with extraordinary diligence to the task of shaping the destiny of the Kennedy sons.

In the preface to his book *Our Day and Generation*, Senator Edward Kennedy wonderingly recalled his mother's constant attention. "She could spot a hole in a sock a hundred miles away," he wrote. "She could catch an error in our grammar,

or sense a wandering eye at the grace before our meals."
But Rose Kennedy was devoted to the development of her
children's minds even more than to the development of their
moral and social roles. She encouraged their intellectual
development by example. Wrote Senator Kennedy:

> She could diagram a sentence, bisect an angle in geometry,
> or conjugate a Latin verb.... She could recite "The Mid-
> night Ride of Paul Revere," name the capital of any nation
> in the world, and bring alive the history of every place we
> went.

Mrs. Kennedy also taught her children by what Max Lerner,
in his book *Ted and the Kennedy Legend*, called her "incessant
drilling"—through games of information and quizzes from
the daily newspaper. While she applied herself with equal
fervor to shaping up her daughters morally and intellectually, her maternal mission was especially intense with her
sons, because Joe Kennedy had special hopes for them. To
fulfill Joe's goals for their manhood, she had to raise these
boys, said Mrs. Kennedy, "as perfectly as possible."

The two generations of women that have followed Mrs.
Kennedy's have had increasing difficulty finding so complete
a reward in the matriarchal role. The ready-made environment of a woman's life and its primarily vicarious power
are not as comfortably or willingly assumed by all mothers,
especially younger ones. "My son's accomplishments give
me a great deal of joy," said the mother of a seven-year-old
boy. "But I also have a great many interests and needs that
are purely independent of him, and as he grows older, I'm
consciously trying to develop more."

A particularly striking example of generational change in
women's visions of themselves is seen in a family even more
royal than the Kennedys', that of Prince Charles and Princess

Diana. At the age of twenty, Diana stepped into a life that, in terms of a woman's function in the world, is a complete throwback to Victorian times. From the earliest moments of her marriage it was clear that the Princess of Wales was assuming her role with some difficulty. Although she dutifully became pregnant almost immediately, she was photographed wearing a bikini well into her pregnancy, which is hardly the costume of a future queen. One wonders how, after having successfully given birth to a son (English queens were once divorced or beheaded for giving birth to daughters), she will negotiate the traditional demands of regal motherhood with the desires of an independent and assertive young woman.

To raise "great" sons has not been the mission of every mother. Neither society nor most women really expected such grand results from the nurturing of less princely boys. Yet, once again, in my interviews I found that it was the rare man of accomplishment who did not connect his achievements in some way or other to his mother's influence, even if it had simply meant capitulating to her generally more elaborate design for his destiny. The majority of sons who had attended Ivy League colleges told me that they had done so primarily "for my mother." As one man said, "I would have been just as happy at a less superstar school but she was so thrilled and triumphant about my being accepted at Yale that I wouldn't have dared to turn it down."

What bears repeating in this man's story was that, like many sons, once he found himself in the prestigious environment of his mother's dreams, he did extremely well there. When it works, a mother's vision of her son's magnificent future *can* be the most certain guarantee that he'll achieve it. Her dreams can be a definite help, not a handicap. As Freud said, a son who is his mother's special pride will retain for all of his life "the feeling of a conquerer."

The French novelist Romain Gary declared that his mother's unwavering confidence in his superiority not only made him believe no goal was beyond him; he even felt insulated from dangers that threaten the lives of less adored sons.

> I knew myself destined to reach those dizzy heights so clearly visible to my mother's eyes. In the darkest moments of the war, in the thick of battle, I always faced peril with a feeling of invincibility. Nothing could happen to me, because I was her happy ending. . . . I always saw myself as *her* victory.

Today, M. Gary's portrait of his mother does seem rather dated because of her total sublimation. Yet perhaps one of the most surprising results of my research was that, in spite of modern arguments about how women must be freed from the constrictions of full-time child care so as to avoid such sublimation, some women were very angry when their husbands attempted to release them from these tasks. Instead of regarding the husband's interest as an overdue gesture toward egalitarian parenting, the wife viewed his attempt as only another imposition of male dominance.

"It's not that I don't want help with taking care of my little boy," a thirty-four-year-old mother of three older daughters explained. "Believe me, as an only boy, my son's pretty spoiled and quite a handful. But if my husband's helping me out once in a while when he gets the urge means that he's always entitled to tell me how to handle things with my son, then I'd rather go on doing everything myself."

Responses like these do not come from women who are part of more modern, two-career marriages, in which the expectation exists that both parents share authority outside the home as well as responsibilities inside it. They are more likely to come from women who are part of more traditional marriages, where there are still very clearly delineated areas of authority and where a mother has little faith in her ability to achieve status in any other way. In such a family, when a husband does occasionally take over his son's care, he automatically becomes an expert in the role, as a consequence of the male's allegedly greater wisdom and significance. That his wife will view this help as an intrusion is therefore understandable.

Furthermore, the power of the mother role can make a woman feel more powerful in her marriage. Part of interpreting the world for a son often means defining what kind of person his father is, especially if his father is not around very much to influence the son's opinion. Inside more traditionally constructed homes, it may be important for a woman to retain this one-upmanship over her husband. Thus, it is not simply that a woman is being old-fashioned when she hangs on to the conventional image of mother. Rather, as a study on women and power by the British sociologists Margaret Stacey and Marion Price concluded, until a woman can achieve power in the larger society, giving up her traditional role to a husband will feel more like a loss than a gain.

Over and over I was to hear stories that confirmed that women felt that sons were theirs to manage and that a husband's "help" was an assault on their domain. Sonya, a woman whose son had recently been accepted at Harvard, said in a voice flat with rage, "I've spent the last ten years preparing Larry for Harvard. I supervised his study habits; I guided his choice of courses in high school; I even planned every extracurricular experience around how he would look to an admissions committee. My husband never took part in any of it. But all of a sudden, when Larry started applying to colleges, there his father was, determined to 'help' him. He guided Larry in filling out every question on the application and then insisted on taking him to Cambridge for the interview. Oh sure," she said bitterly, anticipating my next question, "I went along too, but it wasn't my victory anymore. My husband had taken over. What's more, I suddenly felt like the least important person in the car."

Such accounts of maternal possessiveness reinforce the idea of how the potential for excess exists when the family is a woman's major power base. But if a mother is tempted to impose her own needs on her son's life, she may also teach him unfortunate lessons about male accountability in the process. The sense of masculine control over women deepens as a son grows to understand that he can manipulate his mother's emotions and that her devotion remains constant. When his mother is displeased, an impassioned hug and an effusive "I love you so much, Mommy!" guarantee her unqualified forgiveness. It is the rare son, however "liberated" he may want to be, who does not develop a set of expectations about his ability to soothe an angry woman by offering her an apology and physical expressions of his love.

The dynamic between men and women as lovers seems most often to have its roots in the female loyalty and magnanimous care that a mother has raised her son to expect from women. Several men I interviewed admitted to being "stunned" when a woman walked out on them because of a transgression. "I *told* her I was sorry," one thirty-year-old man said in amazement, "and she still wouldn't forgive me; wouldn't even give me another chance!" Nothing in this man's background had prepared him for the idea that women do not always give men another chance. Nor, of course, do women who later enter into relationships with such men always understand the expectations that have been set up by the all-forgiving women who preceded them in their lovers' lives.

It will be a long time before even the most enlightened mother and her sons can escape the immediate and potential pitfalls of the distribution of power in the mother-son bond. A great many imbalances in the larger society must be redressed before that can happen. Until then, mothers perhaps can do no more than remain aware of the temptation to use their sons' dependency on them as an opportunity to assert personal dominance. At the same time, they must carefully examine the messages they communicate to their sons about love and responsibility. It is no service to a son to make him feel that he can manipulate his mother and that his mother lives only for his success. A mother's love should not lead a son to perceive of himself as all-powerful. Nonetheless, that does remain a hazard that is central to the issue of raising a child who belongs to the more "powerful" sex.

Sons and Lovers Revisited

"You getting to be," she said, putting her hand beneath his chin and holding his face away from her, "a right big boy. You going to be a mighty fine man, you know that?"... And he knew again... that she was telling him today something that he must remember and understand tomorrow. He watched her face, his heart swollen with love for her. . . .

"Yes, Ma," he said, hoping that she would realize, despite his stammering tongue, the depth of his passion to please her.

James Baldwin wrote these lines over thirty years ago in his autobiographical novel, *Go Tell It on the Mountain*.

Many mothers and sons are similarly tongue-tied in the face of the sometimes overwhelming love they feel for each other. When the mother's eyes shine with an awareness that is not only maternal, and a teen-age son's heart beats with a sentiment as sensual as it is adoring, discomfort may hover around the edges of their mutual delight. Conversation halts, becomes heavy with unspoken messages.

These complicated emotional responses often startle mothers and leave them confused about how to behave. "I can't quite date the beginning of my consciously changing the way I touched him," wrote a mother in *Ms.* magazine, under a pseudonym, Amanda Ross, taken to protect her son's privacy, about her relationship with her fifteen-year-old son. "The touches had lost an innocent physical ease and become more conscious gestures, rationed, careful, guarded." Nor, added Ross, had she previously acknowledged that "ongoing sexuality" and "physical longing" were components of her maternal love. However, even women who do accept the sensuality that is woven into the fabric of the mother-son relationship, who unabashedly enjoyed the erotic overtones of breastfeeding and child care, may find themselves becoming uncomfortable as their boys begin to grow into men. This seems to be the time to transform maternity's image into a prim and proper asexual mother from a woman-mother with fully blooming sexual responses.

Despite the advice that therapists like Lily Pincus and Christopher Dare offer mothers about not being afraid to admit the incestuous fantasies these feelings encourage, it was the rare woman who had achieved that freedom with an adolescent son.

"Look," said Hannah, the agitated mother of a thirteen-year-old boy, "I know all about Oedipal attraction, about how Brian may lust after me. But what about what I'm feeling toward him? I'm sometimes so aware of his body! Last summer, he came out of the water and threw himself on my blanket and rubbed his body against mine to make me wet, the way he used to when he was a little boy. His skin was all tan and glistening, and there was that sharp white line around his trunks, AND the trunks suddenly seemed awfully tight, and I was absolutely flooded with sexual response. It terrified me. No one would ever have made me believe I could react that way to my own child."

Hannah described her own mother to me as "saintly," and it was obvious that her problem with reacting erotically to her son had much to do with how unsaintly he was making her feel. Her image of what a mother "should be" made her sexual arousal even more frightening. All the people who appeared at various stages in a woman's sexual development can rise out of the past to color her life with a flush of moral discomfort when she is sexually stirred by her growing boy. Unresolved longings for her father, and perhaps similar feelings for a brother, may fill her thoughts and stir her body. She may remember, too, the boys who made her pulse quicken when she was a teen-ager and how guilty she felt about this arousal.

Irving Markowitz, of the New Jersey family clinic, explained that openness to erotic feelings toward a son begins way back in a woman's life, in her comfort and openness to eroticism long before she ever thought of being a mother. If her concern at base is heavily moralistic, whether because of her educational, or religious, or family background, distress about what she's feeling toward her son can certainly get in the way of their relationship.

Happily, most women are able to accept their current and remembered yearnings without too much moral distress. In fact, they seem to feel delightfully rejuvenated by the interplay of past and present sexual awareness.

"As I watch my son develop," Connie explained, "I feel as if he's taking me back to my own fifteen-year-old self, when sexuality was actually so much more exciting than anything that came later." And, indeed, no matter how aroused we may get in our grown-up beds, the memory of that first discovery of sexual pleasure is often unmatched in intensity. Thus, in reawakening old desire, a son's exploding sexuality may allow his mother to feel like her son's first girl. It is a response that embarrasses but enchants her. "I guess you could say," said Connie, smiling rather sheepishly, "that I always loved my son, but now that he's a teen-ager, I'm madly *in* love with him."

Nevertheless, even women as comfortable about their not-so-maternal feelings as Connie often found themselves questioning whether what they were doing or saying to a thirteen- or fourteen-year-old son was really "appropriate"—a word usually absent from mothers' vocabularies in connection with their sons before they reach this age. In fact, a mother's sense of appropriateness is an important tool for keeping the balance between instinct and expression; it helps her judge when her gesture is loving and when, perhaps, it is too seductive. These remain persistent questions, with elusive answers for mothers of sons.

Not only are we still unclear in our culture about how strong the mother-son tie should be and how long it should continue; we also maintain a strong taboo against incest. No wonder, then, that even the most uninhibited woman will find her step slowed as she hurries to embrace her growing boy. And even when the boy is younger, if she senses that she is about to cross the shadowy line (and allows herself to admit it) between sensual appreciation and sexual titillation, she can be intensely unnerved.

Edith, the mother of an eight-year-old son and a five-year-old daughter, related an experience that was still alarming to her, although it had happened more than a month before our conversation took place. "I'm accustomed to inviting my children into the bedroom when I dress and go out in the evening," she said. "I work a long day, and our time together is scarce. I feel a little less conflicted about going out again if we have this additional time together." She paused a moment and then ruefully added, "To think I always liked the idea that it was such an intimate form of contact. . . . Anyway," she continued with a sigh, "my husband was waiting for me in the living room, and I was in my pantyhose, about to put on my bra. My son was sprawled on my bed, and I looked over at him to say something, the bra still in my hand, and I paused a moment, *just* for a moment, but I caught a glimpse of myself in the mirror, and I was definitely *posing*, in a clearly seductive way. Honestly," she finished, her eyes wide, "I felt as if I were losing my mind."

Edith was playing in what is a fairly common scene in the family drama. To begin with, our intensely youth-focused culture encourages a woman to stay girlish. In her thirties, forties, and even beyond, she may cling to attitudes and actions left over from much earlier days. This can lead a mother to be playful with a son, and the playfulness needs only the slightest shift in emphasis to become coquettish behavior. In addition, entrenched patterns of male-female by-play are not necessarily abandoned because the man in question happens to be the woman's son. If the woman has learned her lesson well—to be flirtatious and teasing with men—she may find herself unable to react differently, particularly if masculine admiration has been her primary source of self-worth. Finally, it is not so easy to sustain the erotic tone of a marriage, even a good and loving one. Wrote Dr. Markowitz, "Many husbands begin to substitute emotional support for sensuality." It was clear to me when talking to mothers of Oedipal and post-Oedipal sons that they found something tremendously satisfying in knowing they not only were adored by their sons, but also played such a vital part in the boys' sensual awareness. It is very, very hard to resist responding to the sweetly thickened atmosphere, if only for an instant of lapsed control.

The French novelist Stendahl painted an extraordinary picture of this atmosphere in his autobiographical novel, *La Vie d'Henri Brulard*.

> I was in love with my mother. . . . I wanted to cover my mother with kisses, and without any clothes on. She loved me passionately and often kissed me; I returned her kisses

with such fervour that she was often forced to go away. I abhorred my father when he came to interrupt our kisses. I always wanted to kiss her bosom.*

For the majority of mothers in my study, the special beauty of that warm climate of mother-son passion was directly related to its forbidden aspects. "Because it's so terribly poignant . . ." a novelist-mother explained softly. "I'm so exquisitely aware of my son's youthful beauty and beginnings of manhood. Every single day I marvel that this young man came from my flesh, and yet every day I know I must try harder to let him go toward other love. It's very beautiful and very sad, the way any rich experience in life has to be."

Almost all of the women in my survey acted on this complex mixture of recognition and regret by beginning to separate from their sons as the boys reached middle childhood. When the sons were somewhere between the ages of eight and eleven, the mother's affection became more verbal than physical, and bedroom doors started to close on any nakedness.

In her *Ms.* article, the pseudonymous Amanda Ross also commented on this change and suggested that it was her son who had subtly invited her to see that it was time to mute certain intimacies. With a clear sigh of loss, she wrote: "I will probably never see Michael's naked body again, except by accident. I don't remember when he started discreetly retiring behind closed doors, appearing only if semiclad." Just as she didn't remember, she said, "when I realized—with a shock of regret and erotic response—that he had developed pubic hair."

Once again, cultural factors influence a mother's self-

*It is worth mentioning that one of Stendahl's biographers, Matthew Josephson, reports that when Freud read this passage, he claimed to be "astonished."

consciousness when she is around an equally self-conscious boy. Today, many women are living as single parents by the time their sons reach adolescence. If there are no lovers in the mother's life, her son's sexuality and loving attention can be especially arousing, as Amanda Ross candidly confirmed. "To have an adolescent son when you are already looking hungrily at the firm bodies of men on the street, noticing and rejecting the pangs you feel at a movie or ad showing romance or tenderness or sexual tension, it is a particularly private pain."

What's more, even a preadolescent boy may mirror attitudes and behaviors that suggest a much older male. As we are a culture that encourages women to stay girlish, so our boys and girls have an erotic awareness that is almost shockingly precocious. The tension between mother and son can quickly increase when he begins to connect her to the jiggling-bosomed females on TV and in the street or the balloon-bottomed temptresses on magazine covers or on the beach. Mothers who are wrestling with inappropriate responses to their sons report being extraordinarily uncomfortable during such moments of the boys' male recognition of other women.

"I hate going to movies with my thirteen-year-old now," a mother complained, "unless they're the PG ones, which of course he never wants to see. I'm conscious of how explicit and stimulating the sex scenes must be for him, and I suddenly want to cover myself up in some baggy smock so that he doesn't superimpose me over those images of 'woman.'" Another mother recalled her twelve-year-old son staring at her hips when she put on a new bikini, until she was so uncomfortable that she covered herself up with a shirt, despite the 90 degree temperature.

Even those women I spoke to who are determined to possess their bodies more fully, who would not be told by any male how their bodies should look or be medically cared for, responded with an almost Pavlovian rush of guilt to the idea that their female figures were stimulating to their sons. It was the rare mother who wasn't discomfited by her son's obvious attraction, or who could allow her political convictions to temper her maternal guilt and fear.

Most therapists agree that boys, more than girls, are overexcited and distressed by the excess of erotica in modern life. The American tendency to turn young girls into sex symbols provokes a boy to desire sexual experience long before he has a remote possibility of achieving it. There floats Brooke Shields, his adolescent peer, on his TV screen, her undulating, tightly jeaned body ostensibly attainable. Unlike a teen-age girl, who can respond to such stimuli merely by copying the look of a seductive nymphet, the boy must respond, according to cultural expectations, by performing sexually. Sexual humiliation as triggered by women, and the resultant anger it arouses in men, seem to be set in motion as impotent desire mounts up inside the frustrated, virginal boy.

In her turn, a mother may be so troubled by the sexual tension surrounding life with her son that she will renounce him well before she really needs to and certainly before she wants to. In addition, the guilt she feels for having contributed to the tension is sometimes projected onto the hapless boy. For example, a mother in a bikini, fearing that she has poor judgment in exposing her body to a sexually preoccupied son, may blame the boy for her distress, defensively snapping at him, as she buttons her robe, "Stop staring at me!" His abrupt and unpredicted expulsion from her loving approval may leave a boy terribly bewildered. Why has he suddenly been exiled? Why is she so angry? Why has she turned so cold? Well into his life a boy may remember the anxiety behind these questions and the dismay occasioned by the unhappy transformation of the love that had, until then, sustained him.

I was able to observe some of these interactions between mothers and sons. The sharpest perspectives, however, came from the vivid recollections of grown sons, who often were trying to place these memories in the context of their adult sexual lives.

"I know a lot of events must have led up to the change in the relationship with my mother," a thirty-five-year-old man began, "but if there was a turning point, at least a symbolic one, it was a morning when I was about ten years old. Up until that time, our Sunday morning routine was that I would take the newspapers into my parents' bedroom. Even before I could read the comics, I'd climb into my father's place while he went into the kitchen to fix pancakes, and my mother and I would look at the paper together. Well, this morning my mother reached across me to get something, and her nightgown slipped off her shoulder and exposed her breast, and I made some silly joke. Her face got all red, and she shoved me hard on the arm and told me to go into the kitchen with my father . . . I was being very rude, and anyway I was too old to get in bed with her anymore. I stood next to the bed for a few minutes before going to my father, and I felt as if she had pushed me out of her life. I was also mortified, because of course on some level I was aware of the deeper sexual undercurrents. From then on, it seems to me, although I knew my mother loved me, there was a distance between us that I was very conscious of and that caused me a lot of pain."

Even when a mother isn't harsh in her retreat, she can upset her son by the transparent excuses for her new behavior. One mother told me, in a voice already nostalgic, how she had snuggled with her son on the sofa when they watched television—until this year. "But now that he's nearly eleven, I've begun to discourage the habit. I have back trouble, so what I usually say is that I need to sit on a straight-backed chair, which just happens to be across the room from the couch."

My interviews with sons convinced me that the messages of such maternal behavior are decidedly mixed and cause considerable confusion. One man, who remembers that his mother became increasingly ill at ease about physical contact as he developed, said he was invariably attracted to women who were warm and expressive, but that after a while he'd pull back, somehow afraid. Analysts tell me that this is a common reaction in men whose mothers sent out puzzling and erratic signals about permissible levels of intimacy. The grown son feels a lingering confusion about how much to trust his own responses—or a partner's. A vague air of danger hovers around the letting down of his sexual guard, and, perhaps more important, he may continue to associate sexual feelings and intimacy with guilt.

A mother's exaggerated fear of acting seductive to her son may cause them much separate and shared discomfort. It is safe to say, however, that greater problems will arise if a mother weaves seduction into the allegedly "normal" routines of their daily life. This is remarkably easy to do. The intensity of the mother-son bond creates the possibility for its subtle corruption and can tempt a woman to exaggerate its intimacy. All the while, no matter how her actions are perceived by others, she may tell herself and her increasingly bewildered son that she is only being a good and devoted mother and has nothing but his best interests at heart.

In his study of maternal overprotection, David Levy found that one set of actions clearly distinguished overprotective mothers from others: they breastfed their sons and slept in the same bed with them long past the conventional time for discontinuing such actions. Wrote Levy: "Regardless of their physician's advice or the criticism of neighbors," they helped the boys with baths or dressing far beyond the point when society condones such care. Many well-known men knew such close connections. A biographer of the industrialist H. L. Hunt reports that he was breastfed until he was seven. Thomas Wolfe, whose parents were separated, was breastfed until he was four years old and slept in his mother's bed until he was nine. Elizabeth Nowell, Wolfe's agent and biographer, wrote that his "prolonged infantile relationship affected Wolfe's entire character and life. He was always trying to escape from it, and yet was always reverting to it, either with his mother herself or to substitutes for her." It is very difficult for such sons to mature emotionally.

Less than 3 percent of the men in my study recalled unquestionably provocative experiences with their mothers. For them, what was especially frustrating was never really being sure of their mothers' motives or, indeed, whether there were any. Thus, the boy felt guilty both about what was going on and about daring to suspect that something was. One man told me how his mother would always check his appearance before he went off to school. "Neatness counted a lot with her." He smiled rather grimly. "She'd hitch up my pants, tighten my belt, and then, just before releasing me, she'd pat my genitals, sometimes give them a little squeeze. There was a certain look on her face that scared the hell out of me, but it wasn't until I was in junior high school that I was able to end the routine. And even then I never said what I was actually thinking; I just insisted I was too old to be checked out anymore. The truth is, for years I blamed myself for somehow inducing her to behave like that."

It is quite common for a boy, who still needs the security of his mother's approval and affection, to blame himself for his mother's apparent arousal, thereby adding another layer of guilt to his already burdened psyche. It is as if the son tells himself that his mother won't hate him for his secret suspicions if he holds himself responsible for creating them. Also, because he still needs her so desperately, he cannot perceive her as the one to blame, because then he might have to reject her.

In recent years, there have been some artistic renditions of incest that place the experience in a rather benign light. For example, in the quite beautiful French film *Murmur of the Heart*, directed by Louis Malle, a young mother and her sensitive fifteen-year-old son go away together to a resort. One night, the mother has too much to drink, and the boy, bursting with the fires and torments of adolescence, makes love to her. Afterward, in a genuinely moving scene, the mother tenderly tells her son that their lovemaking will remain a beautiful secret for them to share but never to repeat. Without apparent trauma to the boy, their lives as mother and son resume.

Off screen, incest between a mother and her son, even when it does not involve actual intercourse, is not experienced this gently or lightly. Both mother and son suffer enormous guilt, and the boy's healthy emotional development is likely to be seriously short-circuited. In the opinion of many experts, mother-son sex is an even more damaging form of incest than father-daughter incest. For one thing, as Susan Forward explained, such incest generally takes place in a loving context; the boy is seduced, not taken by force, so he feels even guiltier about his own role. He does not have "the mitigating excuse of having been violated." Also, while a girl's being violated by her father is obviously a hideous abuse of parental power, the father has not been the child's earliest and principal caretaker. His embrace does not reawaken infant memories, the way that a mother's does.

For this reason a daughter has a somewhat better chance of maintaining her sense of self, even though she suffers great emotional pain. When a boy is taken into his mother's arms, he is re-experiencing his infancy. There is a blurring of time and feeling that can cause the boy grievous regression.

Fortunately, only a small percentage of mothers and sons are truly incestuous or come even perilously close to being so. However, I discovered a curious aspect to the issue in which a woman seems to use her *horror* of incest as a way of rationalizing her subtly seductive behavior. As I conducted my research, I became aware that there were certain women who exuded a sensuousness when they were around their sons that was absolutely missing from their personalities at other times. A warm, earthy mother, playfully teasing her fifteen-year-old boy when we all dined together, became, in a private follow-up interview, a sternly sensible woman, totally devoid of sensuality.

A woman with conflicts about adult sexuality may rely on her genuine abhorrence of incest to assure herself that, however flirtatious she is with her son, she's not heading toward dangerous territory. Because he *is* her own son, there is neither the possibility nor the terror of sublimation and sexual surrender. She seems to tell herself (much the way some women do in their relationships with homosexual men) that with this male it is "safe" to feel sensual.

Yet even when the sexual overtones in the bond are under control, a mother may respond to her son with the possessiveness of a lover. The significance attached to having a son makes it very difficult for her to share him willingly or allow him to respond to someone else with equal affection. Any other female, even a teacher or a grandmother, may be perceived by the mother as a competitor, causing her to tighten her grip on her son's life, although her better instincts tell her to let him go.

With the dubious gift of hindsight, Sandra, a mother who works part time in her husband's office, recalled how she "actually chose baby sitters my son disliked, just to avoid using a woman I knew he was growing attached to. I told myself she wasn't competent, but I knew deep down that it wasn't really true, or even if it were, that it wasn't my real reason for not using her. I can't believe I sacrificed Billy's contentment for my own fear about sharing his love." In his study of overprotection, David Levy reported the ultimate statement of the need to remain the "only woman" in a son's world. A concerned but obviously ambivalent mother brought her troubled little boy to a female psychiatrist for treatment. After several productive visits, she told the doctor, with an air of consummate sacrifice, that she hoped her devotion to her son was appreciated. "I'm letting him come even though I know he likes you."

There is no doubt that the greatest rivalry a woman will feel for her son's attention involves a female lover. A romantic interest that diverts his devotion from her can chill a mother's heart to the point where she sometimes covertly, but other times quite directly, makes her son choose between the images of love. General Douglas MacArthur's mother moved close to West Point when he was a cadet so that she could see him daily. The two strolled together every afternoon along the school's Flirtation Walk, much to the amusement of the other cadets, who were walking arm in arm with their girlfriends. MacArthur did not marry until he was in his forties, and the marriage ended soon and badly. He did not marry again until he was fifty-seven, and then wedded a woman his mother, as her own life approached its end, had chosen as her successor. Andrew Carnegie's mother extracted a promise early in her son's life that he wouldn't marry during her lifetime, and he was faithful to the vow. The industrialist married only after his mother's death, when he was fifty-two years old.

In my interviews, I was struck by the tenacity of a son's worry over his mother's displacement. Years after he marries, a man may still fret over whether he has taken something from his mother by loving his wife.

"I simply can't get beyond this fixed image of myself as first and foremost her son," a man in his mid-thirties explained. "Deep down, I feel disloyal every time I put my wife's interests ahead of hers." He shook his head in amazement at this resolutely irrational response. I was to hear many variations of his dream: "My wife and I go out to dinner, and suddenly I turn around and see my mother sitting in the back seat. Just sort of grimly sitting there, staring at us."

A mother does not even have to be in direct competition for her son's affections to compete with any other woman who tries to enter his life. Many psychiatrists believe that a mother's exaggerated devotion and sacrifice can be as emotionally constricting as her rejection would have been. At least with rejection, they say, the boy is aware of the conflict; with enough strength and will, he has a chance to best it and not allow it to color his feelings toward other women. It takes a long time to become aware of the subtle distortions created by too much love, and by then their effects on the son's perspective may be too deep-rooted to correct.

Although psychiatry defines the problem, Romain Gary made the theory come alive:

> It is wrong to have been loved so much so early. . . . You believe that it is your due, that the world owes it to you, and you keep looking, thirsting, summoning. . . . In your mother's love, life makes you a promise at the dawn of life that it will never keep. Leftovers, cold tidbits, that's what you'll find. . . . Wherever you go, you carry within you the poison of comparisons, and you spend your days waiting for something you have already had, and will never have again.

Although Mme. Gary lived vicariously through her son's accomplishments, she was, unlike some other mothers, not at all jealous of his sexual conquests. Indeed, she trained Romain to be a lover. Somewhat surprisingly, I was to discover this was true of a number of women.

One woman had been an acquaintance of mine some years ago. I remembered her son as a shy and quiet boy. She told me proudly how much the boy had changed. At nineteen, he was outgoing, handsome, and a "real ladykiller." The summer before, she reported with a delighted smile, "I think he screwed every girl over sixteen near our beach house. It got to be a contest, to see if August could top July."

I was incredulous that this woman, whom I had always considered a kind, serious person, could find sexual exploitation of other women attractive. How could she allow, no less encourage, her son's morning-after braggadocio? "We always had breakfast together on the terrace, and he'd fill me in on the highlights of the night before."

Perhaps a mother deflects incestuous yearnings through such projection, or maybe she's compensating for unresolved feelings about female power and aggression. Whatever function it serves for her, one point is clear. The titillation the son feels in sharing his erotic life with his mother will reflect itself, as all aspects of his sexual response to her do, in his attitude toward sex and love in later life. Whether she consciously means to do so, she may be fostering in him a contempt for women. They are only objects for his sexual pleasure, to be used and then discarded, while he returns home to the only woman who commands his respect.

Psychiatrists cite the "madonna-whore" complex when they discuss men's adjustment to women lovers. The young man sitting in the morning sunlight with his mother, spinning tales of an erotic night, is an extreme example of the phenomenon in which men separate women into contrasting categories. In the course of his development, it is common for a boy to create this division in order to make sexual feelings safe. There are good girls (like his mother), whom he cannot allow to excite him, and bad girls, who he decides are different enough from his mother to be permissible objects for his sexual desire.

As a man matures, he must fuse the responses of devotion and desire so that he can enjoy sex with a woman he also admires. For a not inconsiderable number of men, this fusion is never made completely. The renowned psychiatrist Lawrence Kubie saw this syndrome as responsible not only for essentially meaningless sex, but for most infidelity in marriage, as well. There are certain men, he wrote, "in whom the incest taboo on sex is so deep-seated that it can be shared only extralegally or in the gutter." The idealized wife becomes like the idealized mother, respected, honored, but not sexually arousing.

Over 30 percent of the men in my study persistently returned to the separation point between sex and love when they described their sexual lives. Usually the distinction was made between finding only "girls," not "women," as objects of their desire. Over and over, to the point where it was disturbingly predictable, men would say something like, "Really, I *worship* my wife, but I can't help it, the young girls turn me on."

The cultural emphasis on external symbols of youth tends to make men find only young women exciting. A taut body and wrinkle-free skin are considered much sexier and physically arousing than a woman's tenderness or accumulated wisdom. A young woman may certainly be tender and wise, but she need not be so for a man to want to make love to her. An older woman, on the other hand, can never meet the cultural stereotype of erotic beauty.

In novels like Richard Stern's *Other Men's Daughters*, otherwise intelligent, reasonable men are obsessively drawn to arrogant coeds, half their age, who have little interest in giving their lovers anything but the pleasure of their bodies. One wonders whether there isn't also something attractive in the young woman's very self-centeredness. After all, no one can accuse a man of looking to a twenty-year-old for a mother's care. One also asks whether the man is demonstrating that he isn't looking for his mother in the tangled sheets when he aggressively "takes" to bed a series of girls for whom he has little feeling. The psychotherapist Lillian Rubin, in her book *Intimate Strangers*, reinforced the idea that many men see sex in terms of madonna or whore. They are men, wrote Dr. Rubin, who find that "sex is easier, less riddled with conflict, when it comes without emotional attachment . . . who can experience their sexuality fully only with a woman with whom there is no emotional connection."

Of course, few men readily see the underlying roots of their sexual behavior. Even the sophisticated Romain Gary naïvely offered to his readers as "proof" that he had never been incestuously attracted to his mother the fact that older women never appealed to him. No matter how advanced he himself became in years, he said, he always remained "peculiarly sensitive to the tender attractions of youth."

An intriguing variation of this race away from mother-love is currently reported by marriage counselors. They are seeing an increasing number of men who are unfaithful after marriage, although they were contentedly monogamous when their wives were live-in mates. One young man I spoke to told me in a resentful, very angry voice, "My friends all warned me marriage would ruin things, but I just couldn't see how a piece of paper could make a difference. Well, Christ, does it ever! She acts like a 'wife' now, and it completely turns me off. I'm always itchy for other women, and I never once felt like that in the whole three years we lived together."

The professional view of this phenomenon is that a woman who becomes a wife seems, in the framework of marriage, too much like Mother. In the labyrinthine world of Oedipal confusion and conflict, marriage itself becomes the sexual turnoff.

If admitting to "secret" sexual longings for her son can free a mother of the compulsion to act them out, then a grown son may be helped to be a responsible partner to other women by admitting that his mother is always present, in some sense, when he takes, or chooses not to take, another woman in his arms. Once again, the artist seems to lead the way in such awareness. The novelist John Fowles, discussing the roots of fiction, wrote:

> I think the drive to write fiction is mainly a Freudian one. Male novelists, anyway, are really all chasing a kind of lost figure—they're haunted by the idea of the unattainable female, and of course the prime unattainable female is always the mother. The attitudes of most male novelists towards their heroines practically always reflect some sort of attitude towards the mother.

It seems worth repeating that the traditional way in which mothers have regarded sons is as beloved possessions. The proprietary sense is extremely hard to shake, even for women who do not wish to hang on to their sons as they move into the world or to take credit for the successes they achieve there.

Those of us who want to raise sons who are willing to take responsibility in relationships with other women know we must first cut the strings that keep them tied to us. I remember meeting a professor who admired my son, and feeling the impulse to preen and thank him for appreciating the wonderful results of my mothering. I kept silent, because I understood that my son's achievements and his teacher's praise had very little, if anything, to do with me, and that pretending they did was to make him seem a child and demean us both.

How then should a mother respond to the young man who fills her with such pride and so deep a sense of accomplishment? The exultant sense of ownership lingers even as she tries to keep it a secret.

With no real model formed yet of modern mother-son love, with no game plan to help in avoiding old and new pitfalls, mothers often feel they are making up the rules as they go along to a future they can't be sure of. It will help us maneuver if we remember that the erotic attraction between mothers and sons is normal. The danger lies not in thinking, but in acting. Indeed, many analysts reiterate that sensing his mother's admiration of his developing masculinity assures a son that he will grow up to be a man whom other women can love.

When Mother's Little Boy Becomes the Man of the House

In what has since been viewed as a definitive paper on the subject of parenthood, the psychologist E. E. LeMasters described it as a time of crisis. Parents may feel overwhelmed by unfamiliar emotions and responses; old ways of behaving seem inadequate, and there is little information with which to create new ones. A baby forces his mother and father to become grownups, to take what Dr. LeMasters sympathetically called "a last painful step into the adult world."

As there are stories about being a mother, and particularly about mothering sons, so there are many about fathering sons. Mainly these tales are happy; they speak of masculine pride, the perpetuation of lineage, and the exultation of passing on a man's cultural power. Recall the proud soliloquy the hero sings in the Rodgers and Hammerstein musical *Carousel* to celebrate the imminent birth of "My Boy Bill," the son who will stand "tall and strong" as he follows his father's path into manhood. Rarely, except in serious literature, do we get more than brief references to bleaker stories, and even these are offered in a manner that belies the emotions that spawned them. A mother will joke about a husband feeling neglected after his son arrives, or a father will mockingly compare his teen-age boy's lithe body to his own. The tone is light and we are left laughing, but paternal discomfort and its malignant effects hover in the wings of family life.

As we move further in the re-examination of sex roles, we see that for many men the idea of becoming a father is fraught with tension. To begin with, there is an awesome sense of accountability. As the playwright William Gibson wrote in his memoirs, *A Mass for the Dead*, "To these boys whom I invited into the world, I am answerable for every item in my life."

Fathers-to-be, and men whose sons had been born recently, told me about dreams as troublesome as those their wives had experienced during pregnancy. Their terrifying fantasies were filled with images of being annihilated by stronger men or being abandoned by their wives for reasons they could not understand. They also spoke of feeling more dependent during the nine months of pregnancy, particularly if they were waiting for a first child.

Not only are the nine months emotionally taxing for fathers-to-be; they can be physically upsetting as well. W. H. Trehowan, a psychiatrist, compared the general health of men whose wives had recently given birth with that of men whose wives had not been pregnant during the same period. The differences in well-being were dramatic. As their wives' pregnancies developed, the husbands frequently suffered such ailments as loss of appetite, headaches, nausea, and unusually severe colds.

Fathering a son can be particularly stressful, because, as William Gibson suggested, there seems to be a special seriousness to the responsibility of raising a boy and being his guide in the masculine world. My research indicated that even the most modern father responds to his little girl's needs differently from the way he does to a son's. He feels that he is there to protect his daughter more than to act as her mentor, and he does not identify as closely with the choices she will make in her life. What's more, most fathers in my study, even those who already had highly successful daughters, retained the belief that a daughter's career would one day be put aside for marriage and family. Therefore, a sense of urgency about preparing a daughter for professional success did not seem as great to these husbands-turned-fathers. Finally, men's attitudes about fatherhood are clearly affected by the sense that a son's life expands the father's own place in the world.

"I'm sure it's very anachronistic," a new father told me about his son. "After all, more and more daughters will probably keep their own name when they marry, for example, so the family 'line' will continue. But I'm still conditioned to the idea of son as standard bearer, and that does add a special identification and tension to my response to him."

A father's welcome to his son, or lack of it, has an enormous effect on the relationship between the boy and his mother. The father's response is also crucial to the question of whether he will be seriously displaced by his son in his wife's affections. Many men are quickly able to enjoy their new image of role model for a boy. They are not intimidated or resentful of the idea that, as fathers, they will teach their sons many lessons about what it means to be male. And, indeed, even in a world of changing sex roles, a son absorbs his father's messages about manhood and picks up his attitudes on such issues as responsibility for his actions, male competence, the expression of feelings, and relationships with women. When a man is willing to assume the task of male mentor and is open to his wife's feelings about what that should mean, not only is the wife's experience of motherhood enriched, but her pleasure in her marriage is heightened.

"My husband seems so much gentler, so much more dependable now that we have a son," one woman reported. Other women concurred with the idea that the boys they had married seemed suddenly to have matured now that they had boys of their own to father.

Yet, startlingly, four times as many women as those cited above believed that a son placed some strain on a marriage rather than enriching it. When the strain was most extreme, the reason seemed to be that the birth of a son was experienced by the father as the birth of a male rival. Whether this rivalry had to do with unconscious memories of a man's own mother or was directly related to his attachment to his wife, problems of competition could be severe, often lasting long past the usual period of adjustment experienced right after a baby's birth. Such problems seemed to be especially acute when the couple had waited longer than usual to become parents.

One woman I spoke to credited the eight years of her deliberately childless marriage with her husband's persistent difficulty in adapting to fatherhood. Although she accepted some responsibility for his jealousy and fears, after three years of catering to them she felt she was approaching the point of having to choose between her husband and her son. She had no question as to what that choice would be.

"My son's healthy development is more important to me than my husband's arrested development. I can't go on anymore humoring his childish concept of 'his rights.'" Another woman said in angry echo, "My eleven-year-old son has always been a threat to his father. I've had to fight to have his needs properly met every step of the way." She added, "I know I've lost respect for my husband in ways that might never have happened if we hadn't had a son."

A great number of the women I spoke to shared this woman's feeling that a son's presence had revealed aspects of the husband's character she would have preferred not to see. The women's voices were full of contempt as they described their husbands' rivalry with their sons.

"My husband is so competitive with our son. He argues with him about issues he knows nothing about. It's a constant battle over power and supremacy. I *never* saw that side of him with our daughters." Or, as a successful businesswoman told me with even more hostility, "He makes these godawful jokes about our fifteen-year-old son's ostensible sex life that I think are disgustingly inappropriate and sexist. God knows what he thinks he's accomplishing—establishing his macho-ness maybe, or living vicariously through imagining an adolescent's adventures—but I find it revolting. I can't believe that what I thought was a relatively liberated man has been hiding this primitive level of chauvinism."

A son's adolescence appears to be a peak period of stress for fathers. As tension begins to surface over new issues of age-appropriate discipline or freedom, or how a boy should be directed in his life, the marital balance may undergo sudden and shocking changes.

"The arguments we began to have around my son's adolescence were harbingers of increased discord that quickly led to divorce," a woman carefully explained, and added, "Of course, our marriage was always delicate, but until it was injected with those problems of adolescence, we could pretend we were on firm ground. Unfortunately, the reality of my son's conflicts with his father punctured the false reality of my marriage. After that I had to face the truth, and once I did, I had to find the courage to do something about it."

Yet even in marriages where a mother does not feel so repelled by her husband's resentments that she concentrates all her loyalty and affection on her son, the boy's adolescence can engender rivalry between father and son. Fathers often find themselves challenged by even a beloved son's moving clearly into manhood. Father and son will identify with each other, to be sure, and share concerns about such qualities as virility and attractiveness, but the son is climbing, and the father, wrote the sociologist Kenneth Keniston, "has many intimations that he has begun a gradual descent." At best, this presents a difficult family situation, but it is exacerbated if the mother and son find themselves (perhaps partially owing to the edginess between father and son) coming together in new and newly intimate ways.

In adolescence a son is indeed trying to let go of that glorious but childish dependence on his mother, and he often finds the courage and energy to do so by adding different dimensions to their relationship—"manly" dimensions that, at the very least, add a new level of reciprocity to their contact with one another. As the boy whom a mother has nurtured and protected all these years tries out his masculine power, he can, for example, begin to take on the role of her protector.

I interviewed three mothers at one woman's house, and we were all invited to join her family for dinner. She drank a bit too much wine and began a rambling story that bored everyone at the table. Eventually she became aware that attention had lagged, and she apologized, looking shy and very vulnerable. Her fifteen-year-old son, as bored as any of us, turned to look at her, and the air between them seemed charged with a fierce rush of empathetic connection.

"No, Mom, I'm really interested," he said heartily, putting his arm around her shoulders. "Go on, please, finish the story."

He wanted to save her pride, and later she told me that his sensitivity to her distress and his attempts to soothe it were a source of unimagined wonder to her. Increasingly, he saw her needs as a person, as a woman, separate from his need of her as his mother. Her protective response toward him mixed with his sweetly budding concern for her and created that fusion of extraordinary power which is so difficult to match even in a happy marriage.

After all, the years of everyday life and familiarity inevitably erode the precious newness of adoring discovery. When these delights are offered again by a son, few women can resist them. It's no wonder, then, that a father may feel particularly jealous at this time. But the stress may become severe if he senses that it is not just his wife's girlish impulses that make her son's love sometimes seem more appealing than his. If the man has not brought his displacement on himself, by being distant or antagonistic, it is understandable that he will be extremely disturbed if he feels that his wife genuinely and continually finds her son more rewarding company, especially if her pleasure has erotic overtones.

The sight of an unresponsive wife acting sensually toward a son can seriously estrange a man from his family. The father tries to cope with his anger, and the son feels the guilt and fear of Oedipal retribution. Almost all of the men I interviewed who remembered sexual suggestiveness in their mothers' attention affirmed this response. They had been haunted by a sense of foreboding all through adolescence. Even if a father does not actively express his displeasure, a son seems to tell himself that his father must surely rebel at some point and turn on the young interloper to claim violently what is rightly his, the woman who is both wife and mother.

Perhaps the most exaggerated literary example of this threatening, triangular conflict is depicted in *Portnoy's Complaint*. When Alex Portnoy's mother pulls on her stockings provocatively in front of her husband and son, Alex looks away. "Not for me, but for the sake of the poor man, my father!" Another time, Portnoy's mother addresses him as "lover" on the phone while his father meekly waits his turn to speak.

"Her lover, she calls me," Alex thinks in horror . . . "while her husband is listening in on the extension!"

Portnoy also speculates about what would happen if he really did "tumble all at once onto the rug with his Mommy, what would Daddy do? Pour a bucket of boiling water on the raging, maddened couple? Would he draw his knife, or would he go off to the other room, and watch television until they were finished?"

The psychiatrist Alexander Lowen shared a personal memory to help illuminate this complex interplay and its effects on a son's life. His unhappy mother, he said, often turned to him instead of his father for help. In Dr. Lowen's opinion, her husband's support might have required some sexual response from her. "My mother enticed me into an intimate relationship . . . at the same time that she rejected my sexuality. Having made me ashamed and guilty about my sexual feelings for her, she used my guilt to harness me into the role of her savior." Lowen added that he will be forever grateful to his father for not "overreacting." Had he shown jealousy or hostility, "I would have been destroyed." Lowen went on to say that, despite his father's attitude, "for a long while, I could not dissociate my sexuality from a sense of guilt, or the feeling of obligation toward women. Only if I 'saved' women could I be sexual."

Many of the men I spoke to were more like Alex Portnoy than Alexander Lowen, and their recollections of easily vanquished fathers suggested an undercurrent of contempt. Yet there was no triumph in Oedipal victory. When he sees his father's capitulation, a son realizes that he has lost the support of his mentor. How can he model himself on an object of disdain?

Such a son often seems grudging and bitter, as well as

dependent and narcissistic. The lack of a male role model who makes being an adult seem appealing can apparently prevent a son from fully maturing, regardless of his age. Experts say that a man like this also very likely fears a woman's love, seeing it as a force that reduces male power and leaves men weak and ineffectual. Look, he unconsciously thinks, at what love did to his father.

There do not have to be elements of incest in the relationship between mother and son to upset the family balance or rob a son of his father. Emotional gratification comes from a variety of nonsexual relationships, and a woman can make it very clear to her husband that such fulfillment now most often comes from her son.

Indeed, one of the most surprising findings of my research was that even in good marriages a husband must make an extra effort to keep his wife's affection after a son is born. Once again, the degree varied considerably, but every mother I spoke with seemed to have experienced some kind of shift in her feelings from her husband to her son. Largely this was because those girlhood dreams of the perfect man — one who is sensitive, caring, and appreciative of her talents — apparently has a new chance to be realized. A woman will project her dreams onto the man she marries, but even the best of unions will inevitably be a disappointment, if for no other reason than that a husband has been shaped by another woman's mothering. With her son, however, comes the heady and exciting possibility of really fulfilling her girlish fantasies. All her disappointments, the erosions of her self-worth, pain from past lovers and from the lover-turned-husband, may now be healed by the male who has been taught from infancy to see her special virtues and fully to appreciate her worth.

Women frequently admitted that they did not try quite as hard to keep a marriage vital after their sons began to grow up. The mother may simply have found herself devoting more of her energy to the male child's exciting potential, or she may have cultivated companionable interests with him that she had never shared or even sought with her husband. Many women who had returned to school, for example, said they discussed their courses with college-age sons much more often than they did with their husbands. "My husband's a very bright man" was a typical response, "but he really couldn't care less about English literature or philosophy. My son and I keep exchanging particularly beautiful lines of poetry, and sometimes we sit up half the night arguing some philosophical theory . . . I find it deliciously stimulating."

Other women delighted in the eager comradeship of teenage sons at jazz concerts or experimental theater productions, activities their husbands at best merely tolerated. ("My husband fell sound asleep at the one Beckett play I forced him to see. He was black and blue from my poking him awake all through the evening.") Whatever the shared interest, what is significant was how the sons had become their mothers' emotional and intellectual mates.

Occasionally, the perception of a son as the perfect man or ideal companion runs much deeper and is less abstract than the mother has allowed herself to realize. It is often during the son's late adolescence that the mother first confronts the true dimensions of her ambition — and what she sees may bring her up short. For as her beloved little boy's body becomes more muscular and he shoots up past her own height, as the smooth chest and arms suddenly develop hair, the mother may have to acknowledge that her son, not her husband, is the man she would have liked to marry.

"When my son went to college," Rhoda, an especially thoughtful woman in her early forties, told me, "my marriage went flat. I had to face the fact that, outside of our commitment to the family, my husband and I had little in common. At first, I was furious with him and picked on him for habits and characteristics I'd overlooked for eighteen years. I made constant demands on him to change and be 'different,' and of course he was angry and confused. Obviously, what was really going on was that I felt he wasn't providing me with the same things my son had. But, of course, while my son was around, I'd never asked him to."

Rhoda eventually sought professional help for her anxiety and discontent, and claims now to be at a more peaceful stage with her husband while working harder to reclaim some of the vitality of their earlier relationship. It is a shift that will probably benefit her son rather than making him feel deprived. Beyond the idea of paternal retribution, understandably, many sons experience considerable anguish if they sense that they are the source of their parents' marital discord. A son may question whether he is merely the innocent recipient of his mother's immoderate devotion or whether he had actually conspired with her to keep all her attention for himself.

"I'm beginning to realize," said a college senior, "that the major role my father played was to team my mother and myself against him. We used to tease him about his various foibles in a way that was supposedly affectionate. But deep down, I knew we were being condescending and exclusionary, using him to show off our shared and ostensibly sharper wit."

Although both his parents had died years ago, another man unhappily remembered, "My mother was always putting my father down. He'd say something, and she'd wave him away as if he couldn't possibly have anything worthwhile to contribute. I hated to see him take all that crap, but if I tried to defend him, my mother would turn on me. The message she was sending out was more than clear: if I tried to build up my relationship with my father, I might lose all the constant indulgence I'd come to depend on from her. I was too willingly seduced by then to risk it."

It was interesting, if troubling, to discover that not only did these sons regret the loss of a masculine role model; they also felt cheated in their emotional development. One man who was about to become a father himself expressed enormous frustration at not being able to share this momentous event with his father, or to feel some sense of continuity in the experience.

"I never got a clue from him on *how* to be a father; I don't know what it *meant* to him to be a father . . . or, more specifically, to be my father."

Other sons held their mothers primarily responsible for the dimness of their fathers' image, even though, unlike the husbands of women who ignored or deprecated them, the fathers were often held up as objects of momentous respect.

"My dad was *not* a passive figure," said one man. "He was really quite imposing, so much so that my mother convinced me I needed her to stand between us. She was always 'fixing' things so that I could get his permission to buy or do something. At the time, it seemed great to have a constant friend in court, and I'm sure I exploited it, but I understand, now that it's too late, that Mom wasn't a shield between Dad and me, but a wall."

Whether a son blames himself or his mother for his father's disaffection, there is little doubt that he pays a substantial price for replacing his father in his mother's life. Meanwhile, a husband who feels displaced by his son can use her devotion to the boy to distress and control her.

"My husband manipulates my love for our son to keep me in line," a mother announced in our discussion group, and all around the room heads snapped to attention.

"I don't think he always realizes what he's doing," another woman offered, "although sometimes I *know* it's deliberate. But it's clear he's figured out the best way to get at me is through Teddy. He'll pick on him, instead of me, any time he really wants to hurt me or get me to back down in some conflict."

If a woman's resentment of her husband's attempts at control is great, she may strike back with a comparable weapon, using her relationship with her son to diminish further the father in his eyes. Some sons' comments indicate what a threat this can be to their own masculine esteem. In the words of a son drawn by the cartoonist and playwright Jules Feiffer, "I grew up to have my father's walk, my father's speech patterns, my father's posture, my father's opinions . . . and my mother's contempt for my father."

A woman who continually turns to her son instead of her husband may create a host of problems for her son. But the hazards of a son's being the "man" in his mother's house are potentially much greater when a family splits up. To begin with, there is an even stronger temptation for the mother to overinvest in a son when he is the only active male presence around.

"I am not saying that mothers should be prevented from loving their young," Romain Gary wrote in his memoirs, *Promise at Dawn.* "I am only saying that they should have someone else to love as well . . . If my mother had had a husband or lover, I would not have spent my days dying of thirst beside so many fountains."

M. Gary suggests that a model of female love that is so obsessive makes it difficult for a son ever to be satisfied with women who seem to offer less consuming passions. Or, sensing in himself a vulnerability to such total dependence on a woman's love, the son may resist any relationship that promises to re-create that powerful connection, preferring distance to "dangerous" closeness.

In homes where mother and son live together without a father, the pleasures of a maturing relationship may also become distorted. Instead of gradually becoming a more equal partner in the relationship, a son may be asked to be more mature than is psychologically possible at a given age.

The situation I observed most often was that of a son being asked to supply masculine support to his mother at an age when he still needed her maternal support. If the mother is a relatively immature and dependent person, the son's needs are not always met, no matter how much she adores him.

"My mother was very warm, but very childlike," a thirty-five-year-old man recollected, "and extremely dependent on my father. For a long time after their divorce, when I was nine, she was absolutely terrified of being alone. Of course, her anxiety about being in the house without Dad always transmitted itself to me. I'd hear noises and see shadows in my room all night and sometimes be really scared out of my head. But I would never have dreamed of going to her for reassurance, because I knew how frightened she was herself. More often than not, my solution was a delaying tactic, one I felt she wanted as much as I did. I'd stay up in the living room with her, way past my bedtime, pretending, in some childish desire to reassure *her*, that *I* was particularly energetic and cheerful."

I heard many similar stories from grown sons. In fact, a son may often be asked to behave both as a surrogate husband and a surrogate father, with the mother acting as if she were her own son's beloved child.

The philosopher and Nobel-laureate writer Elias Canetti provided an autobiographical example. Canetti recalled that, only seven years old when his father died, he moved into his father's bed to give his mother comfort.

As long as I heard her crying, I didn't fall asleep; when she had slept a bit and then awoke, her soft crying woke me up. . . . I felt she was relying on me, she spoke to me as to no other person, and although she never said anything to me about it, I sensed her despair and the danger she was in. I took it upon myself to get her through the night, I was the weight that hung to her when she could no longer stand the torment and wanted to cast away her life.

Modern literature is full of stories in which mothers who faced their solitude much more courageously than Canetti's mother nevertheless found themselves seeking a level of caring from their sons that seemed unavailable from adult males. In her novel *The Middle Ground*, for example, Margaret Drabble described an unhappy telephone conversation between her heroine, Kate, and a current lover. Kate's teenage son, who had been quietly watching her outburst of tears and temper, said firmly when she hung up, "Mum, why don't you just tell them all to leave you alone?" Drabble commented, "The voice of common sense reached her, and she did what Mark said. She abandoned them because Mark said so."

Many women I interviewed had reached this well-insulated point in their lives with teen-age sons. For the son who so often seems more rewarding and delightful company than a husband, they explain, is perfection itself when compared with many, even most, single men.

"He's so aware and understanding of my moods," one mother said about her fifteen-year-old son in a voice full of feeling. "He invariably anticipates my being sad or anxious and does something loving to make me feel better. The other night I was really feeling down, overtired, lonely, but I thought I had put on a relatively cheerful front at dinner. Anyway, my son went off to band practice, and about an hour later he called to say he'd noticed I looked sad at dinner, that he was sorry he had to be out, and he just wanted to tell me how great I was and that he loved me. I'm astounded," she said, "after meeting so many men who are emotional cripples, that he can be so open to his feelings and so sensitive to mine. I'm enormously proud that he's my son, but I have to admit that knowing it's possible for a man to be like this makes me unwilling to settle for less."

As I listened to such testimonials to a son's superior sensitivity, I became more and more aware of how necessary it is for women to remember that a sensitive young boy is *not* a man yet and, more important, is not the mother's man. But it *is* very difficult for many women to resist the attractions of a son's consideration and concern. "I can bitch to my son at the end of the day about all its little murders and insults without his getting that bored, glazed look in his eyes that a date invariably gets when you dare to admit some need. He really cares about me, worries about me," said a woman in my discussion group. Another mother brought tears to everyone's eyes when she described how she had recently fallen asleep while reading and half awoke to see her fourteen-year-old son gently taking the book from her hand and then turning off the light. "Then he tried to adjust my pillow, which had gotten scrunched up, and finally he bent down and patted my cheek and kissed me on the forehead, the way I used to when I tucked him in. I was absolutely wiped out by his tenderness."

The comparison of a son with other men stands out most intensely to a mother when she has been seriously hurt by a lover. Chillingly disappointed, she may reach out for the boy's dependable warmth.

"A man I cared for very much walked out on me this year," forty-four-year-old Suzanne told me. "I was devastated. He had seemed so perfect—not like anyone I'd ever been involved with before—someone I could really trust, and who appreciated who I was. And then—zap—he was gone, off with a younger woman I hadn't even known was on the scene. I don't know what I felt worse about, losing him or feeling like such a fool. My friends weren't much help, at least not in the way I wanted them to be. It seems they'd all noticed things about my lover that I'd chosen to ignore, and now that he was gone they were tempering their sympathy with a lot of self-righteous wisdom about my blindness and warnings about how I should behave in the future. Only my thirteen-year-old son just listened to how I felt, and I never had to worry that I'd lose face with him, because it's such a given how much he loves and admires me. Do you know how rare that kind of security is for a woman my age with any other male person?"

Once again Suzanne seemed to forget that the "male person" she admired so much was her own son. But if a mother seeks solace from her son that is inappropriate to his age and to their relationship, it will often be because she is aware that her own middle age culturally discredits her.

"It's not that I only feel upset about growing older," I was told by a social worker approaching forty. "In all sorts of ways I'm much better than I've ever been before. But when I'm thrown over for a younger woman—as I've been twice in less than two years—it's hard not to feel in some way diminished. I can't believe there aren't *some* men around who want a woman instead of a playmate, but I'm not sure how many more times I can go through the pain of thinking I've found one and then finding I was wrong."

Even when women successfully struggle against the impulse to have a son fill the emotional emptiness in their lives, the temptation to lean on a loving young son for more concrete assistance is great. Life can be hard and worrisome for a woman on her own, and, as one mother said, "little things become very symbolic. Just being able to ask him to fix a broken table or carry the garbage out on a snowy night makes me feel more secure, as if I'm not so totally alone." Sherrye Henry recalled that almost immediately after her divorce, when her son was still quite a little boy, he took over family finances, giving advice to his mother and older sisters. She could not recall whether she had actually encouraged this or whether her son stepped spontaneously into the role, but the pattern seemed, she said, completely and delightfully "natural."

Certainly it can be a positive experience for a son to feel he is making a genuine contribution to family life with his mother, as long as his mother makes sure that he isn't submerging too many of his autonomous drives. "My mother needed me" was a phrase I heard repeatedly from men as they explained why they had never gone to summer camp or away to college or even taken part in a young man's usual social activities. A shy forty-year-old bachelor named Marty, whose widowed mother had died shortly before our conversation, was only beginning to develop independent social and intellectual interests. He explained that his father had died when he was eleven and that immediately afterward "I began to do all the shopping and cooking during the week. I have a younger sister who my mother picked up from a play group on her way home from work. She was so exhausted from the traveling and the long day that it was a wonderful treat for her to come home to the table set and dinner already cooked. I don't remember consciously resenting the time it took. I *do* remember, though, feeling that a lot was passing me by. It was a lonely and troublesome feeling."

That Marty remained so involved with his mother into his adult life reflects Kenneth Keniston's view that for sons who are very closely bound to their mothers, "growing up comes to mean abandoning a woman who will suffer as a result." The psychiatrist Ann Dally reinforced what might otherwise seem male bias on Keniston's part when she wrote that it is not uncommon for women to use "every kind of excuse and emotional blackmail to keep their children close by." I found this practice particularly prevalent among mothers who felt that they had been discarded by their husbands. To be "abandoned" by a son as well seemed simply more than they could bear.

Nevertheless, an impressive number of single mothers *had* begun to step out of their sons' lives once the boys reached mid-adolescence, allowing their boys, even prodding them, to have their own experiences. One teen-ager, who had been urged the summer before to travel with his mother instead of going to sailing camp, was now being encouraged to enroll in the sailing program. I interviewed Andrea just after she had seen her son off on the bus that would take him to camp in New England. I'd offered to go to her apartment, but she declined. "I don't think I want to be surrounded by the remnants of his leavetaking so quickly," she said, and we agreed to meet at a hotel near the bus station.

"We had a glorious time last summer," Andrea began, "but I realized he was almost my mirror image in tastes and attitudes. I started to wonder, am I really giving him a chance to form his own identity, or is he just astonishingly susceptible to my influence? I've simply got to give him more room to discover himself on his own, but, oh boy, is it hard."

The bar began to fill up as the work day ended, and our waiter hovered impatiently over our table. Even though our glasses were virtually untouched, Andrea ordered us another round. She smiled before continuing the conversation. "I'll do just about anything to prolong going back to that empty apartment and the realization that it will be eight weeks before Josh comes back into it, maybe as a different person."

Interestingly, not every woman finds it a struggle to let go of her son after a divorce. Sometimes a father's disappearance from a mother's life causes her to turn away from her son—particularly if he resembles the husband too closely. As one grown son recalled, "My mother was so bitter toward my father that when I did anything that in any way reminded her of him, she'd absolutely freeze up. It used to drive me crazy." In an unmistakably difficult attempt at honesty, a mother said, "Duane's looking and behaving so much like his father as he grows older that I'm beginning to be terribly tense around him. I love my son deeply, but he's a constant reminder of my loss, of what never died for me, even though the marriage was destroyed."

In the minds of most experts I talked to, such a confusing mixture of affection and acrimony can also seriously hinder an adult son from forming satisfactory relationships with women. He may hold himself back from intimacy with lovers out of fear of the quixotic rejection he senses underneath their declarations of love.

It is vital for mothers to realize that asking a son to respond to their own disappointments in, or expectations from, other men presents a formidable obstacle to the boy. Replacing a father in his mother's affection when his father is still part of the family burdens him with guilt and anxiety and robs him of a vital relationship. To be the "man" in his mother's house when there is no father can bind a son to his mother in ways that will make it impossible for him to seek and find his own place in the outside world. Thus, the mother who wishes her son to have the fullest possible life of his own can probably do no better than to rid herself of the notion that only a man can make her life worthwhile. In learning to rely on herself emotionally, a mother does herself a great service and teaches her son a valuable lesson about life and love.

VARIATIONS ON A THEME

Feminist Mothers

All fixed, fast frozen relations, with their train of venerable prejudices and opinions are swept away. . . . All that is solid melts into air, all that is holy is profaned, and man is at last compelled to face, with his sober sense, his real condition of life.

—Karl Marx

It may seem odd to quote Marx as an introduction to a chapter on feminist mothers, but these words accurately describe the cold, clear look many women are beginning to take at "the real conditions" of motherhood; in particular, of mothering sons.

Marx was referring to how capitalism has torn through the myths society was based on during his lifetime. Similarly, we now find women confronting the idea that there is a mythology about motherhood that has served in large part (if not primarily) to justify their oppression. As this "holy" institution is "profaned" by a new awareness, there emerges a wide range of female response.

Sometimes a mother's anger wells up so intensely that it explodes. Sometimes her sadness is so deep that it engulfs all other joy. Sometimes, perhaps worst of all, women are ripped through with shame at how meekly they accepted the subjugation fostered by the myth.

The myths of a culture function at two levels, as established "norms" of behavior and as attitudes so firmly entrenched that we rarely question their validity. To question is to make the first chip in the wall that upholds the belief system, which is how the current women's rebellion took shape. Why, women began to ask some twenty years ago, must they be mothers? Why should they center their entire lives on a child's development? It immediately became clear that the gospel which idealizes motherhood had entrapped the female sex and finally had to be challenged.

It is astonishing to go back and examine some of the sermons that appeared in the social science literature of the fifties and early sixties. Here is a particularly good example, from a textbook on deviance. "Childlessness is perceived to be associated with irresponsibility, unnaturalness, immaturity, emotional instability . . . psychological maladjustment, and generally unsatisfactory mental health."

If women had confined their reading to less academic material, they could have found such articles as one, by Amaury de Reincort, that appeared in *The New York Times*. De Reincort, a man, advised a woman with a son that she "should see in him a human being who is potentially more individual than she, and to whose creative potential everything should be sacrificed, including her own power and influence over him."

The snare of maternity is broad and enveloping. Not only are women told they must have children; they are told that if they have sons, there is only one suitable way to mother, one that steadily erodes any notion they may have of a separate self, with independent needs and desires. There *were* other articles acknowledging the possibility that at some point a son might release his mother from full-time servitude, leaving her free to lead a less sublimated life. Unfortunately, a great many women discovered that the years of ignoring an independent image of themselves made independence more a curse than a gift. How can a woman contemplate becoming someone she hardly remembers, particularly if she feels ineffectual without the support of her traditional role?

It is this waste of individuality that arouses the deepest feminist anger. The ability to conceive seems to consign a woman to a life of powerlessness and exploitation. It is as if the very act of reproduction forces her to relinquish her separate identity. Many young women, brought up in a value system influenced by feminism, are clearly deciding it is not "safe" to have a child. As they head toward the business or professional world, armed with fine educations and well-honed ambitions, they know that corporations don't encourage pregnancy in up-and-coming executives. What's more, stepping off the career track to have a baby will result in their losing ground with male peers. Recently *The New York Times* reported on the tenth reunion of the first class of Princeton University that graduated women. A poll of the class of 1973 showed "the median salary for men in the class to be $46,000 and that for women, $33,000." According to the *Times* report, the women attributed the discrepancy largely to "having taken time off to bear children and see them through infancy."

It is not surprising, then, that Judith Bardwick, a psychologist, could report that

> while the birth rate has fallen among women of all classes and ethnic groups, it has fallen most sharply among middle-class, educated women. Whether or not they call themselves "feminists," their priorities are the same as feminists. The overriding characteristic of college women who declare themselves proliberationist tends to be their desire for independence, self-sufficiency, and freedom from external con-

trol. They are not interested in raising children, because they associate motherhood with women's dependence, loss of options, deference to others, and low status.

This line of thought should not be dismissed as extremist rhetoric (and therefore not to be taken seriously): it has considerable support from many professionals, like Dr. Bardwick, who have no feminist ax to grind. For example, the sociologists Louis and Rose Coser wrote a metaphorical analysis of the "greedy" family in which they explained that the social institution called the family insists on such total submission to its needs from a mother that she is swallowed up whole, her autonomous drives quickly gulped down as she applies all her energy to appeasing its gluttony. The authors went on to say that the longer a mother feeds this hunger, the greater the family's claim on her life. In order to justify how she has lived her life so far, to quiet her own hunger for personal fulfillment, the mother must frantically continue to serve. If she has lost touch with the possibility of any other identity besides that of "mother," her admitting that this way was a mistake is a denial of her very existence.

Since the belief persists that a mother is supposed to serve her sons with particular dedication, I was not surprised to discover that the self-versus-other dilemma that defines motherhood was at its most pressing when the "other" was a male child. Most women reported that their husbands were especially uneasy about their abandoning full-time care of a son to pursue a career and that male bosses were more critical of working mothers if the child left at home was a boy. Although it is difficult to measure the degree of a mother's objectivity in noting such a bias, this was a common perception.

"The 'good old boy' network begins at birth," a mother told me in frustration. "Whether it's because men think it's a masculine right to have a full-time mother, or they honestly believe a little boy needs more supervision, I don't know. But I actually feel penalized professionally because I have sons, and almost every woman I know in the same situation does too."

Julia quickly corroborated this statement. "Look," she said, "as long as men see a woman's 'real work' as being a good mother and raising successful sons, we're not going to be taken seriously by a whole lot of employers." For three years, while teaching mathematics as an adjunct professor, Julia had been regularly applying for full-time work. Each semester she had been turned down, because the chairman of the department couldn't reconcile Julia's "personal obligations" with the demands of the job, no matter how much she protested that she could manage both. Recently Julia learned that a colleague who has a daughter the same age as one of her sons had been given the appointment. When Julia confronted the chairman, he said his decision had been influenced by the other woman's having only one child; Julia has two. She was convinced, however, that it was the gender of her children that was the deciding factor.

"He mumbled something about it being easier to make emergency arrangements for a single child if child-care problems came up, but that's bullshit. What he really meant was what he'd already said a dozen times, that my first obligation was to those 'little guys,' to see that they grow up to be 'men who'll make their mama proud.' Christ!" she nearly shouted. "Can you believe anyone still talks like that?"

Whenever women spoke on this subject, they invariably arrived at the highly troublesome issue of how feminist resentment is stirred by, or comes in conflict with, mothering sons.

"Sometimes," said Julia, "I am totally enraged at my sons

for inspiring such chauvinism in my boss and for causing me to suffer its effects. I know it's irrational, but I feel they've forced me out of my career, that their supposedly special needs have entrapped me."

Other mothers with sons spoke of career problems that were self-induced rather than imposed on them, but they did note parallels with Julia's experience. Many had short-circuited a career, and certainly their pleasure in one, because of guilt about depriving their sons of the "right" to a full-time mother. In her book *Between the Lines*, K. C. Coles described the frustrations she experienced in trying to counter the traditional view of a mother's proper place.

> In the evening, I take my son to the pediatrician, who's still asking only for my husband's occupation and first name. The nurse prescribes some medication for the finger that has turned a bright shade of green; the finger that was smashed in the door and then got infected because the bandage wasn't changed often enough. The child has a full-time father and a full-time sitter, both fully capable of washing fingers and changing bandages. But who is ridden with guilt about the green finger? Who does the nurse believe should be arrested immediately for child abuse?

The belief in male entitlement continues to run as deep as a woman's fear of her son's wrath over maternal "mistakes." Some research legitimates this anxiety. Experts in adoption told me that many more girls than boys grow up wanting to seek out their natural mothers. The adoption counselors generally agreed that the ability to identify with the dilemma of that unhappily pregnant woman served to temper a daughter's bitterness about having been abandoned. Boys, on the other hand, seemed to blame their natural mothers for having given them up, and generally remained so unforgiving as not to wish to seek them out.

One can also speculate that the potential emotionalism of such a reunion might be enough to make a male wish to avoid it.

Be that as it may, sons do seem to create problems for women who are trying to balance their love for a particular male child with their own accumulated resentments toward men and a male-supremacist society. As the first flush of motherhood fades, a woman may feel conflicting emotions that create anguish both for herself and for her son—the unwitting victim. Sometimes a mother is truly astonished by the intensity of her ambivalence, which may not erupt until the son's adolescence. Then, at the onset of those physical changes which turn a little boy into a "man," long-buried feminist rage emerges to battle with mother love.

About 5 percent of the women felt such extreme antagonism that they caused their sons to suffer simply because they were male.

"I resent having to love him," Lora told me in a tense voice. "I left his father five years ago, and every experience I've had since then with a man has been a total disaster. And here I am, with a growing son. No matter how much I try to see him as my child, rather than male child, there's a barrier rising between us as he grows up that I feel I can never scale; that, to be really honest, given the way I feel about men, I don't think I want to scale."

Patrick is the sixteen-year-old son of a woman I have known for several years and whom I've watched become increasingly militant in her antimale politics. It was Patrick's psychiatrist who called my attention to the way the boy always dressed in baggy clothes, never the tight jeans and open shirts that are fashionable among his peers. It takes no great insight to sense that he was trying to cover up his maleness, in the same way young girls cover up large bosoms with shapeless smocks when they are not ready for womanhood. I had thought that these attempts at camouflage were unconscious, but as Patrick and I walked along a beach one summer afternoon, he let me know he was quite psychologically aware for a boy his age.

"I'm not going to invite any more of my mother's contempt than I already have. As soon as I can, I'll cut out and live by myself, and then I won't have to hide that I have a penis. Look," he finished with a deep sigh, "she hates men, she really hates men, so I guess I don't blame her for having trouble loving me, even though I don't think I'm all those sexist things she despises. I don't blame her, but it sure stinks."

While the response of both Lora and Patrick's mother was an extreme and minority one, other patterns emerged in the conflict between feminism and raising sons. For some women, when the liberated future first beckoned them away from their kitchens, there was a tendency toward overstatement. Previous generations of mothers had made sons their entire raison d'être, but these feminist mothers would now allow a son to be only a tangential part of an excitingly diverse life. Even women who were less adamantly political believed such an attitude was in their sons', as well as their own, best interests. Boys who had not been indulged wouldn't grow up to be the emotional parasites that women bitterly resent and often reject.

Over the years mothers shifted from totally home-bound and child-centered lives to spending much more time and attention on experiences outside the home. However, great conflict arises about how to organize such diversified lives. As K. C. Coles wrote, a man can function well in personal and professional roles, because

> the definition of a good father is different; he may be caught
> between conflicting demands of home and work, but he

isn't considered a "bad" father if he doesn't bake cookies or help out at the school. Nobody says, "See, I told you so: now that he's gone to work, his kids have gone to pot." Or else, "Now that he's had a baby, his career is shot."

It is understandable that a woman will become extraordinarily frustrated by her lack of options if she has been so steeped in traditional values as to view child-bearing as an inevitable factor of married life, or if she gives in to her desire to be a mother before considering what effect that may have on her professional growth.

"I look at my seven-year-old son," Jenny told me, "and I want to scream. I adore him, but I'm dying to get back into my advertising career, which was just beginning to take off when I quit to have a baby. But we live in the suburbs, and it's a forty-five-minute commute to the city, and I won't be earning enough at the beginning to pay for competent full-time help. Plus, I have a husband who wouldn't dream of really pitching in to the extent that I could count on him to stay home if Jimmy got sick and the sitter, if I can find one, couldn't come. No, it's not going to be easy to manage any sort of serious career."

Since we live in a society where very little assistance is given to working mothers, mothers who return to or begin careers will indeed often find themselves dependent on haphazard child-care arrangements. A feminist mother attempts to broaden the horizons of her world and to play two roles at once, but she often finds that something has to give. An ever-changing set of caretakers or a hodgepodge of after-school activities are staples in the lives of children whose mothers are by no means unaware of the children's best interests. Rather, the children seem unavoidably caught between the rigid demands of their mothers' work and the dearth of dependable options for child care.

Although the feminist mothers of daughters I spoke to faced these struggles, the feminist mothers of sons seemed more likely to discount the stress their sons might be feeling as a result of unsatisfactory caretaking arrangements. Perhaps they were attempting to reverse the offensive idea of a male's special rights, or perhaps the belief in male supremacy runs so deep that any man, even a little boy, seemed to them invincible.

I saw this assumption proved terribly wrong much too often. I will never forget the visit I paid to the divorced mother of a seven-year-old boy. Allison enjoyed great success in a sales career, but her job required considerable traveling. Since her ex-husband had moved to another state, the burden of child care was totally hers to bear. Allison had had a difficult time finding a housekeeper willing to take over full-time responsibility for her son during her frequent absences. Within eighteen months, she had made and ended six separate child-care arrangements. Although she admitted that she found the situation troublesome, she assured me that Kieran didn't seem to mind the stream of housekeepers or his mother's constant comings and goings. I was therefore totally unprepared for the little boy's outburst during my interview with his mother.

Kieran was sitting in a corner of the room where we were speaking, erecting an elaborate construction from a building kit. Allison had just told me, with a "here we go again" smile, that her current housekeeper had called in her resignation, and that it was going to be difficult to find someone reliable to replace her before Allison's next trip to the West Coast, less than two weeks away. I glanced over at Kieran and saw that his eyes were fixed on us. Abruptly, he jumped to his feet and began kicking wildly at the half-finished structure, sending the pieces flying around the room with such force that both Allison and I had to duck. As his mother moved out to try to calm him down, the boy started to beat at his chest and face, running in little circles around the room, screaming, "I don't want to know any more ladies! I can't stand it! I can't stand any more people!" As I watched Kieran, I wondered whether, mixed with his anger with his mother, was equal rage with himself. Was he turning on himself in this manner because he had come to see himself as being in his mother's way?

Days later, a very troubled Allison talked in our group about how she had been looking at some problems that she hadn't been willing to confront before this incident. The mothers began to discuss how awesome it is to rethink some of the most basic premises of a culture, such as what a mother owes her son or whether home and family are a woman's ultimate achievement. It is immensely difficult to make the still-tentative values of a contemporary woman's life coexist with these deep-rooted convictions. Yet this is exactly what women like Allison are trying to accomplish.

Slowly, there began to emerge in the group a sense that, in the continuum of change, there are actually several levels of transition, and that choosing to have a life outside of the home is only the first step. Indeed, the difficulties can become increasingly refined as a mother commits herself to a dual existence. Even if she has a supportive partner, even if she has an understanding employer, even if she has a perfect child-care situation, she is not yet out of the woods. For she is still caught between the model of being a mother to a son, what a son looks to her for, and the reality that she can be only so much to so many people. When, as in most cases, ideal support systems do not exist, frustrations of mother and son are bitterly compounded.

It became clear to me as I talked with women that there was another reason for their tendency to deny the unsettling effects their feminist sentiments and actions may have had on a son's equanimity. As females trained to take less than full responsibility for their actions, to crave approval, and to see themselves as giving and unselfish, they found the idea of sacrificing a son's sense of security for their own independent goals was, once again, almost impossible to accept. To live with this conflict, a woman like Allison may need to tell herself that her son does not feel any stress from her expanded life. When Allison ruefully said to the assembled group of women, "I told myself stories to give myself courage," there was an immediate hum of sympathy from the other mothers.

While it *is* enormously distressing to admit that a son may feel he is being asked to pay a price for his mother's freedom, professional opinion supports the view that a woman can evaluate her choices realistically only when she has made such an admission. Giving up the need to be a perfect mother will allow her to judge honestly what compromises with her emotional and physical availability to her son are safe to make, and to deal with his negative feelings in a helpful way. It is interesting that only when a mother did confront her son's distress directly was she best able to reassure the boy that he remained crucially important to her, even though other people and matters competed for her attention.

A quite different set of rationalizations was expressed by Julia, the frustrated mathematics professor, with her long-time, very vocal hostility toward male behavior. Julia, whose sons were growing into middle childhood, said, "I know it can't be good for their self-image to hear such bad-mouthing about men." She admitted that it is a virtual insult to the intelligence of these bright little boys to assume that they will not pick up her disdain for their grown-up counterparts. Certainly, if a mother remains the principal interpreter of her son's world and if she seems to despise everything he represents, the son will have great difficulty in adjusting to it.

Realizing this, even the most ardent feminists appear to be engaging in re-evaluation. One branch leader of a prominent feminist organization told me that she was "laying down quite restrictive conversational rules when my ten-year-old son is around. It suddenly dawned on me that he was becoming very defensive and edgy around my more militant friends, and that not only were they making him feel unhappy by ignoring him or being critical, but I might be perpetuating the very state I'm trying to buck. How can he not grow up to be hostile toward women, if they always seem so hostile to him?"

Such uncertainty invites considerable anxiety on a mother's part when she tries to monitor her son's response to her transitions as he himself grows up. In addition, the level of anxiety always rises sharply when not everyone experiencing a changing order agrees that change is an improvement over the past. For this reason, I found considerable stress between mothers and sons when the mother's feminist impulses developed later in both of their lives. In such cases, each needed to reshape already established patterns of relating. As his mother's horizon broadened beyond him, a son often worried about how secure his position would be inside the wider landscape. Consequently, the son's belligerence seemed, in many cases, to keep pace with his mother's delight in her new persona.

Doris went back to work when her son was twelve, and was promoted a year later to an important executive position. She found her son (as I did during an interview with him), relentlessly hostile about her new image, which was altered in midstream.

"The irony is," Doris told me, "I was always a stronger personality than my husband. I just played the game of pretending I wasn't. As long as I did play it, nobody minded my taking over all kinds of family responsibilities. But now that I've achieved some public success, and genuinely feel more confident, both my husband and my son are unbelievably resentful."

Doris was denying the reality of her life as it was seen by both her son *and* her husband. She did not allow herself to face just how difficult it can be for a man when his wife of some years changes from the unthreatening girl he married to an independent woman. He is uncomfortable about shifting gears to accommodate the needs of a woman when he has been conditioned to assume that she would devote herself entirely to *his* needs. From his point of view, it may look as though he did not have a chance to give informed consent to her bewildering metamorphosis. It is unfortunate that the man a woman loves, and who loves her, cannot help her to expand her horizons and may even attempt to hold her back. Once again, however, women seem better able to deal with the resistance of a mate if they understand that, in spite of his accomplishments and physical maturity, a husband may be as much a frightened boy as his son. As the protagonist of Francine du Plessix Gray's novel *Lovers and Tyrants* lamented:

> You fill me with guilt, eternal boy, you too aren't loved the way you'd wish to be, you'd have done better with a wife who peeled your apple, mended your clothes, worried about your silver and your china.... But I with my searches, my nightmares, my causes... what a burden I must be.

To the son who watches his mother evolve, it may seem that the maternal rug is being abruptly pulled out from under his feet. One morning his mother is waiting for him in the kitchen with his favorite hot breakfast; next, he's being hurriedly instructed to pour himself a dish of cold cereal, because she's on her way to a new job or to law school. Actually it is less where his mother is going that may bother the son than how different she has become from the other mothers he has always identified her with, who remain comfortably unchanged. Many of the teen-age sons I interviewed shared a laundry list of complaints about the less-than-conventional behavior of their mothers.

"She never wears anything but pants," a fifteen-year-old complained, echoing a criticism high on the list of most of his peers. "I mean, no matter what's going on in school, she always wears jeans or pants. I can't remember when I saw her in a dress. It really bothers me sometimes, when all the other mothers are dressed up."

Similar grievances were muttered about mothers who "cursed a lot" or who "always write letters to the town newspaper complaining about feminist stuff." However, it was most disturbing of all to these sons when their mothers' complaints were directed at them, when the boy's own behavior was suddenly and contemptuously labeled by his mother as "sexist." Somewhat to my surprise, I found a good number of women beginning to worry about the implications of their son's retaliatory grumblings, to the point where they paused in their critical tracks. Their zeal for change remained undiminished, but they were beginning to question whether the price their son paid, as well as the toll such maternal passion took on their relationship, may in some instances have been too high.

"My fourteen-year-old son has several attitudes that are absolutely repugnant to me," one mother said, "but I can only go so far in trying to alter them, if he resists, without making him into my enemy."

She described a recent incident that had intensified these misgivings. Coming home from work, she'd found her son and a friend poring over a copy of *Playboy*, making all the depressingly predictable jokes.

"They kept it up, and I overheard them from the kitchen,

where I was preparing dinner, and I just kept getting more and more incensed, until I seemed to be propelled into the living room—where I gave them both my most impassioned lecture about objectifying women and the evils of sexism. My son's friend kept inching his way toward the door and quickly got the hell out of range of my attack. After he left, my son really let *me* have it. His eyes were filled with tears, but he spoke very clearly and made me feel like some madwoman shouting her paranoia at innocent strangers. He told me I dump my ideas on his life so much, he was afraid to bring anyone home, and that I had no right to embarrass him in front of his friends, even if I didn't like them. Well, of course he's right about that, but also *do* I have the right to impose my beliefs on him when my values are still so different from the dominant culture's? And it's obviously a culture that holds some attraction for him."

It is evident that a mother who asks this sort of question still believes that a son's needs and wishes should guide her own behavior. Intellectually, she knows that her son's reading *Playboy* in front of her, when he knows how much it offends her, is provocative and insulting. Another mother, more secure in her feminism and less in need of her son's approval, might have thought of alternative ways of coping. She might have felt it appropriate for her son to exercise the same discretion to her awareness of his sexuality as she practiced in her behavior toward him. At the very least, she might have let him know that he would be more respectful of her needs if he read a magazine she found distasteful in the privacy of his own room.

After all, it is not the "right" of a son to have a mother who follows the instructions of a culture in raising him. When a boy's basic needs for security have been met, he tends to come to this understanding as he matures. One young man named Alex, whose mother is the outspoken leader of many crusading groups, told me, "I used to think it was terrible that I didn't have a mother who stayed home and made chocolate chip cookies and was always available to me, but that simply wasn't the mother I had. After a while, I stopped feeling sorry for myself, and then I was better able to appreciate her for who she was. I realized that I had no more right to a traditional mother than I had to a fat mother or a thin mother or a healthy mother. Once I thought of it that way, we were able to work out a pretty good relationship."

Nevertheless, a great number of women feel themselves trapped by history and are not able to be so rational about the effects of their feminist mothering. This may be true even when a son appears to be taking that upbringing in stride. Mary Kay Blakely, in *The New York Times*, discussed her decision not to buy toy guns for her little boy. As he eagerly unwrapped the gifts at his seventh birthday party, she thought, "In spite of his apparent contentment, in twenty years, in his group-therapy sessions, what will his 'unhappy childhood' stories be? He asked for a cap gun, nobody got him a cap gun. Nobody would. . . . There are things he wanted, he will tell the therapist, that we didn't give him. A gun. What else?"

As such a son moves into a world peopled, for the most part, by boys raised very differently from himself, a mother wonders whether he will be able to hold his own. Even a determined feminist like the writer Jane Lazarre wrote that, although her son at six "is passionate about dolls and cooking, delicate drawings, flowers and imaginary stories about winged swans who carry little boys to magical lands above the clouds and bring them home in time for dinner," she knows that he has a "desire to be like his father and his brother, to find a meeting ground, to translate the natural and interior sense of his masculinity into external and easily accessible terms." Troubled about his masculine dilemma, she wrote sadly, "I may encourage his growing involvement in baseball, which he clearly appropriates from his brother and friends without any authentic interest of his own, appropriates because he yearns to be a boy too, to be a man. I may even buy him a toy gun, if he begs me enough."

Anxiety about a son's atypical sensitivity and gentleness extends to the point where more than a few mothers (to their own dismay) found themselves wondering whether the "feminine" qualities they had nurtured in their sons would put them at a disadvantage, not just with other boys, but with a strong, assertive girl. Traditionally, mothers have always worried that a precious son's mate would not appreciate him enough. But it is ironic that the very woman who is trying to become a more powerful person herself, and to teach her son to accept women as strong, independent people, will be troubled by such male-oriented maternal concerns.

"The political part of me applauds these confident, assertive young women I see growing up around me," the mother of a sixteen-year-old boy said, "but the protective instinct in me wonders if the trusting, guileless boy I've raised is any match for such a female; whether the wrong one won't walk all over him."

Even the "right" girl may distress a mother caught between her political beliefs and her old-fashioned maternal perceptions. Irma Badillo is the wife of former New York congressman Herman Badillo, and at one time held an important job in the New York State governor's office. I remember hearing Mrs. Badillo speak at a NOW meeting on the family. The Badillos' son, newly out of medical school and recently married, had turned down a residency at the hospital of his choice to take another post in the city where his wife had been granted an important fellowship. Initially,

Mrs. Badillo had been nonplussed about her son's making concessions to his wife's career, even though she was proud of her daughter-in-law and applauded her ambition.

When such bewildering juxtapositions of feminist and maternal responses became the subject of discussion in my women's group, some intriguing conclusions were reached that helped to explain them. It appears that, deep down, many women are not really certain that qualities like empathy and cooperation, which seem part of the female character, are positive traits to pass on to sons. Under the shiny new layers of feminist pride lies the old attitude that masculine traits or activities are better than those of women. Certainly, mothers still pay more attention to helping daughters be like boys than they do the reverse. For instance, even a cursory review of various school systems reveals that mothers agitate more to get their daughters admitted to a shop class or a ball team than they do to get sons into a sewing or dance group.

Yet if true social and personal equity is to exist, men must see as much value in being like women as women see in being like men. There is mounting professional support for this view. The psychologist Helen Lewis entreats us to become a society where males are not afraid to "affirm the existential truth that is female," and Dr. Judith Bardwick agrees that "a broad range of feeling and experience [should be] part of everyone's expectation about living." It seems inarguable that such a vision of a man's life has enormous potential for liberating a son from the pain we know is often attached to growing up male. That men have felt compelled to make a wrenching split from their mothers, and that their mothers have, though reluctantly, encouraged the break in the name of masculinity, indicates that sons must benefit if the definition of man is allowed to include and to affirm its feminine source. When female self-esteem genuinely catches up with feminist conviction, perhaps more women will feel free to nurture the feminine side of their sons. Then they will really believe that it is in his best interests, that it will make him stronger, not weaker, and more of, rather than less of, a man.

Some women are already engaged in this emotional exchange. Their goals for their sons are quite specific and clearly related to what they see as the strengths, not the weaknesses, of a woman's life.

"I want my son to be able to claim and name his feelings in the way women have always been allowed to do," one mother said. "It's not just allowing him to cry when he's hurt; it's encouraging him to acknowledge and talk to me about a whole range of feelings, sadness, fear, loneliness. I'm convinced that the reason men are so frozen or anxious is that there's this enormous build-up of unshaped feelings that have never been looked at, that seem overwhelming just because they're so amorphous."

To avoid this masculine heritage, many mothers make deliberate attempts to draw out their sons' responses in situations where an emotional response from a female would naturally be forthcoming. Laurie, for example, told of taking her seven-year-old son to visit his very old grandmother in a nursing home.

"No one with an ounce of sensitivity, including a seven-year-old boy, could resist being moved by the sight of those passive old people sitting in wheelchairs and rockers, while sun and sound poured in from the outside world, where life was so actively going on. On the way home, I told my son something of my own response, and in seconds he was pouring out his jumbled feelings, which badly needed sorting out *and* validation. I think if I hadn't said anything, he never would have opened up. Each time something like this happens, when I help him understand and respect his inner life, I feel I've done him an enormous service."

Although traditional fathers may still encourage a stiff-upper-lip upbringing for sons, helping a boy to develop a vocabulary of feeling *is* singularly important. Counselors who lead consciousness-raising groups for men report that one of the earliest and most shocking realizations grown men come to, when they try to break out of emotional constraints, is that they *have* no vocabulary of feeling. Even in these groups which have come together through men's mutual desire for intimacy, many will speak for a long time in the formal, functional, detached language of the public world. Often men will use language to block emotion, letting glib abstractions act as a shield against attempts at intimacy.

If he is taught as a boy to express feelings, a man will escape the conditioning that has imprisoned his fellows in rationality and objectivity. With this in mind, many a mother is trying, as one woman explained, "to get my son to respect what he senses about what he's seeing as much as he respects clear-cut information and evidence, so that his intellectual life is richer." This mother also believes that if her son sees no shame in revealing his inner life, he will accept similar revelations from other children and, in doing so, will be able to develop the trust and intimacy of true friendship. After I watched her eight-year-old son play with a group of other boys on several occasions, I found her assessment excitingly accurate. The boys seemed to have arrived at a level of companionship that I have rarely observed. They *were* very young, but they seemed entirely free of that guarded, competitive tension that so often reduces male friendships to the brash camaraderie once described by Margaret Mead as "that terrible bang on the back."

When mothers spoke about this issue of friendship, the conversation invariably branched out to the goal of raising sons who would also know how to be friends with women.

"If we're ever going to really discard the notion that girls are only sexual partners rather than full people, we have to broaden our areas of contact," a woman announced firmly. She saw, as others see, that the first step toward this goal is presenting the model of a woman who has many independent interests. Not nearly as self-conscious as nonfeminist mothers about sharing activities with growing sons, these mothers and sons seem to become closer friends as the boy himself grows into a more mature and interesting person.

Each time I met a mother and son who genuinely seemed to enjoy each other without being either too needy or too smothering, I was immensely encouraged. This, I realized, was a harbinger of real social change. There are very important implications in a boy's learning that friendship has no gender and that love combines very nicely with mutual respect.

Social scientists have told me that the idea of male supremacy led many men to marry women they actually held in little intellectual regard. The growing divorce rate leads these theorists to believe that over time a lack of intellectual companionship between a couple is so great a deficiency that love cannot survive. Sons of feminists refuse even to contemplate such a lack. The son of the broadcaster Marlene Sanders and the public television executive Jerry Toobin told me, "I have never made a conscious distinction between what qualities I like in a man or a woman." When Jeff described his parents, it was immediately evident that his responses were never sex-linked. His father, like his mother, was "sensitive," "creative," and "witty." His mother, like his father, was described as "strong," "kind," "loyal," and "brilliant." "I admire my mother's mind enormously," he said easily and, with the same note of pride, began to tell me about his girlfriend, who was entering the Harvard Business School.

In a recent study of the values of young college men, the prominent sociologist Mirra Komarovsky made it clear that Jeff's delightful response is not unique (how much more delightful!). Seventy percent of the men she queried no longer believed that they had to be the smarter sex, or that a woman who was "brainy" was unfeminine. Dr. Komarovsky concluded that the need for "male superiority is giving way to the idea of companionship between equals." She interlaced her data with comments from some of the young men, such as "What I love about this girl is that she is on my level, that I can *never* speak over her head!" In fact, the majority of the subjects in Dr. Komarovsky's study were outraged at the very idea of a woman "playing dumb" to seem more desirable. They found nothing cute or complimentary in such deception; rather, they labeled it "dishonest" and, interestingly, "condescending."

Contemporary families are clearly undergoing important changes, and I am convinced that among the major architects of these changes are mothers who can lovingly apply feminist convictions to raising their sons. But even the most triumphant feminist mother, beaming with a sense of accomplishment as she observes her liberated son, usually admits that there is no greater contributor to such success than a feminist husband.

"It simply takes the issue completely out of the realm of propaganda," Marlene Sanders said. "A son *sees* a man who is tender, who uses his mind instead of his fists to prove a point, who spends a good deal of time, without embarrassment, in 'feminine' pursuits. But even more important," she added, after a thoughtful pause, "he's also being given his father's approval for being that kind of male."

How vital this last point is came home to me many, many

times as I listened to men blame their fathers for helping to enforce the sex-role status quo. Whether it was the son refusing to play football or wanting to write poetry, the youth's attempt to break free of the traditional masculine role was often greeted with a father's destructive hostility.

"I always wrote my thoughts and feelings down in a journal," said a man in his early thirties. "My father really hated it, it seemed so weird to him for me to stay by myself writing instead of playing with other boys. One Saturday afternoon when I was about twelve, I was sitting in the dining room, pouring my latest set of despairs onto those welcoming white pages, when Dad suddenly grabbed my journal out of my hands and ripped out all the pages in one thick tear. He called me a faggot kid and said I should get my ass outside and do what normal boys do on a weekend afternoon. Later he apologized (my mother prodded him into it), and he even bought me a new journal—although you would have thought he was handing me something pornographic, that's how gingerly he touched it—but I never really used it in the same way as the first one. I spent a lot more time outside with the other boys, usually just sort of walking through things, but at least I didn't have to experience my father's anger and rejection."

Some years ago, the sociologist David Riesman said that people often try to prepare their children for a world that no longer exists. One hopes that as men and women proceed into the future, anachronistic fathers will understand that feminist mothers not only have raised sons particularly well equipped to handle the challenges of a new world but have helped to shape its necessarily diverse definitions of family life.

Homosexual Sons and Lesbian Mothers

"I have been perfectly happy the way I am. If my mother was responsible for it, I am grateful." These are the calm, considered words of the writer Christopher Isherwood, speaking about his homosexuality. They can be liberating words indeed for mothers who for so long have been held primarily responsible for their son's sexual "deviance." As boy reaches out to boy, the remonstrances of society and psychiatry induce a mother to bow her head in shame and heartache, pleading mea culpa. She invested too heavily in her son's life, they say; she hovered too closely about him while he was growing up. She tried too hard to control him. She was too seductive.

These accusations die hard. Even today, among the most liberated women, who staunchly defend the right to sexual preference, having a homosexual son seems the most alarming possibility for a mother. Whether traditional or feminist in outlook, women are patently worried about this prospect.

On the one hand, a feminist mother may be committed to the concept of androgyny, which "reminds us," wrote Judith Bardwick, "that most people are both feminine and masculine in their interests and traits, although not necessarily to an equal extent." On the other hand, however, the mother is plagued by such socialized beliefs as that a little boy should play with trucks, not dolls, and should not cry if he is sad.

"I am acutely conscious of my desire to feminize him," confessed the feminist Jane Lazarre about her six-year-old son, and she worried about "what sort of human being would result" from such an upbringing. Without doubt a fear that is deeply buried in many women is that too much "feminizing" will unduly influence a boy toward homosexuality.

It seems to me, from my interviews, that such anxiety in relation to daughters is far less common. Women do not seem to worry that a daughter who is allowed to give vent to masculine interests and activities will become a lesbian. While there are many reasons for this discrepancy, one major explanation is the tenacious, self-effacing belief that a boy who takes on girlish qualities gives up more than he gains. Whatever the reason for her anxiety, no experience was as traumatic to the mother of a son, short of serious illness, than discovering that he was engaged in some form of homosexual activity.

"Last week, I came home early from my office," a mother reported sorrowfully, "and I heard noises from my thirteen-year-old son's bedroom. I thought something might be wrong, because it was his regular day to work on the school newspaper, so without thinking about it, I hurried upstairs, calling his name but not waiting for an answer before opening his door. There was this flurry of activity from the direction of his bed, and covers were hurriedly pulled over heads. I was startled; it seemed much too soon to be involved with sexual issues. But in a matter of seconds, I would have given anything to see some cute little girl in the bed, because the person I did see was his closest buddy, a boy I'd known all his life, and whom I would have sworn was as 'normal' as I'd thought my own son was up until that moment. I absolutely panicked. I ran down the hall to my bedroom for refuge, hearing my poor kid's anguished voice calling after me."

In my study, about 10 percent of the mothers of heterosexual sons said they had known or suspected that the boy had experimented with homosexuality at some point in his life. Time, and often some counseling, had convinced these women that the episodes were not an unusual experience in growing up. During the actual phase, however, their despair had been as intense as that of the woman who went flying down the hall to try to escape the irrefutable proof of her "failure." In the most terrible of ways they felt they had failed in society's designated role of custodian to a son's destiny.

The chances are, of course, that a son will return from his detour from the heterosexual mainstream. The fact that he has been stirred by a member of his own sex does not necessarily make a boy a confirmed homesexual. In 1948, Alfred Kinsey made that point very clear in his seminal study of male sexuality. Of the 5300 males in his research group, not including the 4 percent who were exclusively homosexual, there were these percentages:

37% experienced homosexual orgasm some time after puberty;
13% felt homosexual urges without acting on them;
25% had more than incidental homosexual experience at some point after their sixteenth year;
18% had at least as much homosexual as heterosexual experience during at least one three-year period after the age of sixteen.

Many elements in a young boy's world can stir homosexual yearnings. For example, the books he reads in English class are frequently filled with the heroic adventures and keen friendships of men and boys. As Martin Green, a literary critic, pointed out, in the stories of Kipling and Dumas "the principal value celebrated is the comradeship of a band of brothers — typically brothers-in-arms . . . or three musketeers." He continued, "Often women are absent, and when they are present, they are thematically minor." Many classic writings also celebrate the sensual beauty of young men. Without being homosexual novels in any way, such books reveal what Professor Green calls a "homoerotic sensibility." Witness Leo Tolstoy's *Sevastopol*, in which a young man is described as "slender, broad-shouldered," with eyes that were "limpid." He was, wrote Tolstoy, "the most charming and most sympathetic youth possible to see, and one looked away from him reluctantly."

But what if the son's phase of homosexual sensibility and attraction doesn't pass? What if he seems more, not less, stirred by other males as he moves into young manhood? Then how easy is it for a mother really to accept the idea that her son is a homosexual? One point at least is certain: nothing will work against her acceptance more than if she believes that homosexuality is always, by definition, a pathological condition. If she sees her son as "sick," a mother will be far more susceptible to the excruciating pain of self-indictment. This, in turn, is often followed by an intense and alienating rage toward the boy for choosing a way of life that has caused her to suffer so acutely.

The further I got in my research on this most sensitive aspect of the relationship between a son and his mother, the more convinced I became of the dangers of surrendering to traditional psychoanalytic theory. Meek capitulation to definitions of disease or guilt can create terrible conflict in a relationship that has already been gravely challenged. If, when a mother discovers the nature of her homosexual son's sexual life, she is flooded with sorrow and shame, she communicates a devastating message to her son. The implication is clear that what she has just learned about him is so bad that it has erased all the pride she ever held in him. Without doubt, this will be a mortal blow to the son's self-esteem.

Understanding this, a growing number of psychotherapists who work with homosexual men are entreating mothers to re-examine traditional attitudes about homosexuality. They also urge women not to blame themselves for their sons' sexual choice. One of these therapists, Dr. George Weinberger, wrote that "the observation that homosexuals are raised by parents showing every conceivable pattern of traits is well-documented," and he offered as a specific illustration the popular scapegoat of the "dominant and closebinding mother." Dr. Weinberger pointed out that Jewish mothers proverbially fit this stereotype, so "one would expect more homosexuality among Jews than in most groups if the theory was right." In fact, there is "a lower incidence of homosexuality among Jews than in the country at large."

A recent follow-up study from the Kinsey Institute supports the view that homosexuality does not always originate with the mother. The director of the Kinsey project, Dr. Alan Bell, stated that his findings clearly suggest a mother's influences on a son's sexual preference are "of small magnitude, and thus much exaggerated in psychoanalytic theory"; that, at best, sexual preference is "dependent on other, subsequent experiences."

This is not meant to imply that the psychiatric profession will soon decide that a mother has no effect on the psychosexual development of her son or that homosexuality is never a sign of maladjustment. There is ample anecdotal evidence for both of these assumptions. The homosexual poet Rainer Maria Rilke was raised by a mother who dressed him in girl's clothes, tied his hair with ribbons, and kept him tightly bound to her side. The Beat poet Allen Ginsberg, although publicly affirming his homosexual nature, commented, "From childhood on, I had been mainly shut off from relationships with women, possibly due to the fact that my own mother was, from my early childhood, in a state of great suffering, frightening to me."

Ginsberg went on to describe a trance state he had fallen into, well after his mother's death, in which he "experienced a very poignant memory of my mother's self, and how much I had lost in my distance from her and my distance from other friendly girls. For I had denied most of my feelings for them out of old fear." Ginsberg also recalled the sexual confusion of his old friend Jack Kerouac, the Beat novelist, who was "very mixed up sexually. . . . He had a lot of trouble with attachment to his mother and his mother's dependence on him."

These are familiar refrains. I also found other patterns in the lives of homosexual sons that seemed equally significant to mothers concerned about their influence on a son's sexual preference.

Mirko is the strikingly handsome American son of Greek immigrant parents, who are justly proud of his success as a composer and orchestra conductor. Mirko's parents have never acknowledged his homosexuality, although he has lived with the same lover for twelve years. While he regrets nothing about his sexual choice, he recently has begun to wonder whether his mother didn't help "detour" him from the more traditional route by her apparently enormous resistance to the idea of him as a sexual being.

"The atmosphere in my home was awesomely nonsexual," Mirko explained. "I'm certain that the combination of the church, my culture, which absolutely reveres a man's mother, and my mother's intractable purity made me terrified of the kinds of sexual thoughts boys normally have about women or their mothers. I remember very clearly the first time I had erotic thoughts about my mother. She'd been describing a movie she'd seen with Charles Boyer, and I suddenly began to fantasize a very sexy scene between him and my mother, in the vernacular of my age, 'doing things' to each other. I shut the thoughts off as you'd shut off a faucet, and for a long time I didn't really let any sexual feelings surface. All my passion went into my music."

Mirko went on to explain that his mother's image of a "powerful Virgin Mary" was in confusing contrast with the girls he was attracted to when sexual fantasies and feelings finally flowed again.

"When I was about eighteen, my cousin brought her roommate home from college. I was fascinated by her. She came from New York and was kind of earthy and warm and seemed very free. My mother, who scrutinized every girl I ever brought home until they absolutely squirmed with discomfort, detested this particular girl immediately. When she went back to school, I was icily told by my mother that I had disappointed her greatly by taking up with such a slut. Rather than further incur her distaste, I gave up any idea of pursuing the relationship. It was just one more person who hadn't lived up to the maternal saintly standards."

Mirko now thinks that his mother's discomfort with sexuality in general, and "mine in particular," encouraged an already existing leaning toward homosexuality. "She was so much warmer and approving of my male friends than she ever was of women. Because it was inconceivable to her that I would have male lovers, she didn't feel threatened by my friendship with them, so she didn't make the same kind of judgments and demands. Consequently, I was getting the message that my male friends were acceptable and my female friends were not. How much that reinforced what I'm sure was already my dominant interest, I don't know, but considering my need for her approval, it was certainly a factor. I remember how fantastic it seemed when I brought my first male lover home for dinner, and my mother was so warm and welcoming. I couldn't believe how great it was not to feel pulled apart."

Christopher Isherwood suggested a similarly roundabout influence on his own homosexuality. He wrote that even after he told his mother he was homosexual, she "thought it was some sort of pose, a mental game I played. She was always polite to the young men I brought to the house, and in one or two cases, she genuinely liked them. But I believe her imagination refused to accept the fact that I was actually having sex with them. Sometimes my mother's attitude made me furious. I think it helped confirm me in my homosexuality. I had to prove to her that there really is such a thing as a homosexual."

For most of the mothers I interviewed, the issue seemed to center on whether a son met the criteria of homosexuality. Nowhere in human response has it been possible to see more intense denial than in the mother who fiercely denies that her son is homosexual. It was intriguing to read a letter from Freud on this matter written to a worried mother in America:

> I gather from your letter that your son is a homosexual. I am most impressed by the fact that you do not mention this term yourself in your information about him. May I question you, why you avoid it?

Freud went on to explain to the mother that, while he considered homosexuality a form of arrested development, and while

> homosexuality is assuredly no advantage . . . it is nothing to be ashamed of, no vice, no degradation. Many highly respectable individuals of ancient and modern times have been homosexuals, several of the greatest among them (Plato, Michelangelo, Leonardo da Vinci, etc.).

Today, when even Freud's idea of "arrested development" is being questioned, a woman thoroughly devoted to her son's happiness will often still deny what she sees, because of her terror of the truth. Unfortunately, once again this means that she will also refuse to accept the tacit requests for support and affirmation that the boy tentatively and sometimes quite desperately makes of her.

A mother named Mona, ironically herself a psychologist, looked back in utter amazement at her once tenacious refusal to recognize fact. "I created a series of rationalizations I would have laughed someone out of my office for," she told me, and described a Christmas vacation during her son's second year at college, when he brought a friend home for a visit. "You would have had to be blind not to see they were 'a couple,'" she said. "But I sat there at dinner, making stupid jokes about the girls back at school and not letting someone trap them into marriage before they graduated. I was absolutely manic in my need to deny."

In her discreetly autobiographical novel, *Consenting Adult*, Laura Hobson wrote of a mother whose seventeen-year-old son forces her to face what she has been desperately trying to ignore. His letter to her is written from boarding school:

> Dear Mama,
> I'm sorry about all the rows during vacation, and I have something to tell you that I guess I better not put off any longer. . . . You see, I am a homosexual. I have fought it for months, and maybe years, but it just grows truer.

176 VARIATIONS ON A THEME

In the novel, the mother's feelings follow the pattern I found repeated by almost every mother who had a homosexual son. The first explosion of shock, which left a residue of fury and self-blame, soon turned into agonizing attempts to understand how this had happened, and finally developed into a gradual acceptance of the idea that a son has the right to live in the manner he feels suits him best. Many more mothers of homosexual sons arrived at this acceptance than I would have thought possible.

Such recognition of a son's sexual rights is vital to his self-esteem. For, although psychiatrists are questioning the responsibility the mother should take for his choice, my interviews with homosexual sons convinced me that a mother's acceptance is absolutely crucial to the way he feels about his decision. The title of Laura Hobson's novel, *Consenting Adult*, is taken from the historic 1957 Wolfenden Report, published in England, which held that the state should not police sexual acts between consenting adults. It also implies what every openly homosexual son I spoke to agreed with: that a mother is the second most important consenting adult, after his lover. Dr. George Weinberger movingly confirmed this. He said that homosexuals invariably ask each other, "What did your mother say when you told her?" The doctor also suggested that no gesture more clearly predicts the son's future peace and self-acceptance than to have his mother say, "I'm glad you told me."

Dr. Weinberger came to other significant conclusions on the subject of maternal acceptance of homosexuality: The underlying issue has nothing to do with homosexuality.

It has to do with allegiance. Anyone's child, heterosexual or homosexual, is likely to cherish the thought that, in an emergency, the parent would rush to his defense. When could loyalty be more opportune than now—from the point of view of the young homosexual . . . who finds society scornful and disappointing?

Indeed, for the mothers in my study, it was maternal allegiance and the continued wish to nurture that overcame the self-centered wish to deny. Mona, the psychologist, who had come around to the point where she was president of a parents gay-rights group, said, "It was a question of recognizing that I was sacrificing giving Gregg the help he needed to break with convention, to meet my need for society's approval. Either way, he was heading for an alternative life. The question was, would he do it alone, or with the support of my love behind him?"

For Mona, the turning point came after a night of restless dreams filled by Gregg's sad, lonely face. "I have some awareness of dream interpretation, of course," she said, "but you didn't really have to be very sophisticated to know what I was wrestling with symbolically. I woke up knowing how much pain I was causing Gregg by shutting him off during what was undoubtedly his life's greatest struggle. By midafternoon I had worked through enough of my feelings to be able to call him at school and ask him to come home and talk. I could tell by the sudden tension in his voice that he knew very well what I was referring to, so I quickly told him that I loved him and that I would always love him, and then we both started to cry, and he said he'd catch the next plane home."

Mona changed. She had moved, not without great anguish, from refusal to acceptance of her son's sexual orientation. In *Consenting Adult*, the fictional mother makes a similar journey. At one point toward the end of the novel, she muses, "Once she had thought only, if Jeff could change. Now she saw that it was she who had to change."

Unfortunately, in *Consenting Adult*, in my own study, and

apparently in the general population, one person who does not so easily shift from refusal to acceptance is a homosexual son's father. Before Mona's son returned to school he had asked her to lay the groundwork for a talk with his father like the one he and she had had. Not without design on Mona's part, her husband had been away on a business trip when she invited Gregg to come home.

"It was a very difficult request," Mona said. "It sounds outrageous, but I really had no idea what thoughts had gone through my husband's head all these years. We'd never once voiced our concerns to each other. But I did as Gregg asked, and *when* I did, you'd have thought I told him it was raining outside; he just nodded and left the room on some excuse. Obviously he could not handle hearing the truth."

In his novel *A Boy's Own Story*, Edmund White painted a similar portrait of a father's refusal to acknowledge his son's homosexuality. The young protagonist, who is away at boarding school, writes to his father to request that he pay for psychiatric help. The boy desperately wants to be "cured" of the feelings he has come to believe are ugly and sick.

> In my letter to my father, I used the word homosexuality, thereby breaking a taboo and forcing two responses from him: silence and the money I wanted. Much later my step-mother told me I'd caused my father weeks of sleepless despair and that at first he had chosen to believe I wasn't really a homosexual at all, merely a poseur hoping to appear "interesting." Dad never asked me later if I'd been cured. He was no doubt afraid to know the answer.... Certainly he and I never discussed my problem. Indeed, horror of the subject led to a blackout on all talk about my private life.

In Mona's case, she begged her husband to call Gregg and give him at least some hope of the support and acceptance he wanted, but she couldn't get him to do so. "He

told me he simply couldn't talk to him about it; it would
only end badly for them both. He loved him no less, but
he would not acknowledge this part of Gregg's life. I had
to tell that to Gregg, and of course it was profoundly disappointing to him, but he's made an adjustment. He realizes
how difficult it is for men of his father's generation to accept
the idea of homosexuality into their own lives. Maybe it
will never get better than it is right now. I hope not for
both their sakes, and," she added soberly, "for the sake of
my marriage. When there's something so profoundly important that you can never share, there's no way of not
losing an important level of intimacy."

Actually, Gregg and Mona are comparatively lucky. For
some fathers, the news of a son's homosexuality creates such
fear and revulsion that emotional and even physical violence
erupts.

"My father literally beat me up," reported a twenty-three-
year-old man. "I couldn't fight back. For one thing, I'm a
lot frailer than he is, and for another, it's just inconceivable
in our relationship that I would ever raise a hand to him;
just as till that morning the reverse would also have been
impossible to imagine. I couldn't really believe what was
happening, even while I stood there taking his punches and
hearing my mother screaming for him to stop. In fact, when
he did stop, it wasn't much better, because then he began
to lash out at Mom, cursing at her with incredibly vicious
abuse, blaming her for making me turn into this 'freak.' "

Statistics indicate that a significant number of marriages
break up because of a son who is gay, as frustrated husbands
make accusations against their wives. Some fathers find it impossible to "forgive" a son or his mother for what they perceive
to be a shameful perversion, one that mocks and rocks the
foundation of the father's own masculinity. (Because of the
same sex identification, it appears that a daughter's homosexuality, while painful, may be less threatening to a man.)

There is a certain irony to a father's blaming his wife for a son's homosexuality, for among the current theories on the causes of homosexuality is the suggestion that a father may have more of an influence on such decisions than a mother does. Some theorists speculate that some men turn away from women not through fear of the female sex, but through the fear of, and lack of identification with, masculine power. Such theories build on the idea of Oedipal retribution. They indicate that if a boy is sufficiently afraid of the father's wrath during the Oedipal period, and therefore does not transfer his identification to his father from his mother, he may not be able to form relationships with women. Unconsciously he may worry that if he does, a stronger man will punish him.

Although the recent Kinsey Report does not specifically support this theory, it does conclude that homosexual men generally have poorer relationships with their fathers than do heterosexual men. While it states that parental influence on homosexuality is still relatively "limited," the report does show that a poor father-son relationship is more of an influence on homosexual development than a poor relationship between mother and son.

The major point the Kinsey Report makes, however, one that people like Dr. Weinberger support, is that a homosexual orientation is basically of biological origin. It is determined not by any particular variation of family pathology, but by a genetic "precursor that parents cannot control." From his earliest days, a homosexual son heads toward other men for emotional and physical fulfillment, revealing signs of "gender nonconformity." He will know the sense of being different that every man in my study recalled having known in his childhood. Such sons may play the same games that other little boys do, and they may grow up to date girls as actively as their classmates, but the delights of heterosexual manhood tend to elude them.

It is important to note that the Kinsey Report also disproves the theory of heterosexual trauma as the deciding factor in the making of an alternative sexual choice. The men in their study were generally quite comfortable heterosexually when they were growing up, as were most of the men I interviewed. The difference was simply that these activities seemed not to be much fun in comparison with later homosexual pleasures.

Equally interesting is the fact that homosexual feelings invariably begin to stir long before homosexual experience. With puberty still years off (most men say before they were ten), a boy seems to sense he is moving along a divergent path. Although he may worry about its pitfalls, he gradually becomes more convinced that it is a journey he wants to, has no choice but to, make.

Christopher Isherwood offered an illustration of this commitment to his destiny.

> There was no question at all in my mind about homosexuality [he wrote]. It was like a choice which my mind and body had definitely made. I was quite willing to agree that I might become heterosexual if I had decided to. I tried it a couple of times. It was quite workable. But I preferred boys, and I already knew that I could fall in love with them.

Such testimony was frequently corroborated by men like Mirko, who remembered that, as a teen-ager, he felt more affection for other boys than for girls.

"I had a real desire to touch them and hug them," he told me, "in a way I never felt toward girls even when they evoked some lust." He also remembered how, even in early childhood, he would cajole his father's friends to take him on their laps when they visited. "I'd wriggle around in delight, certainly understanding that on some primitive level our bodies touching like that was sexually exciting."

In *A Boy's Own Story*, the young man similarly remembers:

> I was possessed with a yearning for the company of men, for their look, touch and smell, and nothing transfixed me more than the sight of a man shaving and dressing, sumptuous rites. It was men, not women, who struck me as foreign and desirable.

For Mirko, like Mona's son, Gregg, and many other young men, the first experience of homosexual love took place in college. When he is away from home and the family's moral constraints, the boy's confrontation with the sexual self can begin. Even then, however, it is usually a very gradual process, and the first admitted attraction is often toward a boy who is unequivocally "straight."

"Perhaps," mused one insightful man, "because after all those years of repression, we aren't ready to have fantasy so abruptly become real. With a straight roommate or friend, we can explore our feelings, test them out in our heads, without the terror of having actually to commit ourselves to their implications."

Whatever the reason for such tentative progressions, many homosexual men ruefully recounted nights, like that remembered by a lawyer named Arthur, of "lying in bed, nearly choking with desire, while my poor jock roommate lay innocently sleeping across the room. I'd get up in the morning as stiff as if I'd run fifty miles, from the strain of keeping myself from touching him."

Edmund White's young hero paints his own picture of painful restraint when describing Tommy, his teen-age friend and secret passion.

> Sometimes, after he fell asleep at night, I'd study the composition of grays poised on the pale lozenge of his pillow,

those grays that constituted a face, and I'd dream he was
awakening, rising to kiss me, the grays blushing with fire
and warmth—but then he'd move, and I'd realize that what
I'd taken to be his face was in fact a fold in the sheet. I'd
listen for his breath to quicken. I'd look for his sealed eyes
to glint, I'd wait for his hot, strong hand to reach across
the chasm between the beds to grab me—but none of that
happened.

As one reads or hears such stories, one has no way of
knowing whether they prove the idea of a biological or
psychological root of homosexuality. As the theoretical dis-
cussions of sexual preference continue, however, a growing
number of homosexual men, as well as their mothers, feel
less and less need to join in.

"My only problem is making the best life I can as a
homosexual man," said Arthur, "but that's no different than
if I were a heterosexual. I don't view my homosexuality as
a handicap, so why should I blame my mother or anyone
else for the fact that I am one?"

We can look again to Freud for corroboration of the idea
that many emotional problems exist outside the realm of
sexual preference and that mental health or illness can exist
whether a person is gay or straight. Despite his belief that
homosexuality was "arrested development," Freud wrote the
mother who worried about her son that psychoanalysis would
be valuable only if the son were "unhappy, neurotic, torn
by conflicts, inhibited in his social life." Then, indeed,
"analysis may bring him harmony, peace of mind, full ef-
ficiency, *whether* [italics mine] he remains a homosexual or
gets changed."

As the mothers of homosexuals come to accept the idea
that their sons can be contented with an alternative way of
life, they seem to give themselves the absolution necessary
for enjoying their own continuing part in that life.

"It's really irrelevant to me, now, how he 'got that way,'" a mother said at one of Mona's parents' meetings. "The important thing is, he is still a lovely person, living as productive a life as I could ever have wished for him, only in a less conventional context. So why should I really blame myself? Look," she continued heatedly, "I have friends whose kids are living in many ways as untraditionally. They're unmarried mothers; they walk away from ten years of college and graduate school to live in Vermont and throw pots . . . Nobody expects these women to go around forever apologizing for their mistakes or to turn away from their kids to prove some point about the sanctity of convention."

In this era, which is becoming more accepting of diversity and not quite so ready to label it illness, other untraditional mother-and-son relationships exist, those between lesbian mothers and their heterosexual sons. This is a far more controversial situation for most people and for society as a whole. Will a boy be psychologically damaged, become sexually confused, if he is raised by a lesbian mother? The evidence that exists is on the side of the more liberal view. Unless a mother is filled with anger toward men, her sexual preference for other women does not seem to preclude her raising an emotionally and sexually secure son.

My own observations of this situation are reinforced by the scientifically controlled data that are slowly emerging. In one study by Martha Kirkpatrick, a psychiatrist at the UCLA Medical School, of two groups of children raised by either divorced heterosexual or homosexual mothers, both sets of children experienced the same kinds of problems. These problems apparently result from broken marriages, rather than from the lesbian mothers' breaks with convention. Most closely applicable to the discussion of a predisposition to homosexuality is another study of children raised by homosexual mothers, conducted by Dr. Richard Green of the State University of New York. It indicates that the sons showed no "confusion of gender." Some other research contradicts Dr. Green to the extent that it suggests a tendency on the part of some sons of lesbian mothers to become bisexual (a variation that is itself gaining wider cultural acceptance), but the preponderance of the data show that the sons are heterosexual and pick up their cues for maleness outside the home.

What seems to cause the greatest anguish to lesbian mothers is not the worry that they will hurt their sons—they know the depth of their commitment too well to worry about that—but the fear that their sons will grow to hate and reject them when they realize their mothers' true sexual nature. For this reason, lesbian women who are otherwise quite comfortable about their sexuality may become immensely self-conscious around their growing boys. Often they choose to live sexually clandestine lives, having a lover sleep in the guest room on an overnight visit, or never showing the most adored partner any physical affection.

Yet when more courageous mothers have spoken out, their sons were often openly accepting. The responses I heard from sons ranged from "I think it's weird, but she's still my mother, and we love each other. As long as she cools it around my friends, I think it'll be okay with us," to something like pride in a mother with the ability to "live authentically."

"I don't know. I appreciate that she had the guts to do what she wanted to, without worrying about other people's approval," said a seventeen-year-old boy named Chad. "Being 'different' is such a terrible fear for some of the kids I know; my mother and I talk about that, about being strong enough to fight for your convictions, whatever they are. Sure, I'm not pretending I wouldn't rather she showed her gutsiness in a more conventional way, but I certainly wouldn't want her to deny who she was just to fit in. And I really do believe she's helping me be more of an individual myself."

Most mothers who are open about their lesbianism subscribe to this view.

"I can't pretend I wouldn't rather he be heterosexual," a lesbian mother said in response to a hypothetical question about her nine-year-old son. "But that's only because society still has a way to go in really accepting homosexuality, and I know his life will be simpler if he conforms to the norm. On the other hand, I believe I'm presenting a model of personal responsibility, of someone making reasoned, tough choices about her life in every area, choices she's willing to fight for, that will serve him well in the complicated world he's going to be a man in."

What these mothers and sons seem to be doing, most of all, is expanding the definition of "normal" behavior, in a way that seems appropriate to our pluralistic age. As the British psychologists Chris Gosselin and Glenn Wilson stated in their important book, *Sexual Variation*, "Unusual sexual patterns and predilections can be found in anyone. . . . What is more, they can be found in people who otherwise don't feel themselves to be sick or abnormal in any way."

The authors also offered this concluding definition: "That which promotes love, caring and affection between people is normal, while that which divides them is abnormal."

If one uses that measure, having a homosexual son or being a lesbian mother need not be regarded as abnormal. It is far more abnormal to allow society's view of 'deviance' to impinge on the profound feelings mother and son hold for each other.

Not-So-Present Mothers

"Man's love is of man's life a thing apart; 'tis woman's whole existence." So wrote Robert Browning, capturing in a few words the traditional view of women's lives, one that generations of women accepted as accurate and natural. To want more than love, to want also what the psychologists Grace Baruch and Rosalind Barret and the writer Caryl Rivers call "mastery," in their important book, *Lifeprints*, can create intense emotional conflict. This is particularly true for women who, like myself, were socialized before the women's movement took hold. Indeed, perhaps nothing so divides younger and older generations of mothers than the guilt and discomfort the older women feel about seeking self-esteem through mastering activities in the outside world. Even when they are enormously successful there, even when they make an impact on all humanity, as some singular women have managed to do, ambivalence can temper the pride of accomplishment.

In an interview with Oriana Fallaci, Golda Meir, the late prime minister of Israel, said, "After all, it's the woman who gives birth. It's the woman who raises the children. And when a woman doesn't want only to give birth, to raise children . . . when a woman also wants to work, to be somebody . . . well, it's hard. Hard, hard. I know it from personal experience. You're at your job and you think of the children you've left at home. You're at home and you think of the work you're not doing. Such a struggle breaks out in you, your heart goes to pieces."

Mrs. Meir claimed to have "paid a lot" for her success, and that the price largely related to her children. "You see, I know that my children, when they were little, suffered a lot on my account. I left them alone so often. . . . I was never with them when I should have been or would have liked to be. Oh, I remember how happy they were, my children, every time I didn't go to work because of a headache. They jumped and laughed and sang, 'Momma's staying home! Momma has a headache!' I have a great sense of guilt toward Sarah and Menahem."

Indeed, even women who had professional mothers as role models found it difficult freely to admit dreams and aspirations that went beyond maternity. One striking example is the psychiatric social worker and professor Sophie Freud Lowenstein, who is the daughter of a full-time practicing speech therapist and the granddaughter of Sigmund Freud. Dr. Lowenstein said that, despite "this compelling script for achievement, conflicting societal expectations interfered with a clear pursuit of professional goals. Although my work was an emotional necessity for me, I long denied its significance in my life."

It is important to point out that in this chapter I am discussing women for whom working *is* an emotional necessity, whether or not it is also a financial one. Society is generally forgiving of the mother who had to work in order to help support her family but is far less accepting of the woman who chooses to extend her life beyond the role of mother. When this social disapproval is mixed with anxiety about male approval, the mother of a son can be intensely distressed if the boy suffers in any way as a result of her absence from his daily life.

It is apparently for this reason that many women are compelled to deny both their ambition and its possible effects on family life. For instance, one vice president of an advertising agency told me rather sternly, "I have no patience with women who aren't willing to take on double roles. It's a cop-out to settle for family over career, or vice versa. I've raised two sons, and they're fine young men. They've never felt deprived in any way."

Interestingly, the higher a woman climbs professionally, the more defensive she may become about her career commitments. The old value of the selfless, totally devoted wife and mother can make a woman who obviously cares about her career feel uneasy about her female identity. Once again, we can look to women of high achievement as examples of those who felt the need to meet the conventional criteria of a woman's role. Margaret Thatcher regularly extols the virtues of marriage and family and professes little patience with feminists who put personal ambition ahead of traditional rewards. In an interview with the *Daily Mail* of London, Mrs. Thatcher made clear that she hadn't got where she was by being "some strident female. I don't like strident females. I like people who don't run the feminist ticket too hard."

Similarly, Indira Gandhi told Oriana Fallaci that she had "never had the need" to join feminist ranks. She also dismissed the difficulties of combining motherhood and career. "It's not at all hard to reconcile the two things if you organize your time intelligently," she said. Then she hotly denied that she and her husband were separated, even though they had lived far apart from each other for years. As for being a mother, that "had always been the job I liked best. Absolutely. My sons . . . I was crazy about my sons and I think I've done a super job in bringing them up."

Margaret Thatcher and Indira Gandhi notwithstanding, most women who hold political office find it the most difficult of all professions to combine with motherhood. Much of the difficulty has to do with time. While many jobs can be adjusted fairly successfully to meet a child's schedule, the political office holder's life is marked by sudden crises and erratic time demands. She may have to appear at a fundraising dinner or take part in an emergency meeting on an impending bill, though a child needs to be picked up from school or is waiting at home with a sitter. Often, too, a female politician must work in Washington or her state capital, and so must leave her family for days and even weeks at a time. Having to leave her children in this way is a definite hurdle in a mother's running for office.

Ruth Mandel, in her book *In the Running*, about women and politics, cited a typically defensive response of one California candidate to this criticism. She "mentioned in every speech that [her] children are grown," in order not to be seen as "shirking [her] duty as a family woman."

Once a woman has begun to campaign for office, the issue of maternal neglect quickly surfaces. "I thought the big hurdle would be working it out with my husband so that he would be willing to handle things during the week when the legislature was in session and I had to be in Albany," one candidate for the state assembly told me in frustration. "But that's going to be easy, if I ever get past the hostility that greets me every time I make a speech. I keep having to justify 'leaving my little boy' and 'setting such a bad example' for future mothers. No matter how many major issues I raise in a talk, the question-and-answer period seems to be dominated by these personal attacks."

Cynthia Fuchs Epstein, a sociologist and feminist activist, wrote that women like this are caught in a classic double-bind. If the woman "campaigns vigorously, she is apt to be criticized as a neglectful wife and mother; if she claims to be an attentive mother, her ability to devote time and energy to public office is questioned."

Whatever her field of "self-interest," a woman may find that the conditioned belief in maternal availability makes her feel so guilty that she must seek other coping mechanisms to deal with her distress. One response, as common as denial, is to overcompensate furiously the child she has chosen to leave on a regular basis. Congresswoman Pat Schroeder talked of spending several hours, one evening after an exhausting day of politics, mixing, baking, and carefully frosting a cake for a fund-raising event at her son's school. The following evening her son told her that the cake had been "okay," but that "all the rich kids brought money." Mrs. Schroeder admitted to having longed for the option of sending money instead of using up a precious evening baking, but her guilt at being less available than other mothers had propelled her to the kitchen.

On a more serious level, a medical student told me in a low, thoughtful voice, "My mother is a corporation lawyer. I guess it's different today, but when I was little, almost no one I knew had a mother who worked, let alone had as important a job as my mother did. She made a big issue about spending Sundays with me while my Dad played golf or hung out at his health club. I look back at our time together as frenetic. We'd race around from one bit of 'fun' to another, until I was exhausted. Often, I'd wake up on Monday morning feeling the way I do now when I'm hung over. I'd also be depressed about the upcoming week, even though I didn't realize for a while that at the heart of what I was feeling was the incredible contrast between my mother's relentless attention on Sunday and her virtual disappearance from Monday to Friday. She frequently couldn't get home in time even to have dinner with my father and me. I think she and I would have been much better off if she'd been able to accept the fact that she really wanted her career as much as she wanted to be my mother. From where I am today, that seems like a perfectly reasonable admission.

I felt it was true, anyway, as a child. But I think I resented it much more because her denial suggested I *had* been wronged."

Increasing numbers of women, especially younger ones, are admitting that they want both love and work, to be a mother but also to achieve in the outside world. It is an admission both influenced and mirrored by changes in beliefs about a mother's role and what is in a child's best interest. To begin with, there is growing support for the idea that a working mother can be better for a child's successful development than one who is overinvested in his life. Dr. Lowenstein remembered that when her career ambitions were unfulfilled, they "found destructive expression through projecting on my children the unfair and absurd expectation that they would fill my needs for fame and glory."

Mothers of sons who are trying to break the pattern of burdening a son's life with frustrated maternal ambitions are doing so by rethinking what a mother's primary purpose is in regard to a son. Is it to be crucially important to, and protective of, his day-to-day experience? Or is it to prepare him to be an adult, a person who is mature and resilient enough to handle life's inevitable frustration and stress?

Studies of working mothers confirm that, critical voices to the contrary, they value their children and their role as mothers as much as women who have no careers. It is simply their definition of the role that is different. As the psychologist Faye Higier Von Mering concluded from a comparative study, the most striking difference between full- and part-time mothers was that "working mothers saw dealing with frustration as learning to deal with life. Nonworking mothers tended to be more aware of the child's personal gratification needs, and more likely to monitor experience around him."

Thus, one mother, totally invested in her son's life, leaps

into the center of any frustrating situation and attempts to "cushion" it for him. If a teacher bothers him, she immediately telephones the principal of the school for an appointment. If he is not invited to a party, she arranges an elaborate outing to take his mind off being excluded.

On the other hand, Margo, who at thirty-nine is the first female vice president of an international banking corporation, said, "When my thirteen-year-old son complains about his teacher, of course my instinct might be to storm into his classroom and tell the guy to lay off. But I don't feel that's in Charlie's best interest. Nor would it really do very much good in any practical way. So what I would do, what I have done, is let Charlie go on for a while, and then hug him and say I know he must be right about the man, because I trust his judgment, but we all have creeps like that in our lives, and we can't let them control us. Then I move on to other things, and I expect Charles to do the same."

Margaret Drabble, in talking about the effects of her career on her children, told me that it "has been good for their independence," and Pat Schroeder said that her children are "independent and mature" and have been helped by being brought up in an atmosphere that didn't turn them into "hothouse plants," watched over by a nervously attentive mother. The ethic of independence is particularly meaningful for women who only recently have begun to learn to enjoy their own strengths, even though they try not to perpetuate the system of pushing a male child toward an independence he isn't ready to handle. But another reason mothers have for letting their sons take some responsibility for their own lives is that they feel it will help break the traditional male response of expecting a woman to anticipate and fill every masculine need.

"I don't believe in men suffering in silence," said Renée, a physician, "because the other side of that heroic stance is how aggrieved they become when a woman doesn't see their suffering and 'fix' it. I adore my son, but I'm too busy to know every one of his needs without his telling me what they are. I think it's in his best interest to break that historic masculine muteness and speak up for what he wants."

Renée offered an illustration of her son's generally direct approach to his life. When the boy was nine years old the family housekeeper resigned, and Renée and her husband felt that Roger could manage being by himself for the two hours between his return from school and their return from work.

"But after a week or so of coming into the empty apartment, Roger told me he was unhappy with the arrangement and would like me to hire a sitter or a new housekeeper. He said it frightened him to enter an empty set of rooms. He kept hearing noises and seeing shadows at the windows, even though we live fifteen floors up. It was very clear that I had overestimated his readiness for that much independence."

That Renée calmly honored Roger's request for an after-school baby sitter says something else about the relationship the career mother is forging with her child. Because she *does* see her son as a separate person, and because she is *not* totally invested in his life for all of her rewards, she is able to accept her son's fears and problems with relative equanimity. And because a boy like Roger does not feel that his mother will be threatened by his fears (from a sense of her own failure), he is much freer to admit his concerns.

Overall, a successful relationship between a working mother and her son seems to be one in which the mother invites acceptance of her own *and* her son's limitations and strengths. Such a mother does not, in the psychiatrist Ann Dally's words, "falsify experience or indulge in wishful thinking."

A charming publishing executive named Betty, the divorced mother of a seven-year-old, was able to say, quite matter-of-factly, "Perhaps the hardest part of my life involves accepting my own limitations. I can't be a supermother, but I mustn't be too hard on myself. I'm doing the best that I can in all aspects of life, and always trying to do better, but it will never be perfect, and that has to be all right for both Brian and me."

Exactly what does help to make things all right is a fascinating phenomenon. Although a career mother is open about wanting more in her life than her son, she is extraordinarily sensitive to those occasions when his needs should take precedence. Perhaps this is because mothers who are handling dual roles learn to be flexible and to trust their own instincts. Whatever the reason, successful women invariably say they instinctively "know" when a son needs some special attention. This is the day to take off from work; this is the class trip to go along on; this is the school party to attend.

Of course, the freedom to follow these maternal perceptions depends a great deal on the conditions of a mother's job. It was heartening to discover that the vast majority of successful career mothers credited an understanding male employer with their ability to manage motherhood and work. K. C. Coles has written about how difficult it is for women climbing up the corporate ladder to admit to the demands of motherhood. "Somehow it's acceptable to stay home from work if your car breaks down, but not if your child comes down with the flu. It's okay to leave early for an appointment with your shrink or your tax accountant, but not with your child's pediatrician." She called women who are self-conscious about their children "closet mothers [who] are so embarrassed by the fact that their children are showing that they mumble and stumble through their explanations until they come out sounding like excuses."

Most career mothers I talked to were quite open about

their delight in their sons. Pictures of the boys were prominently displayed in their offices, walls were decorated with drawings from nursery school, and desks held hand-crafted boxes from art class. None of the women feigned an emotional disengagement that didn't exist.

"If my son should get sick at day care," said one computer executive, "it would never occur to me not to pick him up rather than ask him to wait in the nurse's office till the end of the day. Nor would I lie about where I was going. On the other hand, I've never had the feeling that my boss would think, 'This is why you can't have women working for you.' Of course," she added with a smile, "he knows my work will be on his desk the next morning, even if it means my staying up all night to do it. Still, I know I simply couldn't have succeeded if I weren't allowed to be forthright about my personal responsibilities."

Interestingly, success itself, as delicious as it is, can strike its own blows to the balance between motherhood and work. Said a foundation executive, "It's easier, certainly, to take a day off now without being worried about a boss's approval. But as my work gets more compelling, I'm more preoccupied with it. It used to be rather simple to set business aside when I came home and really be there for my son. Now I have to force myself to give him my full attention and not just my physical presence."

Because she *is* more distracted at the end of the day, this mother gets up at 6:00 A.M. to breakfast with her son, who has to be at school by eight, even though her own day doesn't begin until ten. There are many such trade-offs in the lives of women trying to reap the benefits of love and work. Mothers may travel out of their way on buses and subways to accompany a teen-age son to school; mothers of younger children frequently go home at lunchtime. "No dinners with clients" and "no evening meetings" are the sorts of restrictions some women build into their job descriptions with apparently little regret, for they see them as realistic limits to lives that hold so much. These mothers also tend to include their children in social events connected to their professional as well as their personal lives. As a result, their sons often are unusually comfortable in adult company.

This is not to suggest, however, that the mothers do not have private lives. Even women who are divorced—and statistically many mothers with successful careers are—develop interests that they do not always share with their children. Although immediately after a divorce a career mother may tend to put her social life on hold so that her son will not have too many changes to deal with at once, after a while she begins to question this aspect of her obligation to her son. Does a mother owe every bit of her personal time to a boy who is already without his parents so much of the time?

"I don't believe in sublimation and sacrifice as a definition of motherhood," Betty said. "After my divorce I used to feel guilty about having a good time without Brian, if it wasn't work-related. But this year, I've taken a brief trip to Paris by myself, and I've gone on a bicycling tour to Vermont with friends. Of course I know Brian missed me, but I believe he also sees me as a person with many interests who is joyous and excited about life. If I can be that way, I hope he will feel he can be, too—much more so, I think, than if I dutifully stayed home with him during vacations or did only child-centered things that made me feel like climbing the walls."

Evidence mounts for the theory that there is no one right way to raise a son or a particular amount of time that should be allotted to the task. The quality-versus-quantity argument is an old one and is easily bent to accommodate a mother's rationalization. But if a woman genuinely wants to provide her son with emotional security, it does seem possible for her to do so even when she has serious, time-consuming career commitments. This is especially true if, as so many women sincerely believe, a mother's principal task is to set a model of self-confident, active adulthood.

Not every woman feels capable of combining her personal needs with the needs of her children. Particularly when the desire is strong to achieve outside the home, motherhood can seem a terrible trap. About 3 percent of the women in my study who had arrived at some significant level of professional success had separated from their children for an extended period in the early stages of their careers.

"I simply needed the time to write my dissertation without one eye on the clock all the time," Suzie, a biology professor at a community college, said. An actress-mother remembered her decision to come to New York City from Chicago, some ten years before, to "see if I could really hack it in the big time." There was no way she felt she could put herself to such a test while taking care of a four-year-old boy, so she left her son with her husband for what was supposed to be six months but stretched to over two years.

It is difficult to document the effects of such separations on the children, although they were usually beneficial for the mother's career. We do know that the taboo against a mother separating herself from her children is still a strong one in this society, and it is the rare boy who will not feel some sense of rejection by a mother who willingly breaks that tradition.

"My son is fifteen years old now," a lawyer told me. "And I only left him for a year when I first started law school, and his father is perfectly capable and responsive. Still, there doesn't seem to be a week that goes by that Billy doesn't make some reference to that year. Usually it's rather oblique, like how awful fourth grade was, which just happens to be the grade he was in at the time. I think he's come to terms with it intellectually, but I can't delude myself that he has emotionally."

As difficult as these breaks with tradition are, separation between mother and son is far more dramatic when it is not temporary, but permanent. A small but increasing number of women are relinquishing not only custody but all contact with their children, their sons more often than their daughters, after a divorce. Or they may simply flee their families, running away from responsibilities that seem to restrict any possibility of self-fulfillment.

In her book *Absentee Mothers*, Patricia Paskowicz, a woman who left her husband and three children, wrote that it is the need for self-realization that triggers the decision of many women to run away from a life of sublimation. However, it is also a reason that society and, often, a child find particularly unacceptable. It is one thing for a child to understand that his mother tried to escape a brutalizing husband or left to seek help for a serious emotional problem, but that she simply envisioned a life without him as a happier life can deeply erode a son's own chances of happiness.

"The fact is, she didn't want me," said Keith, a college freshman. "I know you're not supposed to be your mother's whole world, but her cutting me out of it completely leaves a feeling inside me that's dark and ugly."

Another young man, Michael, recalled how, shortly after his mother left, when he was seven years old, he woke up in the middle of the night, feeling sick. "The room was dark and chilly, and my stomach and head hurt, and I started to cry and call out for my mother. I called and called, and suddenly there was a flash of light, and my father was standing in the doorway in his robe, with this sad, sad look on his face. Up until that moment I had forgotten she was gone. And *in* that moment, I realized I could never call for her anymore. The bleakness of that idea, the terror of it, can't be described."

Both Michael and Keith see their mothers now, but they feel that their relationships with women have been profoundly affected by their sense of maternal deprivation. "I simply can't trust any protestations of love. It's as simple and, I suppose, as banal as that," Keith said. Banal or not, his reaction is well documented, both in the psychoanalytic literature and in the biographies of similarly scarred sons. George Bernard Shaw, for example, had a mother who almost completely rejected him; she went off to London with her three daughters for a period of six years, during which time she never even wrote to the son she left behind with his failure-ridden father.

While Shaw felt that his isolation and despair contributed to his self-sufficiency and to his compensatory intellectual efforts, his emotional development was badly thwarted: "It left me a treacherous brute in matters of true affection."

Mothers and Troubled Sons

It would be impossible to write a book about mothers and sons without touching on a mother's deepest fear, that she will raise a son who finds his life painful, frightening, or joyless. No amount of adult delight can compensate a woman for a son who is home alone because no other child has invited him to join in neighborhood play. The myth of the perfect mother who raises a perfectly successful and contented son pervades the imperfect world all mothers share, and causes women to blame themselves for any isolation and despair their sons experience. Society has always encouraged mothers to believe that their love and attention could and, more important, should guarantee a son's well-being. When a man exhibits unmistakable signs of emotional disturbance, society's emissaries are quick to point their accusing fingers at the woman who raised him.

For example, just after World War II, Dr. Edward Strecker, a leading psychiatrist who had served as an adviser to Secretary of War Henry Stimson, horrified mothers with his widely read book, *Their Mothers' Sons*. In the book, Dr. Strecker angrily charged "Mom" with so crippling her sons that three million of them were found psychologically unfit to serve their country. By creating these "psychoneurotics" through their sins of omission and commission, American mothers had shrunk our armed forces to the point of nearly stilling the very breath of democracy!

Only rarely in my study did I encounter a mother who managed to escape a sense of responsibility for a son's problems. "Intellectually, I know I'm not all that powerful," a frustrated woman commented as she told me about her son's unhappy adolescence. "I know there are a lot of other influences on his life. What's more, I can look at my mother-in-law, who was an absolute witch to my husband when he was growing up, and know that she couldn't be responsible for the sunny soul that he is. And yet I can't shake the idea that it's a mother's behavior that determines a son's contentment and security, that Jay's depressions could have been avoided if I'd been a better mother."

In truth, it is inevitable that some children will falter on the path of growing up, for reasons not completely understood by even the most thoughtful professional, although research on the issue continues. Why are certain children more vulnerable to stress than others? Why does one child easily tolerate an experience that another may find tremendously upsetting? One explanation that is gaining more and more credibility is the significance of inborn temperament.

In their research, Drs. Stella Chess and Alexander Thomas, of New York University Medical Center, have determined that, from the earliest days of life, children show distinct temperamental differences. Some children are extremely adaptable; others are more "difficult," not so easily able to adjust to new situations and more inclined to say no than yes. Others are markedly slow to warm up to new people or experiences, holding back, often in obvious fear, until the terrain or face becomes familiar. One child is easily distracted; another is persistent, refusing to be diverted from an activity no matter how much it frustrates him or how often he is entreated to stop.

A mother does have a profound effect on the quality of a son's life, but she is not omnipotent as a shaping force. As the boy moves out in the larger world, he becomes subject to all sorts of stresses. Depending on what his inherent needs and characteristics are, these other experiences may be more powerful than even his mother's loving influence. The research psychologist Arlene Skolnick, of the Institute of Human Development at Berkeley, reminded mothers that there "is an important difference between influence and control." No matter how dedicated a mother is to her child's happiness, her relationship with him does "not occur in a social vacuum but in the complex world of daily life." A mother does not necessarily control how a child will deal with stresses in the outside environment.

In general, boys are particularly susceptible to environmental stress. To a large extent this is because they tend to be exposed to more stressful situations than girls are. In a study of British primary school children it was found that, as in American society, teachers were much more critical of boys than of girls and much less tolerant of difficult behavior from them. It is for this reason that school problems rank very high on the list of tensions in a son's life. Ironically, this is most often true when the boy is very bright and creative. As the well-known psychiatrist Sula Wolff wrote, "High intelligence is a source of delight to most parents. But exceptionally high intelligence also has its hazards."

Dr. Wolff's judgment is confirmed by the results of the previously cited study, *Cradles of Eminence,* by Victor and Mildred Goertzel, on the early years of famous people, in which three out of every five of the four hundred subjects suffered considerable school-related emotional pain. The majority of these unhappy, often academically unsuccessful students were boys. History is filled with tales of brilliant sons who found school totally incompatible with their natures, and who, as a result, frequently fell victim to a teacher's scorn. Albert Einstein's teachers, for example, reported to his parents that he was "mentally slow, unsociable, and adrift forever in his foolish dreams." Thomas Edison remembered that "I was never able to get along at school. I was always at the foot of my class." Winston Churchill so antagonized the headmaster at the prestigious school his mother had chosen for him that she was forced to withdraw her son and send him instead to a far less select establishment. In that seaside school, run by two gentle women, Churchill was permitted to ignore subjects that bored him and leave his classes to go leaping around the schoolyard when he felt too confined by the classroom.

It is not uncommon for creative, intelligent boys to antagonize school authorities. Teachers often perceive the idiosyncratic interests of these boys as a defiant challenge, and their straying from lessons to original musings as deliberate disruptions of classroom order. The teachers' dislike is often mirrored by the boy's classmates, who find his unusual concerns and atypical responses silly. Their ridicule intensifies the boy's feeling of being hopelessly outside the definition of what a "normal" boy should be, and thus intensifies his sense of isolation. Many of our most creative men were lonely little boys. As Einstein once said, in summing up the richness of his adult life, "I live in that solitude which is painful in youth, but delicious in the years of maturity."

My interviews confirmed that school failure, problems with teachers, and the rejection of peers continue to rank high on the list of difficulties a bright and unconventional son faces. They also confirmed that a son's self-esteem is clearly affected by his mother's reaction to his atypical behavior. As with a homosexual son, if a mother is not the sole force shaping a boy's personality, she does have much to do with how comfortable he is with himself.

I discovered a spectrum of maternal responses to exceptional sons and their difficulties with "fitting in." A woman named Chloe saw her nine-year-old son as "quirky but fascinating," and told me with a grin that "he can't do his spelling, but he reads the entire *New York Times* every morning before he goes to school!" Another mother, Arline, said, with a tense frown, that her twelve-year-old son had "some bizarre obsession with meteorology. He spends hours alone in his room, concocting these elaborate charts that absolutely no one else cares about or could understand." Chloe was able to stand behind her son against a school system that was pushing him to conform. "They keep giving him work that bores him. That's why he loses interest and doesn't try. They should challenge him, not badger him with routine exercises." Arline, on the other hand, was guilty and apologetic when a teacher sternly informed her that her son wasn't living up to his potential and was "emotionally immature."

Being accused of immaturity is another common experience in the life of a bright little boy. His emotional maturity *does* often lag behind his intellectual development, and the discrepancy can be especially annoying to teachers. Although they know that little boys' emotional development is slower than that of girls, the teachers expect this little boy, so clearly above average, not to follow that pattern.

"God! Those expressions—'I'm so *disappointed* in you; I expected so much *more* from you—' bang in my head like a hammer to this day," a young graduate student named Spencer told me. "I was a terribly clumsy little boy. My head always worked much faster than my muscles, and I just couldn't master things like tying my shoes or neat penmanship until way past the time most other kids did. Of course the reason my writing was so awful was that I had too many ideas I was trying to get down, but the end result was that I felt like a dummy. By the time I was in the middle grades, I knew I was smart, and I was filled with anger that I was made to feel so stupid. Thank God my parents stressed my capabilities instead of my failures."

Spencer's recollections seem to illustrate Dr. Wolff's cautionary advice to mothers about exceptional sons needing "at least as much protection and mothering as an average child." From my research, I conclude that there is little doubt that when a mother *is* able to provide the safe shelter such a boy needs, he tends to feel better about himself, even when he experiences the rejection that comes from being different.

One of the more delightful young people I met while conducting my research was a fifteen-year-old boy named Aaron. He is a remarkably gifted musician who composes complex symphonic pieces and plays a variety of music on three instruments.

"I'm a very strange person," Aaron told me calmly. "I always was. When I was in grade school, the other boys really used to get on me; they thought I was a complete flake. I didn't mind too much, though, and by now I don't mind at all. I like spending time on my own interests, and I can always keep myself busy."

Aaron's mother, Cate, and I spoke extensively about raising a boy like her son. Clearly, it was often very difficult, "primarily because I felt incompetent," Cate said. "I'm a bright person, but his mind is so unusual, his way of thinking so challenging to traditional thought... Well," she continued with a smile, "I decided when he was very young that I wasn't going to be able to turn him into a 'normal' little boy, even if I truly wanted to, so it seemed to me that encouraging him in his music was the answer. If he could invest his gifts and feelings in music, he could be different in a positive framework."

From a professional point of view, Cate behaved very wisely. Her attitude also illustrates the point that the extent to which a mother does not blame herself for a son's singularity enables her to keep him from crossing the line between manageable oddness and serious emotional trouble. Cate was able to resist pressuring Aaron to be something other than he is because his gifts are so exceptional. It is as if these gifts were out of her hands, and she was content simply to nurture him with love and appreciation and let him grow as he would.

Louis Koren, a psychiatrist, wrote that "the chief need of children is to be enjoyed." This is perhaps nowhere more evident than with the highly intelligent little boys who find that the conventional delights of childhood escape them. The poet W. H. Auden once wrote that "I think we shall find that all intelligent people are the product of psychological conflict in childhood," and that intellect and especially creativity thrive from a child's trying to "understand the mechanism of the trap" he perceives childhood to be. Nonetheless, Auden's biographer, Humphrey Carpenter, wrote that Constance Auden's obvious delight in Wystan, her last-born son, provided him with "a security that gave him the immense, unshakable self-confidence that was his overriding attribute. . . . To the end of his life, he behaved like a precocious and highly praised youngest child."

To be sure, a gifted, creative child does sometimes seem to perch far too precariously on the edge of illness. Albert Einstein used to chant hymns to the god he had invented. Salvador Dali leaped from the tops of staircases to get the attention of his classmates. Winston Churchill was the despair of his family for his dangerous exploits, one of which resulted in his being bedridden for three months when he was eighteen years old. (He failed to scale an open bridge.)

From my interviews I learned that many mothers encouraged their eccentric sons in the arts, much as Cate did with Aaron. Other sons seemed to gravitate on their own to a world they instinctively felt would not label unconventional behavior alarming or distasteful. Yet even in the comparatively less threatening world of the arts, sons frequently found their creative outlets did not guarantee continuing contentment. The great musician Paderewski took up farming at one period in his career, because he had developed a deep revulsion to the piano. Maurice Chevalier (who had been extremely close to his mother) experienced a period when he couldn't remember the lyrics of even the most familiar songs, and was forced to take a lengthy rest while undergoing psychological treatment. Almost every writer or artist or innovative scientist whom I interviewed cited periods when he had been so deeply depressed, or at a point of such emotional exhaustion, that he felt he might finally cross the line between manageable neurosis and mental illness. All of the men had been in therapy at some point in their lives; in several instances, for prolonged periods of time. Yet only one person had suffered the total debilitation of a mental collapse.

There were similar findings from the Goertzels' study. Very few of the four hundred people who made up their sample had ever reached a state of true psychosis. The doctors speculated about why the dedicated scientist or artist is not usually the person who slips into madness. In an intriguing conclusion, they wrote that it may be because "being psychotic" is too "time-consuming," and the gifted son, intent on developing a powerful interest, simply doesn't "have the time to be mentally ill. The intensity of the drive toward a goal may be too compelling to leave time for the individual to nurse his anxieties to the breaking point."

As if to corroborate this theory, the psychiatrist Milton Erikson explained that there are comparatively few mental breakdowns, and even these are sometimes cured almost miraculously during times of genuine crisis. To illustrate, he told of a patient who had been in a state of catatonia for many years. One night his hospital ward caught fire, and the attendant was too terrified to take charge. Suddenly, the man who had huddled in a corner for so long took the keys from the attendant and "efficiently engineered the evacuation of the ward." Only after the fire had been controlled did he slip back into his catatonic state.

If a state of actual crisis can temper mental illness, perhaps the passionate pursuit of a creative goal sufficiently resembles an ongoing crisis situation so that the highly creative person does not break down, often in spite of his tensions and despair. The playwright Tennessee Williams, who died recently in a tragic accident and whose writing always reflected intense anguish, once articulated an extreme version of this point of view. "To me, it was providential to be an artist," he wrote, "a great act of providence that I was able to turn my borderline psychosis into creativity."

It appears, then, that it is wise to channel a boy's gifts into a creative mode that allows him to impose some artistic form on inner turmoil. But there are many intellectually creative boys who do not have a special talent for artistic expression. I discovered that the route many of these sons take away from their more conventional and often critical peers is lined with books.

"He seems to be spending his entire childhood reading," a mother named Elsie said gloomily. "If he does consent to go somewhere with the family (with another child, forget it), he always has at least one book stuffed in his pocket, like a security blanket. Of course I like the idea that he's learning so much and is so intellectually mature, but I have to admit some of it seems freakish to me. Sometimes I simply can't stand it when he gets lost in a book; it seems to be another part of his problem rather than a solution to it."

There is no doubt that reading can be a source of great solace to a sensitive, somewhat isolated little boy. Nearly every grown son I spoke with who had been unhappy as a child recalled the joy of "discovering" the neighborhood library. Nowhere did there seem a more certain escape from internal as well as external tensions. Nonetheless, Elsie's misgivings about her son's constant reading are not entirely off base. Sula Wolff cautioned mothers to remember that there *is* a certain danger to precocious wrestling with books and the ideas they contain. The boy whose reading is well beyond his years is exposed "to a wealth of information from which other children are shielded." Such children "struggle early with questions of morality and matters of life and death. Often they are bewildered by the many concepts and ideas they have to master" and, as a result, "frequently suffer from multiple anxieties."

As the mother of a son whose wit never ceases to delight me, I was interested to discover that many a troubled boy deals with anxiety through the sophisticated defense of humor. Despair has always given birth to humor as an antidote. "The most acutely suffering animal on earth invented laughter," wrote the philosopher Nietzsche, and the playwright Ionesco said, "The comic alone is able to give us the strength to bear the tragedy of existence."

Yet a son who handles conflict through humor may upset his mother. Even though she may recognize humor as a useful weapon against sadness, there is something very poignant about his mockery, particularly when it is aimed at his own uncomfortable world. As a writer named Patsy told me about her son, "I know his sense of the ridiculous helps him not to take his problems too seriously, but on the other hand, sometimes it seems very sad to me that there's clearly so much pain there for him to deflect."

For some children, a sense of the ridiculous sometimes

takes a self-destructive turn, even if it still functions as a mechanism to help them cope. The psychologists Seymour and Rhoda Lee Fisher researched the family dynamics that seemed to keep turning up in the lives of children who were sent to them for behavioral problems that often involved an exaggerated silliness at home or in school. Even in therapy, said the doctors,

> these children often prove to be really funny. . . . They delight in mimicking, satirizing, doing things backward and upside down. They enjoy initiating the unexpected and magnifying contradictions. They contrive kidding imitations of their parents, especially of their mothers. . . . [They seem to] want to render everything absurd. It is as if they are forever on stage trying to convert life into a string of foolish jokes.

Most of the patients the doctors wrote about in their research report were boys. In attempting to understand their behavior, the Fishers made a comparative study of the early lives of people who had grown up to be professional comedians. Again, the vast majority of their subjects were men. The research revealed that while many of the comedians were growing up, there had been great contradictions between their mothers' expectations of their sons' capacity to handle responsibility and the children's need for nurturing. A mother's temptation to overload a competent, bright little boy with tasks and to expect behavior from him that was beyond his years was apparent in the recollection of the grown sons. That much of a professional comic's repertoire contains jokes about mothers, and women in general, may relate to the Fishers' conclusion that "the comic's relationship with his mother was most likely to have been his largest source of frustration."

Mothers of boys who seem to be constantly acting silly

or outrageous (particularly if their behavior is putting them in conflict with the family or at school) may do well to wonder whether their sons are not responding to unreasonable demands for performance. The Fishers point out the essential absurdity of expecting a child to behave like an adult, which can create a situation where "absurd demands are countered with absurdity."

There are some boys who, though they have a cultivated sense of irony to help them cope, and that irony stays within reasonable bounds, can be especially unhappy growing up. These are the boys who seem to have been born with an unusual ability to identify with the suffering of other people. As the Goertzels pointed out in their study, such boys' "sensitivity to injustice and inequalities, their easily aroused guilt feelings, frequently bring them into disfavor with adults and cause them to be ridiculed by other children." Albert Schweitzer's musical ability was recognized early— he was asked to substitute for the church organist when he was only nine years old—but he was reprimanded by his elders when, because there were so many poor boys in the village who could never own finery, he refused to wear a brand-new suit for the occasion. His peers made continuing fun of him for not taking part in aggressive games or in taunting sport with animals. Wrote the Goertzels, "Early evidences of altruism are not often well received from children, especially from boys."

Especially from boys. Over and over again, in one form or another, the point was reinforced that the normal pains of childhood are exacerbated for boys by the harsh demands of our image of masculinity. I can offer no greater argument for allowing boys to escape that stereotype, and more freely admit their feelings and emotional needs, than to point out where the turning-inward of such sadness and need can lead in its extreme. Four of the mothers in my study had sons who had taken their own lives. In each case, the boy was remembered as always having been acutely aware of the distress of both other children and adults.

"He'd pick up a tone in his grandmother's voice that even I would miss," recalled a woman who was still mourning her son. And the three young men in my study who had attempted suicide remembered the constant pain they always sensed around them, even in the small humiliations so common to a child's life. Said one, "I'd watch a teacher embarrass one of my classmates, and I'd know how stupid and helpless he felt, and I couldn't bear that a person could be so cruel." Still, it is the agony of believing that no one else really comprehends his own suffering that seems to be the motivating force in many an adolescent son's suicide.

There was little doubt in my sampling that male silence had widened the gulf between mother and son. Had these sons been able to break this silence, their mothers might have been able to prevent tragedy. But none of the mothers of suicides in my study had come even close to understanding just how unhappy their sons were. Although there are mothers who are so aloof that they make it impossible for a boy to share his feelings, the women in my research seemed warm and responsive. It was impossible to imagine them not wanting to help their sons in any way they could. That they had not been able to comprehend the degree of their sons' torment, they all agreed, is related to the idea of male stoicism. This idea is so pervasive that it influences a son's reticence and is communicated consciously or unconsciously by the mother herself as she raises her son.

"With my daughter, I would ask questions when she seemed sad, probe a bit and try to get her to talk about what was troubling her. But I realize now that with my son, as soon as he passed the preschool years, my inclination was to distract him from a mood, to short-circuit a 'babyish' flow of tears." With the torturous awareness that she said came "seventeen years too late," this mother added that, because her son was so exceptional, she did not pay the same kind of attention to his behavior that she would have to the behavior of a son who was destructively acting out his aggressions. Her conclusion is totally substantiated by the literature on troubled children. It is the aggressive child, not the obedient one, who claims our concern.

Perhaps it is this imprisoning goodness that causes a boy, when he does attempt suicide, often to be especially dramatic. Statistics show that while more girls make suicide attempts, boys' efforts are more violent and more often "successful."

One of the young men in my study who had not been successful looked back on his adolescent attempt at suicide with the analytic insight that comes with a newly earned doctorate in psychology.

"I took great pride in the scheme I concocted," he began. "I spent months planning it and experimenting to see that it would work." (That it did work is chillingly affirmed by the scars still visible on his wrists.) On his fifteenth birthday, he tied razor blades to his wrists and stood in front of his mother as she prepared dinner, slowly swinging his arms back and forth so that the blades cut into his veins, while she watched, too frozen with fear to move. Having her watch was for him an integral part of the experience.

"It sounds absurdly theatrical now," he said with a sad smile, "but at the time it was vitally important to have her really see how unhappy I was, even though in her eyes I was such a success. I had been feeling more and more alienated from reality. I felt like a shit; she bragged about me to her friends. I needed her to help me, but I was ashamed to tell her that her prized son needed help. Finally, it seemed that the only way to break through the image of me I couldn't live up to was to die and have her see it happen."

Fortunately, his father came into the room and, in a desperately inspired lunge, was able to swing his son's arms above his head and hold them until the boy's body relaxed and crumpled to the floor.

Statistics show that many suicide attempts occur when a severely emotionally inhibited child first goes away to college. Many experts believe that the years of blocking off feelings, and the resulting lack of introspection, leave such young people unprepared for coping with the experiences and excitements to which they are suddenly exposed. Since males are taught to fear emotional responses, a troubled son may be especially overwhelmed by them. Confrontations with unfamiliar situations and people can challenge his fragile equanimity and may result in such terror of being engulfed by new sensations that he attempts literally to deaden himself.

There are less terrible responses to emotional distress and the common inability of boys to communicate it that nonetheless bring a mother unimaginable pain. Rather than take his life, a troubled son may take to the road, running away from unhappiness that he thinks no one at home cares about. A growing sense of alienation from his family lessens the chance that the boy will talk about what's troubling him without considerable encouragement. Everyone who deals with troubled children says that empathetic understanding of how their lives appear to them is crucial to their recovery. Children do not always interpret their parents' behavior in the way it was intended. What seems to a mother to be an attempt to cheer her son up, by minimizing his tentative admission of distress, may seem to a boy to be a rejection and even contempt for his "weakness." As Sula Wolff explained, "Only when the child feels that he is being understood on his own level will he be able to communicate with increasing freedom and frankness."

If this kind of communication continues to be denied in family life, a boy may indeed begin to feel that his only solution is flight. Although the stuffing of a backpack and a plunge into the night may seem to be an impulsive response to yet another row over grades or a sloppy room, what actually propels him is much more complicated. When he does go, almost nothing short of suicide so nearly destroys a mother's sanity than the sight of his untouched bed, morning after morning after morning.

"I thought I would simply not survive," Peggy, the mother of a recently returned fourteen-year-old, told me quietly. "My son was gone for almost four weeks without a word. I was certain he had died and that he'd done so in the most horrible way possible. Sometimes, my mind would seem on fire, with images of him crying, suffering, being in terrible pain. And always, that deep, indescribably terrifying certainty that I would never see him, dead or alive, again. Even now," she added, closing her eyes for a moment, "even now that he's back and we're pulling ourselves together, I still can't approach his room without being washed over with panic. I hear his voice behind the door, and yet I'm sure when I open it that I'm going to be assaulted by the silence, by the vacant space . . ."

Peggy's family now is in therapy together, trying to open up the lines of communication so that her son will never again feel so alone that he will run away from home. Yet she is also learning that there are limits to her ability to make him trouble-free while he *is* at home. As Arlene Skolnick wrote, "Just as we have come to accept that there are limits to growth and to our natural resources, it is time we lowered our expectations about the perfectability of family life."

Actually, there is no guarantee that even if we were able to create the perfect environment for a son, he would grow up to be a totally successful and happy man. Research indicates that there is a very weak correlation between a happy childhood and contentment as an adult. In one longitudinal investigation conducted at the University of California's Institute for Human Development, two hundred children were studied from infancy until their teens and then were seen again at the age of thirty. The hypothesis was that an unhappy childhood would make for an unhappy adult, and a happy child would remain happy into maturity. Two thirds of the predictions failed to come true. Unhappy children were often successfully coping adults. Trouble-free children frequently became nervous, anxious, and immature thirty-year-olds. Interestingly, adult unhappiness was common among men who as boys had been popular heroes, leaders in sports that physically and socially awkward boys could never hope to master.

This is in no way meant to suggest that mothers should not attempt to ease the distress of a young son's life. Like Peggy, they would do well to examine what they may be doing that intensifies a son's problems and, where it is possible, to monitor their own behavior so that good will and love have a chance to help him. Nonetheless, it is important to accept a son as the separate person he is, with dark as well as lighter sides to his childhood.

It is more possible for a person to cope with suffering if he believes he will eventually overcome it. Arlene Skolnick reported that the literature on children who can handle even severe childhood trauma suggests that "self-esteem and a sense of competence may not depend on whether we experience good or bad events, but rather on whether we perceive some control over what happens to us." Thus, it seems that a mother can be most helpful to an unhappy son if she encourages him to believe that, with her love and help, he will gain real competence (as opposed to the automatic, isolated, imposed competence of the male role) in coping with his sadness and in gaining enough control over events so that he has a better chance at happiness. To transmit this faith, however, a mother truly has to believe it, and she can do so only by finally removing herself from the absolute center of her son's suffering. Freed from oppressive responsibility for his every tear and for his sense of estrangement, she will be better able to encourage a troubled son toward self-accepting manhood.

While no man can be viewed in isolation from his mother if we are truly to understand him, there are certain troubled sons (undoubtedly constitutionally flawed) who defy anyone's attempts to find a correlation between their interaction with their mothers and the dangerous kinds of men they become. I don't mean to suggest that certain attitudes or behaviors in a mother will produce a pathologically ill son, no matter what his genetic make-up. Yet the biographical literature on certain disturbed and destructive sons and their relationships with their mothers is fascinating and compelling.

Some of the most violent men of our century have virtually sanctified their mothers. When Al Capone's father died, early in the gangster's notorious career, he brought his mother to live with him in Chicago. With profits made from his crimes, he built a luxurious house for both of them that was a source of continuing pride to his mother, despite its fortresslike atmosphere (it had walls a foot thick, and the windows were barred tightly with narrow steel rods). When Teresa Capone grew nostalgic for old friends in Brooklyn, her son saw to it that she visited the shabby neighborhood in splendor. His New York cronies shepherded the elderly woman around in a bulletproof Cadillac driven by a uniformed chauffeur, who had an additional bodyguard riding beside him in the front seat.

When Capone was finally convicted for tax evasion, his mother visited him in prison, bringing a huge platter of his favorite macaroni and cheese with tomato sauce. Later, when he was sent to Alcatraz on other, more serious charges, Capone amused himself by learning to read music and play the banjo, skills he then employed to compose a sentimental song called "Mother." In her turn, his mother went to her death insisting, "Al's a good boy."

Adolf Hitler is perhaps the most dramatic example of the relation between pathology and filial love. He and his mother were extraordinarily and exclusively attached to one another, to the extent that even other family members felt intrusive. As a young man, the person who would later order the execution of millions nursed his cancer-stricken mother with a dedication that attending physicians found awe-inspiring. Clad in a blue apron, he scrubbed his mother's floors after ministering to her bodily needs. And at night he moved his bed into the kitchen to be close enough to her to hear in case she called. This dedication to another person did not extend to anyone else in Hitler's life. Albert Speer, Hitler's chief architect and his armaments minister, described his leader as a man who

> could not respond to friendship. Instinctively, he repelled it. The normal sympathies that normal men enjoy were just not in him. At the core, in the place of where the heart should be, Hitler was a hollow man. . . . We who were really close to him, or thought we were all came to sense this. . . . We were all, all of us, simply projections of his own gigantic ego.

Related patterns of mother fixation and lack of real feeling for others can be found in many of Hitler's evil peers. Their mothers apparently remained blind to the horrifying behavior of their sons in the outside world. As a little boy, Joseph Goebbels was bitter toward everyone but his mother. When he was twelve years old, he articulated his disgust for humanity in a diary entry: "As soon as I am with a person for three days, I don't like him any longer, and if I am with him for a whole week, I hate him like the plague. I have learned to despise the human being from the bottom of my soul." Only his mother was able to sustain his love, and she in turn refused to acknowledge that he might be flawed in any way.

There are also horrifying puzzles to be found in the lives of men whose acts of violence are individual rather than global. For instance, there are many complex theories about why men rape, but one postulates that certain men who harbor deep anger toward their mothers idealize her image rather than admit their sense of maternal deprivation. When other women fall short of her idealized image, as they inevitably must, the mentally twisted man will explode in a vicious act of rage and "retribution." According to a related theory, some men who rape appear to be inordinately sensitive to a woman's scorn, real or imagined, which can in many cases be traced to the bitter memory, once again real or imagined, of a mother's mockery. This kind of man is obsessively sensitive to a woman's "putting him down." Her amusement at his attempt to impress her can be quelled only by turning her laughter into terror.

In some rapists we see the most grotesque example of how emotionally impotent men blame women (mothers?) for their own failures. Clearly there is a world of darkness a mentally ill son inhabits that breeds its own evil. How such a son interprets his relationship with his mother must be seen in the context of all of his distorted perceptions about life.

For the majority of women who mother sons, and sons who become men under their guiding hands, cause and effect, though still limited, is more easily understandable. One conclusion about a mother's influence on her son's emotional problems is unmistakable. By not romanticizing the idea of his childhood and how happy it should be, she will do much to help him become a fully experiencing, self-aware man, who will not hold women responsible for his emotional pain or think less of himself for experiencing it.

Mothers and Successful Sons

"All I am and ever hope to be, I owe to this wonderful woman who is my mother." So says the successful businessman, the political victor, proudly paying homage to the woman who shaped his ambition. The audience's eyes fill with tears at a picture as old as the idea of family.

This is not the entire story, however. Much more may lie behind the smiles on the faces of that man and his mother. The relationship between them is so complex that it is virtually impossible to know where the eye deceives. At what point does rationalization or fantasy or denial color truth? Is the mother, standing in her son's shadow, really happy in that subordinate position? Is the son really feeling guilt and resentment about his mother's sacrifice? Is her devotion a burden he feels he may never escape, no matter how much higher he climbs on the ladder of her expectations?

Many such questions arise as one talks with "successful" sons and reads about others. His mother appears to be the single most important force in a man's worldly success, but how that success is defined, and how satisfying he finds it, varies as much as the complexities of the interaction between mothers and sons. We know that sons like the fictional Alex Portnoy, with their literary wails and whines, illustrate the profound discomfort a son may feel when he suspects he has not fully satisfied his mother's dreams. As such a son pushes on to become the next Einstein or Shakespeare, there is a frenetic quality to his quest, which may be a reflection of his fragile self-esteem. As the analyst Gregory Rochlin commented, "The hope to excel, the fantasy of being perfect persists." And yet, he continued, no matter how much the son achieves, public applause may not satisfy him, for there is always the possibility of the primary failure, "the deep apprehension, held in repression, of disappointing one's mother."

Of course, much of this psychic pain depends on the definition of success that has been handed down from mother to son. Many sons come to feel that it is primarily the trappings of traditional success — money, power, and prestige — that matter to their mothers most of all. In an interview about a play he wrote on this corrosive theme of family life, Jules Feiffer recalled that, with his own mother, "there was always the sense that the quality of my work was of less concern than its success." In the play, *Grown Ups*, he depicted a son's bitter frustration over his mother's insatiable goals. No matter how the son triumphs, his mother lusts for more. When, for instance, he tells her that he has interviewed Henry Kissinger as an assignment for his prestigious job on *The New York Times*, his mother responds that she is looking forward to the day when her son will be so important that Henry Kissinger will want to interview *him*.

Obviously, much of the desire for her son's achievement relates to the limits society has placed on a woman's own success. Although most of the mothers of successful sons in my study were more benign than the women in Jules Feiffer's real and created lives, they seemed to be women who, in a later generation, would probably have had careers of their own. As a result, they often had a ferocious need to push

224 VARIATIONS ON A THEME

their sons through doors that were closed to them. This was particularly true of the mothers of men in professions like medicine. A surprising number of physicians reported that, while they welcomed the tangible rewards of their vocation, they might have pursued other careers had they felt they had any choice in the matter.

"I just took on my mother's attitude about the desirability of being a doctor," said a fifty-year-old New York ophthalmologist who is now disengaging himself from a Park Avenue practice. "It simply never occurred to me that it might not be the right profession for my personality." In midlife, like a large number of other professional men, he is trying to explore his genuine needs for a career. "There should be a way for me to be emotionally satisfied as well as professionally successful," the doctor continued, and then added with a smile, "I would say I want the rest of my life to be my own, and not just my mother's dream."

A strong-minded, ambitious mother can be the decisive factor in a son's career choice. The son is enveloped by her concept of success and her idea of what paths he should take to achieve it. In a way he is captive to her goals, for, as the Goertzels' study on the backgrounds of famous men indicates, rebellion is difficult when a mother is "the focus of both love and authority." Not "progressing" may mean the loss of her approval, her attention, and, the son may fear, her love.

Yet research also confirms that if a mother keeps her desire for control from overwhelming her son, and mixes it with some appreciation for his individual needs, her faith in his exalted destiny may indeed be rewarded—not only by his achievements, but by his ability to enjoy them (perhaps even as much as she does). The author David McCullough wrote in an article, "Mama's Boys," that a loving, ambitious mother can "be of unparalleled benefit to the child. Her warmth and support become all-important, altogether favorable to social, emotional, and intellectual growth."

On the other hand, other people may not find these sons as delightful as their mothers do (which in turn may explain the son's continuing devotion to his mother). In the lives of many men who achieved great political success, for example, there has often been a totally committed mother who created in her son a taste for and expectation of admiration from everyone who crossed his path. Erich Fromm commented that men who seek political careers may be trying to "substitute mass adulation for the uncritical adulation they received from their mothers." Similarly, Sam Janus, a psychologist, and Barbara Bess, a psychiatrist, noted a marked dualism in the lives of male politicians they studied for signs of deviant sexual behavior. On the one hand, the men were dedicated to noble and virtuous goals; on the other, they seemed "impelled to render the world subservient to them . . . to prove their mightiness by imposing their will on others."

There seems little doubt that a cherished son who seeks a political career often has difficulty engaging himself in a personal relationship that asks for true commitment. Although usually a most charming companion, he offers considerable resistance if he senses that more than charm is expected of him.

President Franklin Roosevelt's son James recalled that his father was at "his sparkling best" when there were admiring women with whom he could talk. It was Roosevelt's natural inclination, he wrote, to be "the center of attention," especially with women. Eleanor Roosevelt once reflected that, while her frequent criticism of her husband "sometimes acted as a spur" for what she believed were important decisions, "he might have been happier with a wife who was completely uncritical," the kind of person that she "was

never able to be . . . and so, he had to find it in other people."
This wistful summary of her marriage and of her husband's
expectations concludes with the quietly dramatic statement
"I was one of those who served his purpose."

As might be expected, this self-absorption was well tended
by Roosevelt's mother, Sara. Like many other mothers of
future presidents, she was sure from the time of his infancy
that her son was headed toward greatness. She saved his
baby clothes and early school compositions for what she was
certain would be the scrutiny of historians. There was no
aspect of his experience that was too minor to absorb her
interest. In fact, until he was fourteen they were never
separated for more than a few hours. It was only with the
greatest reluctance that she finally sent him to boarding
school, two years later than most of his contemporaries.

Doris Haber, in a study of presidents and their mothers,
commented on the "obsessive interest" mothers like Mrs.
Roosevelt had in their sons' physical and intellectual development. Of the many illustrations in Roosevelt's life of
such fixed maternal attention, one is particularly memora-
ble. While he was at boarding school Franklin contracted
scarlet fever and, although mending well, was put in quar-
antine. The enforced lack of contact was so painful for his
mother that it is said she located a ladder on the school
grounds and climbed it daily to peer through the window
and gauge her beloved son's progress.

James Roosevelt said that his father "seethed under the
drip-drip of maternal advice, and never ceased resisting his
mother's attempts to tell him what to do." Yet there are
many anecdotes which indicate that, at least early in his
career, Franklin was uncertain about making personal and
professional decisions without his mother's approval. It is
reported that when he was asked to run for the New York
Senate, he told the visiting delegation that he wanted "to

talk with my mother about it first." (The Democratic Party emissary is said to have answered tersely, "Frank, there are men in Poughkeepsie waiting for your answer. They won't like to hear you had to ask your mother!") And when Eleanor Roosevelt and Franklin first fell in love, he was so concerned about his mother finding out that he wrote about Eleanor in code in his diary. When he finally did break the news to his mother, he immediately followed up the announcement with a letter of reassurance: "I am the happiest man in the world. . . . And for you, dear Mummy, you know that nothing can ever change what we have been and will always be to each other."

The marriage of Eleanor and Franklin Roosevelt clearly suffered from his apparent inability to break free of his mother's hold on his life. As a husband, he continued to be primarily a son. In New York City, he and Eleanor lived adjacent to Sara; in Hyde Park, they lived under the same roof; at Campobello, they were next door to each other. In describing the way they lived in the city, Eleanor once said this of her mother-in-law's omnipresence: "You were never quite sure when she would appear, day or night." Nonetheless, her biographer Joseph Lash reported that Eleanor learned early in her marriage not to reveal her "dislike of the arrangement."

Of all the mama's boys who became presidents, Harry Truman may have been the most successful in breaking away from his mother. To be sure, he was thirty-three years old and still living with her when he went off to war in 1917, but he came home to marry Bess Wallace, and their marriage was close and happy. Nonetheless, he was in constant contact with his mother during all the years of his presidency. When the Japanese surrendered in 1945, he called her in Missouri immediately after finishing his victory broadcast to the nation. It is said that Mrs. Truman remarked to a guest when she hung up the telephone, "That was Harry. . . . I knew he'd call. He always calls me after something that happens is over."

Turning to the equally special connection between military leaders and their mothers, the Goertzels noted that an overpossessive mother of a peer-rejected child (especially a mother who dislikes her husband) is most likely to rear . . . a military hero who enjoys the carnage of battle." Some suggest that this is because a son wants to stamp out evil in a world not fit for his revered mother. One may also speculate that he unconsciously wants to deny his softer female-identified side, which he feels other sons have always disdained. Or perhaps he feels that only his heroism can repay his mother for her constant faith and sacrifice.

In any case, in the Goertzels' study, military sons seemed to have enormous difficulty in separating from their mothers or in even wanting to. From the days when she moved to a hotel near West Point, "Pinky" MacArthur followed her son, Douglas, to his various posts of duty. In 1935, when President Roosevelt asked General MacArthur to go to the Philippines to strengthen its defense systems, a major factor in his deciding to undertake the assignment was that his ailing mother was well enough to accompany him. But shortly after they arrived in Manila, Mrs. MacArthur's condition worsened, and she died, leaving her son as bereft an orphan as if he had been a small, helpless boy.

Twenty years after the end of World War II, when Dwight David Eisenhower's top-secret papers were declassified, one, dispatched in May 1944, just weeks before the invasion of France, proved that even the heat of battle could not lessen this son's devotion. The order was for aides to send a Mother's Day greeting to Ida Eisenhower in Kansas.

Another fascinating example of a fierce and tender son is General George S. Patton, Jr. An officer so ruthless that

his nickname was "Blood and Guts," Patton commonly
shouted obscenities at his troops and, in one celebrated case,
even slapped a shell-shocked soldier across the face. He was
a man who, according to his biographer James Wellard,
"had a zest for killing, and felt lost and useless when there
was no battle to fight." Yet the overprotected boy who had
grown into this much-feared general visited his childhood
home, years after his mother's death, and was so moved by
memories of her that he wrote a note of testimony and left
it in a box she had used for prized possessions:

> Darling Mama, I had always prayed to show my love by
> doing something famous for you, to justify what you called
> me when I got back from France, "my hero son." Nothing
> you ever did to me was anything but loving. I have no
> memories but love and devotion. . . . Perhaps this is foolish,
> but I think you understand. I loved and love you very much.
> Your devoted son, George S. Patton, Jr.

Like Patton, Truman, Franklin Roosevelt, and many others, superachieving men are often their mothers' firstborn
or only male child. A firstborn son often enters his mother's
life when she is still in many ways a girl and when her
motherhood shapes her maturity rather than reflects it. It
is an atmosphere that seems to endow the boy with a special
destiny. Said Rebekah Johnson about her son, "Naturally,
I love all my children, but Lyndon was the first, and to me
he was the greatest marvel in the world." But one need look
no further than to Freud himself to see how a son's self-
esteem is nurtured by a young mother's great delight in
him. When he was eighty, Freud wrote to a friend, "Deeply
buried within me there still lives the happy child of Freiberg, the firstborn son of a youthful mother, who received
his first indelible impressions from this air, from this soil."

Sometimes, as in Pablo Casals' case, it is the special talent a mother senses in her son that drives her to devote herself to his development. Noël Coward's mother recognized her son's genius for performing when he was still a very young boy, and concentrated all her energies on ensuring that the world became aware of, and duly rewarded, his gifts. F. Scott Fitzgerald began to write in school, publishing stories and poems in the school newspaper. Of his mother's relentless attention and admiration, he wrote, "I didn't know until I was fifteen that there was anything in the world except me."

At other times it may be the lingering memories of her own childhood that a mother projects on to a new generation. David McCullough discovered that all the mothers in his research on mama's boys were extraordinarily devoted to their own fathers. "As near as can be determined," he wrote, the "mothers of Mama's boys were . . . very much their Papa's girls." Lyndon Johnson's mother, one of McCullough's subjects, was evidence that a father does not have to be a success for his daughter to relate his grandson's achievements to his life. Rebekah Johnson was said to have gravely mourned the fact that her beloved father died without reaching his goal of holding a congressional seat. When her son was born, she immediately claimed to see the same "deep purposefulness and true nobility" in her baby's eyes that she remembered in her father's. In linking her son to her father in this way, she dedicated herself to helping the grandson vindicate his grandfather's failures, to seeing that Lyndon became what his grandfather could not.

To this end, Rebekah Johnson tirelessly drilled her son in his daily lessons, often walking along with him to school to get in some extra time. When he went away to college, she wrote him daily letters to spur him on. He responded to these missives (which often began with "My dearest love" or "My splendid sweet son") with floods of gratitude. "The end of another busy day brought me a letter from you. Your letters always give me more strength, renewed courage, and that bulldog tenacity so essential to the success of any man." Another time he wrote:

> Dearest Mother, Have all of my books arranged before me in preparation for a long evening of study. You can't realize the difference in atmosphere after one of your sweet letters. I know of nothing so stimulating and inspiring to me as one of your encouraging, beautifully written letters. Mother, I love you so. Don't neglect me.

Lady Bird Johnson always recognized the formidable presence of her mother-in-law. Like Eleanor Roosevelt, she undoubtedly knew that little good could come from objecting to a tie that held until the mother's death. This tie, reported Johnson's biographer Robert Caro, kept her "torrents of effusive encouragement and endearment" coming to Lyndon any time she was unable to be close enough to her son to profess her devotion directly.

Still, in all the research conducted on high-achieving men, including my own study, it is clear that no matter how devoted a mother is, it is her own character, rather than her attention, that seems to influence her son's life most of all. There is no greater indicator of a son's success than maternal dedication to learning, particularly if the mother is herself intellectually curious and a prodigious reader, and creates an environment where a son's intelligence can flower. All of the mothers David McCullough studied were women of "great vitality; they were well read, even cultured, and strong-minded. Each was a vivid personality in her own right."

To be sure, both Martha Truman and Rebekah Johnson

taught their sons to read before they entered school, and Mrs. Truman saw to it that the family moved from their Missouri farm to the town of Independence, because the schools there were superior. Nonetheless, these mothers' goals were not simply academic achievement, but rather the encouragment of the same love of learning and sense of purpose that informed their own lives. The poet Robert Graves's mother gave him advice as a young boy that he felt explained his prodigious literary output, even during times of great adversity. "Robert," she said, "this is a great secret, never forget it! Work is far more interesting than play!"

Mothers who are more interested in ideas than in financial rewards, and in creativity more than worldly success, seem to have a high tolerance for their sons' interests, no matter how wide ranging they may be. When Auden developed a passionate interest in lead mining, his mother bought him books like *Machinery for Maliferous Mines*, and did not think him wasteful of his time or peculiar for creating what he remembered as a "private, sacred world, the basic elements of which were a landscape, northern and limestone, and an industry, lead mining."

Victor and Mildred Goertzel's research confirmed that "in homes which cradle eminence, there are strong tendencies to build directly on personal strengths, talents, and aims, rather than to assume there is a large, specific body of knowledge that everyone should possess." Furthermore, the sons in their study were often allowed to take time out from formal education to "have a free period in which to think, to plan, to read unrestrainedly, or to meet an entirely new group of people under novel circumstances." In my interviews, a sizable percentage of high-achieving sons recounted such a period in their own lives, and attributed great significance to its influence on the kind of men they had become.

"My parents were both teachers," James, a book publisher, told me. "One year they both got grants and they wanted to use the money to travel rather than to stay in one place and study. My brother was eight and I was thirteen, and my parents asked if we'd mind missing a year of school. They would do their best to tutor us, they said, but we were taking the chance of having to repeat a grade when the year was over. (We didn't!) I was a little reluctant at first, because, at thirteen, being with your peers is very important. But I really wanted to have that travel opportunity, and it turned out to be extraordinary in every way. I was part of a life that was completely open-ended. It was as if I'd gotten off some narrow track that was taking me to a predetermined future and instead I was seeing myself reflected against a whole world of possibilities. That was the year I became passionately interested in the classics, because they were the easiest books to find in English in foreign bookstores. I had always read before, but my time was so taken up with assignments for school that I hadn't really discovered books as a life source. I'm sure I would never have gone into publishing if it wasn't for what reading came to mean to me that year."

Other sons were allowed to go off on their own to pursue an interest that a mother couldn't help them to develop on home ground. Several musicians told me of being permitted to take part in summer music programs all over the country, and even abroad, at an age many would judge as much too young. In a major study by the psychologist Fred L. Strodbeck, *Talent and Society*, it was shown that the mother who permits her son to leave home for more sophisticated study than his hometown or city offers, or who, like Casals' mother, sacrifices her day-to-day relationship with her husband and even her other children, does much to ensure that her son will be the accomplished man he shows signs of becoming as a child. Indeed, the very notion that one must be willing to sacrifice in order to achieve becomes an integral part of the successful son's value system.

The idea that success means being true *to* a value system also becomes important to high achievers. It is a common characteristic of many men who succeed in complex fields that they respond to a set of inner convictions and truths. As the writer-scientist C. P. Snow said of Albert Einstein, "Einstein continued to work hard at his physics until the end. The curious thing was, he worked in complete disagreement with almost all of his contemporaries."

Mothers of useful, accomplishing men seem to communicate their own convictions to their sons from the earliest days of their lives together. David McCullough reported that Frank Lloyd Wright's mother told her son, "I would have you a man of sense as well as sensibility. . . . If you have to choose, choose truth. . . . Simplicity of heart is just as necessary to an architect as for a farmer or a minister."

One especially provocative conclusion of research in this area is that the mothers of high-minded, achieving sons often possess a host of strong opinions; they do not resemble the carefully neutral image of mother that traditionally has been fashionable. The Goertzels give us an indication of how these mothers shape their sons' destiny. They point out that the "eminent" sons in their study usually came from families that "espoused strong political attitudes . . . were religious liberals with equally strong feelings, or were atheists or agnostics, or espoused unpopular causes, or worked in reform movements, or expressed controversial views in print or on the public platform." Before their sons were even born the women in these families "often found themselves in conflict with the established order and accepted mores." In contrast to the research on troubled sons, which revealed that such sons did not really know what a parent thought or believed, the children in these opinionative homes are more likely to emulate the parent than to be rebels. The brash, critical adolescent who quarrels with his parents, disagrees with them violently about cultural or political matters is not often found in these families. He is more likely to be tagging along after opinionative parents, trying to find out what the excitement is all about.

What seems to happen most often is that a son will extend his mother's beliefs to fit the increased dimensions and opportunities of his own time. Almost all the young men I interviewed who were social activists had mothers who were actively engaged in and concerned about politics and society. Her concerns might be very different from those of the son, sometimes even at the opposite end of the political or moral spectrum; it was her passion that the mother passed on to the boy, not any particular belief. This was very clearly demonstrated in early studies of the first freedom riders who went to the South to work for civil rights. The most dedicated young men were those whose mothers, and often fathers too, were vitally committed to certain causes, even if they were, once again, causes the son had rejected or from which he had strayed.

Moreover, an intelligent mother with strong opinions stirs more than her son's intellect; she stimulates both his curiosity and his energy so that he will one day be an opinion-shaper himself. When one looks at the lives of articulate, innovative thinkers in the arts or sciences, one generally finds in the background a mother who early provided her son with stimulating companionship. The mother of the Victorian writer Lytton Strachey was lovingly remembered by his friend Virginia Woolf as "many-sided, vigorous, adventurous, advanced." Woolf described how Lady Strachey presided over her children's lives:

A little absent-minded, a little erratic, but nevertheless the controller and inspirer of it all, now wandering through the rooms with a book, now teaching the steps of a Highland reel, now working out, with equal intentness, some puzzle in a penny paper which, if solved, would provide her with thirty shillings a week and a workman's cottage for life.

A mother whose intelligence and values are respected can encourage a son's potential even when almost everything else in his life threatens to restrict it. A number of men in my study had fathers who had been abusive or were chronic alcoholics, and several men had grown up in bitter poverty, yet their mothers had been able to heal the wounds left by neglect and indigence. In fact, when there is also a bitter marriage to contend with, the bleakness may serve to fuel a son's ambition, for he wants to make up to his mother for his father's failure. The son will, by his fame and success, put pride back into his mother's life.

The actor James Cagney remembered a childhood with terrible disadvantages. There were seven children in his family. His father was an alcoholic, and they lived in a neighborhood where most boys climbed very early onto a road leading to a prison cell. But, wrote Mr. Cagney, "we had a mother to answer to. . . . We loved her profoundly, and our driving force was to do what she wanted, because we knew how much it meant to her." Thomas Edison, whose mother was not in such personal distress, was still motivated to reward her for the faith that had spurred him on. "With a mother of a different caliber," he eulogized, "I should probably have turned out badly. But her firmness, her sweetness, her goodness, were potent powers to keep me on the right path."

Of all the recent studies of men's development one of the most important is the Grant Study. Researchers at Harvard

University followed the lives of 268 men from the time they were undergraduates until they were middle-aged, some thirty-five years later. Their purpose was to find out why some men adapted to life so much more successfully than did other men with similar gifts and potential. Here the focus was on success that is not career oriented, although almost all of the men in the study had received more than average professional acclaim and monetary reward. The Grant Study attempted to ascertain how men can cope with life's failed dreams as well as those that are fulfilled; how they adjust to life rather than merely achieve.

While a loving mother or mother surrogate was not the only decisive factor in successful adaptation, Dr. George Valliant, who wrote the book analyzing the study's long-awaited results, arrived at some other powerful conclusions about that connection. No matter what degree of material success he achieves, wrote Dr. Valliant, a son who is not sufficiently loved in childhood will suffer these limits on his ability to enjoy his life. "First, he will be unable to play. Second, he will be dependent and lack trust in the universe. Third, he is most likely to be labeled mentally ill. Fourth, he will be without friends."

Another compelling finding of the Grant Study has to do with the ways in which sons may be encouraged toward goals that are more than challenging; they are perhaps dangerous. Males must bear the burden of what Dr. Valliant called "the specter of overachievement." For some men, this becomes particularly perilous.

Several of the clearly dissatisfied men I interviewed seemed unable to cease competing, even though they had achieved great material success by any objective measure. They could not settle for anything less than the top rung, the first place, total leadership. Certain men in Dr. Valliant's report were similarly driven, to a point where, through chance or bad luck, their magnificent potential was wasted. It may be, Dr. Valliant concluded, that, like Icarus, they were men who tried to "fly too close to the sun." Perhaps their goals were too "dangerously high [and they] should have been willing to settle for something closer to mediocrity earlier in their lives. . . . I suspect," he continued, "that for most Grant Study men, one reason that success seemed healthy is that they knew when to stop."

In relating these results to the coping skills and behavior problems of troubled sons, one notices that a man's ability not to take himself too seriously seems to help him realize when he should stop seeking the culturally imposed goals of male success. Mothers who wish to cultivate in their sons a system of defenses against adversity may want to know that those men who had learned to laugh at themselves were among the best-adapted subjects in the Grant Study. Within healthy bounds humor is, in Dr. Valliant's opinion, "one of the truly elegant defenses in the human repertoire. The capacity for humor, like hope, is one of mankind's most potent antidotes for the woes of Pandora's Box."

As we examine the traits and defenses that a mother should nurture in a son to ensure his "success in living," we inevitably come to the primary need, helping him part gently from the security of his early days under her care. For men who have been pushed too early to become achieving males, success rings hollow and failures seem immensely threatening. As the Grant Study concluded, "No whim of fate, no Freudian trauma . . . will be as devastating to the human spirit as the prolonged ambivalent relationship that leaves us unable to say goodbye."

A mother should not worry overmuch about a single failure, one mistake, one unmet need, as she guides her son toward manhood. Given the security of a sustained committed relationship with his mother, a boy will be able to overcome the occasional setbacks on the path to achievement and adjustment. He will leave his childhood behind with reasonable contentment and look to his future with reasonable confidence, for, in the words of Joseph Conrad, he has learned "while young to hope, to love, and to put his trust in life."

Some Final Words

Norman Mailer, about his mother: "If I took a tommy gun and shot up hundreds of people in a shopping mall, she would say, 'They must have said something truly awful to him.'"

The editor and writer Geoffrey Ward, on former governor and presidential candidate, Thomas E. Dewey: "His strong-willed mother . . . was ambitious for him: it was she who made sure that he alone of all 58 of his Owosso classmates was never late or absent in twelve years of schooling. But she was also oddly scornful of his accomplishments, and since neither she nor his wife, Frances, really approved of politics, his victories could never fully be savored and his defeats were all the more nakedly humiliating."

The Argentine writer Jorge Luis Borges, who is blind, on his mother's contributions to this career: "My mother has always had a hospitable mind. She translated Saroyan, Hawthorne, Melville, Woolf, Faulkner. She has always been a companion to me and an understanding and forgiving friend. For years she handled all my secretarial work, answering letters, reading to me, taking down my dictation, and also traveling with me. . . . It was she who quietly and effectively fostered my literary career."

A friend recalling the mother of the deeply troubled, immensely talented actor Montgomery Clift: "Mrs. Clift was a small, slender, rather unobtrusive little lady. But you always knew she was there. You felt her presence and her influence on Monty, because when she was not there, he seemed to blossom and be himself, and the moment she appeared, he would withdraw."

Pablo Casals, about his mother's self-effacing dedication: "She was an exceptional woman! Just think of what she did in Madrid: she studied foreign languages and more or less did the same lessons as I did, partly because she thought it would help my work, but mostly because the deep feeling we had for each other should not be affected by any difference in our education."

These words express the range of responses possible between mothers and sons. On one end, the resolute maternal defender, unwilling to recognize her son's faults, no matter how terrible they may be; the facilitator who puts her own talents and needs in the shadow so that the light may shine more fully on her son. Virginia Woolf once wrote that when she read about some man's striking literary accomplishment, she often suspected he had a mother who was herself a "lost novelist" or "suppressed poet."

The recently deceased writer John Gardner poignantly illustrated the fact that men internalize the idea that women are selflessly here to help them: "If I have any doubts about what a character would say or a room would look like, I ask my wife." His writing always contained her imagination, "page after page after page," informing "everything I do." Mr. Gardner admitted that he probably should have used the names "John and Joan Gardner" on his books, but didn't do so because he felt that modern readers do not respect books that have been co-authored in the same way they respect individual works of art. Most male authors would probably not so readily give credit to their wives, but there is little doubt that such help is often the norm in the lives of grown men who enter the arts.

On the other end of the spectrum is Philip Wylie's terribly

destructive "Mom," the "vain and vicious" woman who masquerades as an angel while she brandishes a fierce and emasculating sword. From Philip Roth's fictional Mrs. Portnoy to the images of a mother offered by sons like writers Henry Miller ("Even the earliest memories of my mother are unhappy ones") and Gore Vidal ("She was a traumatic experience"), it can be seen that the wounds inflicted by such a mother are sharp and lasting.

But portraits like these are fading. Emerging instead is an image of motherhood that is congruent with a changing society, in which being the mother of a son—a role that includes commitment, anxiety, and joy—has not radically altered. All that has changed is the social context within which the feelings of mother and son take shape.

There is a tendency to believe that because women are seeking fuller development of themselves, and because they want more direct, rather than reflected, power, they will feel less for their sons. While in some cases too much divergence from the traditional role of mother does mean less maternal attachment to the child, in most instances no such cause and effect can be shown. There is reason to hope that as women integrate themselves more fully into society, the potential for joy in the mother-son relationship will be greater than ever. This is primarily because the problems that stem from the rigid definitions of sex-role behavior will in large part cease to exist as women and men strike what the psychoanalyst Erik Erikson called a "new balance" between the sexes. That this balance is as liberating to men as it is to women is understood by men who experience social transition. The writer Warren Farrell confirmed the feelings of feminist mothers when he wrote that the gains will be just as profound for men as women when the latter

begin to improve their self-concept through expanding their

roles beyond wife and mother. . . . The fear engendered in a male that he be thought of as female—with all the negative implications—has been the central basis of his need to prove himself masculine. A more positive image of women, held by both sexes, frees a man to display so-called feminine traits without being mocked, and allows him to start displaying human emotions without fear of being called feminine.

As long as sons are unable to break away from the traditional ideas of male and female behavior, they stand a good chance of remaining boys emotionally, even as they continuously and often joylessly engage in proving that they are "real men." The lesson to be learned by sons is that if they continue to fear their need of a woman's love (as well as their own feminine qualities), they will not be able to trust any woman enough to reach out for a vital and nurturing connection with her. Or the years of unexpressed need may build up such tension that a man may suddenly explode from the pressure and compulsively enter into a relationship with any woman who seems willing to mother him. When and if he discovers that this woman has needs of her own, he may become bitterly resentful, lashing out at her in fury or refusing to accept her needs as legitimate. Had the son grown up less constrained by his unresolved attachment to his mother, he might not have been deprived of a potentially rewarding union with a woman.

An important lesson for mothers of sons to learn is that there is no need to deny the contradictions of their role and the rewards they find in it. To love a son profoundly is not the same thing as endowing him with the power to make his mother's life worthwhile. Sophie Freud Lowenstein, who has written so movingly about women's concerns, said that "competence as a mother lies, in my opinion, in how successful one is in viewing one's children as separate from oneself." The fascinating paradox my research revealed is that the very difference of a male child creates that completion of self which makes it so difficult for the mother to separate her own emotional responses to the world from his.

We owe it to ourselves as well as to our sons to make that separation. Erikson offered as a definition of identity "a sense of knowing where one is going," and mothers can know that sense only if they are not dependent on a son's travels to validate the journey of their own lives. Similarly, a mother's becoming less narcissistically involved in her son's life adds richness to her experience of being a mother. Being a mother today requires self-assurance as much as selflessness, and self-assurance can come most fully from a sense of independent worth outside the maternal role.

Yet even as a mother reaches outside that role for personal definition, she remains a sustaining presence in a son's life. The Pulitzer Prize–winning poet Galway Kinnell celebrated that lasting influence in his poem "The Last Hiding Places of Snow."

> I have always felt
> anointed by her love. . . .
>
> So lighted I have believed
> I could wander anywhere,
> among any foulnesses, any contagions,
> I could climb through the entire, empty world
> and find my way back and learn again to be happy.

As men become freer to acknowledge the value of such supportive love, nurturing will undoubtedly cease to be entirely the province of women. To some extent this has always been true. Great men have frequently had qualities traditionally thought of as motherly. For instance, Ernest

Jones often remarked on Freud's "motherliness." Of course, how we look at a future in which men as well as women respect and assume maternal qualities depends, wrote the sociologist Jesse Bernard, "on how one values the principles embodied and symbolized in the role of a mother."

But surely it is a service to sons to teach them to value the characteristics of a good mother. The fusion that exists between mother and son in childhood can achieve no greater transformation than in the synthesis of the feminine and masculine aspects of men and women in adulthood. Even as they welcome each other as separate people, they will retain the mysterious element of the "found half."

Such discovery and resolution is extremely difficult, however, for the son whom fate has prevented from working through primary issues of dependency and identity. James Dean, the gifted actor who died tragically young, once summed up his chaotic emotional life by saying, "My mother died on me when I was nine years old. What does she expect me to do? Do it all alone?"

Men whose mothers died when they were small boys often feel haunted and enraged by this question. Nothing can match the impact of a mother's death in a little boy's life, particularly if he is not old enough to have developed emotional and intellectual resources to cope with the death. Her leaving is to him the ultimate desertion, and he hates her for it. At the same time, in the magical thinking of childhood, he may blame himself for being so "bad" that his mother wanted to leave him, and he may live forever in fear of allowing anyone to get close enough to him to see the evil person he really is.

If a boy has not yet passed through the Oedipal stage, a mother's death can leave him incapable of ever dealing with separation and loss. Michael Balint, a psychoanalyst, coined the term "basic fault" to describe the profound "deficiency state" that results from a son's losing his mother before his Oedipal period. Balint learned that a man who has known such an early disappearance of his mother cannot easily respond to conventional psychoanalytic treatment. He must be allowed to regress to his childhood state, to work through the primary deprivation and stunted development, if he is ever to move on to a successful adult relationship. The son must finally resolve what he has "given up" in order to "begin anew."

Even if a boy is past the Oedipal stage when his mother dies, the effects of her "abandonment" are long-lasting, as James Dean indicated. For one thing, he cannot alter the romantic images of early life. His beloved mother retains forever the mythic quality she had in his childhood, to the extent that it is almost impossible for him to form realistic expectations of other women.

Gregory, a soft-spoken film producer whose mother died when he was eight, explained, "All my memories of my mother are perfect. I only remember her as beautiful, as happy, as warm and loving. She wasn't around long enough for me to see her as a real person, complete with flaws. I'm forty-five years old, and I've been married three times, and I know I'm still looking for the reincarnation of my mother in every woman I meet, someone who will match the magic of the woman who left me at a time when her magic ran so high."

Even if a mother lives out her life span, a mature son finding himself suddenly motherless may feel helpless and confusingly adrift.

"The entire taken-for-granted quality went from my life," Bert, a man in his late forties, told me. "I don't recall ever feeling dependent on my mother once I became an adult, and I feel good about about our relationship, so I'm not eating myself up about what I should have done or said.

But she seemed to ground me to life, provided it with a continuity that her death has shattered. I'm much more conscious now of life's finiteness."

In truth, a man's mother never does really die for him. She is there still, to look to for blessing or to blame for his failures. Rarely does her physical ending erase the memory of the primary fusion of mother and son. In his poem, Galway Kinnell made this eminently clear:

> Even now when I wake at night
> in some room far from everyone,
> the darkness sometimes
> lightens a little, and then,
> because of nothing,
> in spite of nothing,
> in an imaginary daybreak, I see her,
> and for that moment I am still her son
> and I am in the holy land. . . .

BIBLIOGRAPHY

INDEX

Bibliography by Chapter

Introduction

Faber, Doris. *The Mothers of American Presidents*. New York: New American Library, 1968.

Kitzinger, Sheila. *Women As Mothers*. New York: Random House, 1978.

Ehrlich, Richard, ed. *Mothers—100 Mothers of the Famous and the Infamous*. London and New York: Paddington Press Ltd., 1974.

Solotaroff, Theodore. *Writers and Issues*. New York: Signet Books, 1959.

Pregnancy and Birth

Bell, Donald H. *Being a Man*. Lexington, Massachusetts, and Brattleboro, Vermont: Lewis Publishing Co., 1982.

Betts, Doris. *Beasts of the Southern Wild and Other Stories*. New York: Harper & Row, 1970.

Coleman, A., and Coleman, L. *Pregnancy: The Psychological Experience*. New York: Seabury Press, 1971.

Grossman, Frances, Eichler, Lois, and Winichoff, Susan. *Pregnancy, Birth, and Parenthood*. San Francisco, Washington, and London: Jossey-Bass, 1980.

Meyerowitz, J. H., and Feldman, H. "Transition to Parenthood." *Psychiatric Research Reports*, 1966.

Pincus, Lily, and Dare, Christopher. *Secrets in the Family*. New York: Pantheon, 1978.

Rich, Adrienne. *Of Woman Born*. New York: Norton, 1976.

Rochlin, Gregory. *The Masculine Dilemma*. Boston: Little, Brown, 1980.

Stephens, William. *The Oedipus Complex, Cross-Cultural Evidence*. New York: Free Press (Macmillan), 1962.

Oedipal Myths and Misunderstandings

Freud, Sigmund. *The Basic Writings of Sigmund Freud*. Translated and edited by A. A. Brill. New York: Random House, Modern Library, 1956.

————. *Totem and Taboo*. New York: Norton, 1950.

Fromm, Erich. *Greatness and Limitations of Freud's Thought*. New York: Harper & Row, 1980.

Horney, Karen. "The Dread of Woman." *International Journal of Psychoanalysis* 13 (1932).

Kafka, Franz. *The Diaries of Franz Kafka*. New York: Schocken Books, 1948.

Lawrence, D. H. *Sons and Lovers*. New York: Viking Press, 1933.

Lederer, Wolfgang, M.D. *The Fear of Women*. New York: Harvest, HBJ Book, 1968.

Mullahy, Patrick. *Oedipus Myth and Complex*. New York: Grove Press, 1948.

Roth, Henry. *Call It Sleep*. New York: Cooper Square, 1934.

Slater, Philip. *The Glory of Hera*. Boston: Beacon Press, 1968.

Growing Up Male

Bowlby, John. *Attachment and Loss*. vol. 1: *Attachment*. New York: Basic Books, 1969.

————. "Childhood Mourning and Its Implications for Psychiatry." *American Journal of Psychiatry* 118, 1961.

Brooks-Gunn, Jeanne, and Schempp, Wendy Matthews. *He & She, How Children Develop Their Sex-Role Identity*. Englewood Cliffs: Prentice-Hall, 1979.

Chodorow, Nancy. *The Reproduction of Mothering, Psychoanalysis*

and the Sociology of Gender. Berkeley: University of California
Press, 1978.
Goldberg, S., and Lewis, M. "Play Behavior in the Year-old
Infant, Early Sex Differences." *Child Development*, 1969.
Hantover, Jeffrey. "The Social Construction of Masculine Anxi-
ety." *Men in Difficult Times*. Edited by Robert Lewis. Engle-
wood Cliffs: Prentice-Hall, 1981.
Hartley, R. E. "Sex-role Pressures and the Socialization of the
Male Child." *Psychological Reports*, 1959.
Jourard, Sidney. *Disclosing Man to Himself*. New York: Van Nos-
trand, 1968.
Mahler, M. S., "Thoughts about Development and Individua-
tion." *Psychoanalytic Study of the Child* 18 (1963).
Mahler, M. S., Pine, F., and Bergman, A. *The Psychological Birth
of the Human Infant*. New York: Basic Books, 1975.
Mead, Margaret. *Male and Female*. New York: Dell, 1949.
Pincus, Lily, and Dare, Christopher. *Secrets in the Family*. New
York: Pantheon, 1980.
Schafer, R. "Concepts of Self and Identity and the Experience of
Separation-Individuation in Adolescence." *Psychoanalytic Quar-
terly* 43 (1973).

Mother and Son Equal Guilt

Axelrad, Joseph, *Anatole France: A Life Without Illusions*. New
York: Harper & Brothers 1944.
Baker, Russell. *Growing Up*. New York: Congdon and Weed,
1982.
Bart, Pauline. "Portnoy's Mother's Complaint: Depression in
Middle-Aged Women." *Response: A Contemporary Jewish Review*,
no. 18 (Summer 1973).
Bernard, Jesse. *The Future of Motherood*. New York: Dial Press,
1974.
Deutsch, Helen. *Psychology of Women* 2. New York: Grune &
Stratton, 1945.
Goertzel, Victor, and Goertzel, Mildred. *Cradles of Eminence*.
Boston: Little, Brown, 1962.

Heffner, Elaine. *Mothering.* New York: Doubleday, 1978.
Roth, Philip. *Portnoy's Complaint.* New York: Random House, 1969.
Wickes, Frances G. *The Inner World of Childhood.* Englewood Cliffs: Prentice-Hall, 1966.
Winnicott, D. W. *The Maturational Processes and the Facilitating Environment.* New York: International Universities Press, 1965.

Power—The Hidden Agenda

Dally, Ann. *Inventing Motherhood.* New York: Schocken Books, 1983.
de Beauvoir, Simone. *The Second Sex.* Harmondsworth: Penguin, 1972.
Fransella, F., and Frost, K. *On Being a Woman: A Review of Research on How Women See Themselves.* London: Tavistock Publications, 1977.
Freud, Sigmund. "The Psychology of Women." *New Introductory Lectures on Psychoanalysis.* Translated by W. J. H. Sprott. New York: Macmillan, 1933.
Gary, Romain, *Promise at Dawn.* New York: Harper & Brothers, 1961.
Gotti, Richard. "Love and Neurotic Claims." *The American Journal of Psychoanalysis* 42:1 (1982).
Janeway, Elizabeth, *Cross Sections from a Decade of Change.* New York: Morrow, 1982.
Jones, Ernest. *The Life and Work of Sigmund Freud.* New York: Basic Books, 1961.
Kennedy, Edward. *Our Day and Generation: The Words of Edward M. Kennedy.* New York: Simon & Schuster, 1979.
Lerner, Max. *Ted and the Kennedy Legend.* New York: St. Martin's Press, 1982.
Levy, David, M.D. *Maternal Overprotection.* New York: Norton, 1966, 1981.
Mill, John Stuart. *On the Subjection of Women.* New York: Fawcett, 1971.

Miller, Alice. *Prisoners of Childhood*. New York: Basic Books, 1981.
Slater, Philip. *The Pursuit of Loneliness*. New York: Beacon Press, 1976.

Sons and Lovers Revisited

Baldwin, James. *Go Tell It On The Mountain*. New York: Dial Press, 1952.
Erikson, Erik H. *Childhood and Society*. New York: Norton, 1963.
Forward, Susan, and Craig, Buck. *Betrayal of Innocence—Incest and its Devastation*. Harmondsworth, England: Penguin, 1978.
Freud, Sigmund. *A General Introduction to Psychoanalysis*. New York: Liveright, 1935.
Gary, Romain. *Promise at Dawn*. New York: Harper & Brothers, 1961.
Goertzel, Victor, and Goertzel, Mildred. *Cradles of Eminence*. Boston: Little, Brown, 1962.
Kakutani, Michiko. "Where John Fowles Ends and Characters of His Begins," *The New York Times*. October 5, 1982.
Kubie, Lawrence. *Practical and Theoretical Aspects of Psychoanalysis*. Revised edition. New York: International Universities Press, 1975.
Levy, David, M.D. *Maternal Overprotection*. New York: Norton, 1966, 1981.
Lewis, Melvin, and Sarrel, Philip. "Some Psychological Aspects of Seduction, Incest, and Rape in Childhood." *Journal of the American Academy of Child Psychology* 8, October 1969.
Lowen, Alexander. *Fear of Life*. New York: Macmillan, 1980.
Nowell, Elizabeth. *Thomas Wolfe*. New York: Doubleday, 1960.
Parsons, Talcott. *Family, Socializations and Interaction Process*. New York: Free Press (Macmillan), 1955.
Pincus, Lily and Dare, Christopher. *Secrets in the Family*. New York: Pantheon, 1980.
Rochlin, Gregory. *The Masculine Dilemma*. Boston: Little, Brown, 1980.

Rubin, Lillian. *Intimate Strangers*. New York: Harper & Row, 1983.
Ross, Amanda. "Growing Up With My Teenage Son." *Ms.* magazine, July 1981.
Stendahl. *The Life of Henry Brulard*. Translated by Jean Steward and B.C. Knight. New York: Noonday Press, 1958.
Wells, Hal. *The Sensuous Child*. New York: Stein & Day, 1978.

When Mother's Little Boy Becomes the Man of the House

Bibring, Grete. "On the Passing of the Oedipus Complex," in *A Matriarchal Family Setting, Drives, Affects and Behavior: Essays in Honor of Marie Bonaparte*. New York: International Universities Press, 1953.
Biller, Henry B. "The Mother-Child Relationship and the Father–Absent Boy's Personality Development. *Merrill-Palmer Quarterly of Behavior and Development*, vol. 17, no. 3 (1971).
Canetti, Elias. *The Tongue Set Free*. New York: Seabury Press, 1979.
Dally, Ann. *Inventing Motherhood*. New York: Schocken Books, 1983.
Drabble, Margaret. *The Middle Ground*. New York: Knopf, 1980.
Keniston, Kenneth. *The Uncommitted*. New York: Harcourt, Brace and World, 1960.
LeMasters, E. E. "Parenthood As Crisis." *Marriage and Family Living* 19, 1957.
McCord, J.; McCord, W.; and Thurber, E. "Some Effects of Paternal Absence on Male Children." *Journal of Abnormal Social Psychology*, 1959.
Roth, Philip. *Portnoy's Complaint*. New York: Random House, 1969.
Trehowan, W. H. "The Couvade Syndrome." *British Journal of Psychiatry*, 1965.
Wylie, H. L., and Delgado, R. A. "A Pattern of Mother-Son

Relationship Involving the Absence of the Father." *American Journal of Psychiatry*, 1965.

Feminist Mothers

Bardwick, Judith. *In Transition*. New York: Holt, Rinehart, & Winston, 1979.
Blakely, Mary Kay, "Hers" column, *The New York Times*, March 26, 1981.
Coles, K. C. *Between the Lines*. New York: Doubleday, 1982.
Coser, Lewis, and Coser, Rose. "The Housewife and Her 'Greedy' Family." *Greedy Institutions: Patterns of Undivided Commitment*. New York: Free Press (Macmillan) 1974.
de Reincort, Amaury. *The New York Times*, November 10, 1957.
Janeway, Elizabeth. *Man's World, Woman's Place*. New York: Dell, 1971.
Komarovsky, Mirra. *Dilemmas of Masculinity: A Study of College Youth*. New York: Norton, 1976.
————. "Patterns of Self-Disclosure of Male Undergraduates." *Journal of Marriage and the Family* 36:4, 1974.
————. *Women in the Modern World: Their Education and Dilemmas*. Boston: Little, Brown, 1971.
Lewis, Helen Block. *Psychic War in Men and Women*. New York: New York University Press, 1976.
Marx, Karl. *Capital*, vol. 1. New York: International Publishers, 1867.
Mead, Margaret. *Male and Female*. Harmondsworth, England: Penguin, 1950.
Veevers, J. E. "The Violation of Fertility Mores: Voluntary Childlessness as Deviant Behavior." *Deviant Behavior and Societal Reaction*. Edited by Craig Boydell, Carl Grindstaff, and Paul Whitehead. New York: Holt, Rinehart & Winston, 1972.
"Women in Their Place." Paper presented by Sharon Conarton-Kachidurian. American Orthopsychiatric Association. March 24, 1975.

Homosexual Sons and Lesbian Mothers

Beiber, Irving. *A Psychoanalytic Study of Male Homosexuality*. New York: Basic Books, 1962.

Gosselin, Chris, and Wilson, Glenn. *Sexual Variations*. New York: Simon & Schuster, 1980.

Gould, Robert, M.D. "What We Don't Know about Homosexuality." *The New York Times* magazine, February 24, 1974.

Green, Martin. "Homosexuality in Literature." *Salmugundi*. Fall, 1982,–Winter 1983, no. 58–59.

Gunn-Brooks, Jeanne, and Schemp, Wendy Matthews. *He & She*. Englewood Cliffs: Prentice-Hall, 1979.

Hobson, Laura. *Consenting Adult*. New York: Doubleday, 1975.

Jones, Ernest. *The Life and Work of Sigmund Freud*. New York: Basic Books, 1961.

Kinsey, A. C.; Pomeroy, W. B.; and Martin, C. E. *Sexual Behavior in the Human Male*. Philadelphia: W. B. Saunders, 1948.

Lazarre, Jane. *On Loving Men*. New York: Dial Press, 1980.

Lee, J. A. "Going Public: A study in the Sociology of Homosexual Liberation." *Journal of Homosexuality*, 1977.

Leyland, Winston, ed. *Gay Sunshine Interviews*. San Francisco: Gay Sunshine Press, 1978.

Maddox, Brenda. *Married and Gay*. New York: Harcourt, Brace Jovanovich, 1980.

Norton, Joseph. "Male Homosexuality." *Counseling Men*. Monterey: Brooks/Cole Publishing Co., 1980.

Simmons, J. L. *Deviants*. Berkeley: The Glendessary Press, 1969.

Stockard, Jean, and Johnson, M. *Sex Roles*. Englewood Cliffs: Prentice-Hall, 1969.

Thompson, N. L.; McCandless, B. R.; and Strickland, B. R. "Personal Adjustment of Male and Female Homosexuals and Heterosexuals." *Journal of Abnormal Psychology*, 1971.

Weinberger, George, M.D. *Society and the Healthy Homosexual*. New York: St. Martin's Press, 1972.

White, Edmund. *A Boy's Own Story*. New York: Dutton, 1982.

Not-So-Present Mothers

Baruch, Grace, Barnett, Rosaline, and Rivers, Caryl. *Lifeprints*. New York: McGraw-Hill, 1983.
Epstein, C. F. "Women and Power: The Role of Women in Politics in the United States." *Access to Power: Cross-National Studies of Women and Elites*. London: George Allen and Unwin, 1980.
Fallaci, Oriana. *Interview with History*. Boston: Houghton Mifflin, 1976.
Horner, M. "The Motive to Avoid Success and Changing Aspirations of College Women," in J. Bardwick, ed., *Readings on the Psychology of Women*. New York: Harper & Row, 1972.
Lowenstein, Sophie Freud. "The Passion and Challenge of Teaching." *Harvard Educational Review*, vol. 50, no. 1 (February 1980).
Mandel, Ruth. *In the Running: Women As Political Candidates*. New York: Ticknor & Fields, 1981.
Miller, J. B. *Toward a New Psychology of Women*. Boston: Beacon Press, 1976.
Paskowicz, Patricia. *Absentee Mothers*. New York: Universe Books, 1982.
Report on Study by Felton Eearls, M.D., Washington School of Medicine.
Ruddick, Sara, and Daniels, Pamela. *Working It Out*. New York: Pantheon, 1977.
Smith, Liz. *The Mother Book*. New York: Doubleday, 1978
Stacey, Margaret, and Price, Marion. *Women, Power and Politics*. London: Tavistock Publications, 1981.
Von Mering, Faye Higier. "Professional and Non-professional Women As Mothers." *The Journal of Social Psychology*, 1980.
"Working Mothers' Empathy." *Psychology Today*, February 1983.
Wortis, R. "The Acceptance of the Concept of the Maternal Role by Behavioral Scientists: Its Effect on Women." *American Journal of Orthopsychiatry*, 1971.

Mothers and Troubled Sons

Adler, Alfred. *The Problem Child.* New York: Putnam, 1963.

"Adolescence and Stress." Report on NIMH Conference, U.S. Department of Health and Human Services. Rockville, Maryland, 1981.

Allen, Frederick. *Psychotherapy with Children.* New York: Norton, 1942.

Carpenter, Humphrey. *W. H. Auden.* Boston: Houghton Mifflin, 1981.

Chess, S., and Thomas, A. "Temperamental Individuality from Childhood to Adolescence." *Journal of the American Academy of Child Psychiatry* 1 (Spring 1977).

Durkheim, Emile. *Suicide.* Glencoe: Free Press, 1951.

Fisher, Seymour, and Fisher, Rhoda. "Schlemiel Children." *Psychology Today,* September 1980.

Keniston, Kenneth. *The Uncommitted.* New York: Harcourt, Brace & World, 1965.

Lavery, L., and Stone, F. H. "Psychotherapy of a Deprived Child." *Journal of Child Psychology and Psychiatry,* 1965.

Lukas, J. Anthony. "Don't Shoot—We are your Children!" New York: Delta, 1973.

Malcolm, Henry. *Generation of Narcissus.* Boston: Little, Brown, 1971.

Redl, Fritz. *Children Who Hate.* Glencoe, Illinois: Free Press, 1951.

Segal, Julius. *A Child's Journey.* New York: McGraw-Hill, 1978.

Skolnick, Arlene. "The Myth of the Vulnerable Child." *Psychology Today,* February, 1978.

"Special Report on Depression Research." Rockville, Maryland: National Institute of Mental Health, 1981.

Strecker, E., M.D. *Their Mothers' Sons.* Philadelphia: Lippincott, 1946.

"The Bridgewater Study." Bridgewater, Massachusetts: The Center for Diagnosis and Treatment of Sexually Dangerous Persons. Report in *Newsweek,* August 20, 1973.

Wickes, Frances. *The Inner World of Childhood*. Englewood Cliffs: Prentice-Hall, 1927.
Willeford, William. *The Fool and His Scepter*. Chicago: Northwestern University Press, 1969.

Mothers and Successful Sons

French Boyd, Elizabeth. *Bloomsbury Heritage: Their Mothers and Their Aunts*. New York: Taplinger, 1976.
Caro, Robert. *The Path to Power*. New York: Knopf, 1982.
Faber, Doris. *The Mothers of Famous Presidents*. New York: New American Library, 1968.
Janus, Sam, Bess, Barbara, and Saultus, Carol. *A Sexual Profile of Men in Power*. Englewood Cliffs: Prentice-Hall, 1977.
Lash, Joseph. *Love, Eleanor*. New York: Doubleday, 1982.
Leyland, Winston, ed. *Gay Sunshine Interviews*. San Francisco: Gay Sunshine Press, 1978.
McClelland, C. David, et al. *Talent and Society*. New York: Van Nostrand, 1958.
McCullough, David. "Mama's Boys." *Psychology Today*, March 1983.
Rochlin, Gregory. *The Masculine Dilemma*. Boston: Little, Brown, 1980.
Roosevelt, Eleanor. *This is My Story*. New York: Harper & Brothers, 1937.
Roosevelt, James, and Shalett, Sidney. *Affectionately, F.D.R.: A Son's Story of a Lonely Man*. New York: Harcourt, Brace and World, 1959.
Smith, Liz. *The Mother Book*. New York: Doubleday, 1978.
Vaillant, George. *Adaptation to Life*. Boston: Little, Brown, 1977.

Some Final Words

Brenner, Marie. "Mailer Goes Egyptian." *New York Magazine*, March 28, 1983.
Erikson, Erik. *Identity, Youth and Crisis*. New York: Norton, 1968.
Farrell, Warren. *The Liberated Man*. New York: Bantam, 1975.

Kinnell, Galway. *Mortal Acts, Mortal Words*. Boston: Houghton Mifflin, 1980.

Matson, Katinka, *Short Lives: Portraits in Creativity and Self-Destruction*. New York: Morrow, 1980.

Norton, Smith Richard. *Thomas Dewey and His Times*. New York: Simon & Schuster, 1982.

Smelser, Neil, and Erikson, Erik. *Themes of Work and Love in Adulthood*. Cambridge: Harvard University Press, 1980.

Index